KU-778-269

THE GAA
& REVOLUTION
IN IRELAND
1913–1923

HOME FROM FRONGOCH!
WHAT LIFE IN A WELSH DETENTION CAMP IS LIKE.
GAELS! GAELS! GAELS!
CROKE PARK,
GAELIC ATHLETIC ASSOCIATION, LIMITED.

THE GAA & REVOLUTION IN IRELAND 1913–1923

GEARÓID Ó TUATHAIGH
Editor

The Collins Press

First published in 2015 by
The Collins Press
West Link Park
Doughcloyne
Wilton
Cork

Eoghan Corry, Mike Cronin, Paul Darby, Páraic Duffy, Diarmaid Ferriter,
Dónal McAnallen, James McConnel, Richard McElligott, Cormac Moore,
Seán Moran, Gearóid Ó Tuathaigh, Ross O'Carroll, Mark Reynolds, Paul
Rouse have asserted their moral right to be identified as the authors of this
work in accordance with the Irish Copyright and Related Rights Act 2000.

All photos courtesy of GAA Library and Archive unless otherwise credited.

A CIP record for this book is available from the British Library.

Hardback ISBN: 978-1-84889-254-5
PDF eBook ISBN: 978-1-84889-509-6
EPUB eBook ISBN: 978-1-84889-510-2
Kindle ISBN: 978-1-84889-511-9

Design and typesetting by Burns Design
Typeset in Adobe Garamond
Printed in Malta by Gutenberg Press Limited

Contents

Notes on Contributors

Eoghan Corry

Eoghan Corry is a graduate in journalism from Rathmines College and in history from University College Dublin (UCD). The author of several books on sports history in Ireland, as well as on travel, biography and general history, he storylined the original GAA Museum in Croke Park. He is a former Sports Editor of the *Sunday Tribune* and Features Editor of *The Irish Press*. He currently lives a nomadic existence as a travel writer, taking every opportunity to return to the archives to pursue his love of sports history.

Mike Cronin

Professor Mike Cronin is the Academic Director of Boston College in Ireland. He has written widely on the history of sport, and recent publications include *Sport: A Very Short Introduction* (Oxford, 2014) and, with Mark Duncan and Paul Rouse, *The GAA – A People's History* (Cork, 2009). He is currently leading the online historic-newspaper source Century Ireland (www.rte.ie/centuryireland) as part of the Decade of Centenaries.

Paul Darby

Paul Darby is Reader in the Sociology of Sport at the University of Ulster. He is the author of *Gaelic Games, Nationalism and the Irish Diaspora in the United States* (Dublin, 2009) and *Africa, Football and FIFA: Politics, Colonialism and Resistance* (Oxford, 2002). He is the co-editor of *Emigrant Players: Sport and the Irish Diaspora* (Oxford, 2008) and *Soccer and Disaster: International Perspectives* (Oxford, 2005). He sits on the editorial boards of *Soccer & Society* and *SportsWorld: The Journal of Global Sport* and on the advisory board of *Impumelelo: The Interdisciplinary Electronic Journal of African Sports*. A former Antrim senior inter-county footballer, he occasionally turns out for the reserves of Naomh Éanna.

Páraic Duffy

Páraic Duffy is *Ard Stiúrthóir* of the GAA.

Diarmaid Ferriter

Diarmaid Ferriter is Professor of Modern Irish History at UCD. His books include *The Transformation of Ireland 1900–2000* (London, 2004), *Judging Dev: A Reassessment of the Life and Legacy of Éamon de Valera* (Dublin, 2007), *Occasions of Sin: Sex and Society in Modern Ireland* (London, 2009) and *Ambiguous Republic: Ireland in the 1970s* (London, 2012). His most recent book is *A Nation and not a Rabble: The Irish Revolution, 1913–1923* (London, 2015). A regular broadcaster on radio and television, he is also a weekly columnist with *The Irish Times*.

Dónal McAnallen

Dónal McAnallen works as Outreach Officer for the Irish Volunteers Centenary Project at the Cardinal Ó Fiaich Library and Archive, Armagh, and as a part-time lecturer and researcher. He received his BA in history from Queen's University Belfast and his PhD from NUI Galway. He is the joint editor of *The Evolution of the GAA: Ulaidh, Éire agus Eile* (Belfast, 2009) and the author of *The Cups that Cheered: A History of the Sigerson, Fitzgibbon and Higher Education Gaelic Games* (Cork, 2012).

James McConnel

James McConnel is Reader in History at Northumbria University in Newcastle-upon-Tyne. He has published extensively on the subject of John Redmond and Edwardian nationalism in journals such as *Past & Present, English Historical Review, Irish Historical Studies, War in History, The Historical Journal* and others. He is the author of *The Irish Parliamentary Party and the Third Home Rule Crisis* (Dublin, 2013).

Richard McElligott

Dr Richard McElligott lectures in modern Irish history at UCD. He is the author of *Forging a Kingdom: The GAA in Kerry 1884–1934* (Cork, 2013). His research on the GAA and its impact on Irish social, cultural and political life has been published in *Éire-Ireland* and *Irish Economic and Social History*. He edited a special issue of *The International Journal of the History of Sport*, published in late 2015, focusing on Irish sports history. He is also chairman of the Sports History Ireland society.

Cormac Moore

Cormac Moore has an MA in modern Irish history from UCD and is currently pursuing a PhD in sports history at De Montfort University in Leicester. He is the author of *The GAA v Douglas Hyde – The Removal of Ireland's First President as GAA Patron* (Cork, 2012) and *The Irish Soccer Split* (Cork, 2015).

Seán Moran

Seán Moran has been GAA Correspondent of *The Irish Times* since 1994, having previously written on Gaelic games for the *Sunday Tribune* and *The Sunday Times*. A winner of the GAA McNamee Award for national media, he is a frequent contributor on radio and television. He has scripted a number of programmes for television, including the IFTA-award-winning *Breaking Ball* series on RTÉ, which he also co-originated.

Ross O'Carroll

Ross O'Carroll is a secondary school teacher at St Mark's Community School in Dublin. He obtained his MA from UCD, with a thesis on the GAA between 1914 and 1918. When he is not writing about the GAA, he plays both football and hurling for his beloved Kilmacud Crokes and proudly holds county titles in both. He has also represented Dublin at inter-county level. He longs to return to Croke Park on St Patrick's Day for the All-Ireland Club Championship Finals.

Gearóid Ó Tuathaigh

Gearóid Ó Tuathaigh is Professor Emeritus in History at NUI Galway.

Mark Reynolds

Mark Reynolds is the GAA Museum Archivist.

Paul Rouse

Paul Rouse is a lecturer in the School of History and Archives at UCD. He has written extensively on the history of the GAA. His book, *Sport and Ireland: A History*, was published by Oxford University Press in 2015.

Acknowledgments

In preparing this volume for publication, the editor has incurred several significant debts. Firstly, the cooperation, courtesy and general punctuality of the contributors is gratefully acknowledged. A special word of thanks is due to Aogán Ó Fearghail, *Uachtarán Chumann Lúthchleas Gael*, for kindly agreeing to write the Foreword. We are grateful, also, to his predecessor, Liam Ó Néill, for his support for the project at an early stage. The support of the *Ard Stiúrthóir*, Páraic Duffy, was steadfast throughout.

The team at The Collins Press displayed their customary care, consideration and expertise in ensuring that the book was well dressed in going to meet its public. We also thank all who gave permission for the use of images. Cormac Moore would like to thank William Murphy for his help in the production of his chapter.

Two people, in particular, are deserving of special gratitude for their role in the preparation of this book. Lisa Clancy, Director of Communications of the GAA, has shown a singular and constant commitment to this project from the very outset: her advice and assistance at every stage of the process of publication is gratefully acknowledged. The contribution of Mark Reynolds, Archivist of the GAA Museum, has been invaluable. In addition to his own chapter, Mark provided wise counsel on various editorial issues and was mainly responsible for sourcing and providing the captions for the images included in the volume.

Go gcúití Dia a gcineáltas leo ar fad.

List of Abbreviations

AARIR	American Association for the Recognition of the Irish Republic
AC	*The Anglo-Celt*
BMH	Bureau of Military History
BNL	*Belfast News Letter*
CPA	Croke Park Archive
DD	*Dundalk Democrat*
DJ	*Derry Journal*
DORA	Defence of the Realm Act
FJ	*The Freeman's Journal*
FOIF	Friends of Irish Freedom
FS	*Frontier Sentinel*
GPO	General Post Office
IAAC	Irish American Athletic Club
IMA	Irish Military Archives
IN	*The Irish News*
IPP	Irish Parliamentary Party
IRB	Irish Republican Brotherhood
IRFU	Irish Rugby Football Union
IRPDF	Irish Republican Prisoners' Dependants Fund
ISN	*Ireland's Saturday Night*
KRB	Knights of the Red Branch
NAI	National Archives of Ireland
NLI	National Library of Ireland
PRONI	Public Records Office of Northern Ireland
RIC	Royal Irish Constabulary
UCD	University College Dublin
UH	*Ulster Herald*

Foreword / Réamhrá

Thar aon dáta eile i stair na hÉireann, seasann 1916 amach. Tuigeann gach aon duine in Éirinn gur tharla 'rudaí móra' sa bhliain sin, agus aithníonn a lán den phobal i gcoitinne gur fhás an stát seo as an réabhlóid a tharla i 1916. Cuideoidh an leabhar seo go mór linn chun an tréimhse 1913–23 a thuiscint, is tabharfaidh na haistí eolas doimhin dúinn faoi na heachtraí a tharla is na daoine a ghlac páirt sna gluaiseachtaí éagsúla san am. Tá mé cinnte go spreagfaidh an leabhar seo scoláirí eile chun taighde a dhéanamh ar an tréimhse tábhachtach seo i stair na tíre.

I warmly welcome the publication of *The GAA and Revolution in Ireland, 1913–1923*. On behalf of Cumann Lúthchleas Gael, I want to thank Editor Gearóid Ó Tuathaigh, and all the contributors for their scholarly work in this timely production.

This book of essays will add significantly to our knowledge of the formative decade of modern Ireland. GAA membership during this period reflected the mood and make-up of Ireland itself. There were many and varied views and opinions. This book addresses that complex and diverse range of opinions within the GAA during the period. The Association's links and attitudes to nationalism, unionism and republicanism are explored with insightful details of members' involvement in the First World War, the Easter Rebellion of 1916, the War of Independence and civil strife. There are stimulating essays on the Irish Parliamentary Party (IPP), the emergence of Sinn Féin, the role of women, the Irish diaspora, social life in Ireland and the games themselves – their progress and how they were reported. Important pieces on the development of Croke Park and the work of Secretary Luke O'Toole will help students of the period to understand the GAA and its role during these turbulent years. We are very appreciative of all the authors' scholarly work.

Cumann Lúthchleas Gael was born out of the emerging nationalist movement in Ireland. Along with the Gaelic League and various literary and language groups, the GAA was very much part of a movement that sought to preserve and promote distinctive Irish traditions, values and culture, including games. It is therefore no surprise that a great many GAA members were attracted to the emerging movement for Irish independence.

Many involved in the 1916 Rising, and significantly more of those who took part in the subsequent War of Independence, were GAA members. Research at local level in many counties identifies a crossover between membership of the local GAA team and of the local companies of Irish Volunteers. Éamon de Valera, Michael Collins, Arthur Griffith, Harry Boland and other revolutionary leaders frequently appear attending games in Croke Park in photographs of the period. Indeed, many significant Volunteer meetings were held under the old Hogan Stand. The role of the GAA specifically in the revolutionary period has never been fully explored, so this book will certainly help to address that lacuna.

Ireland and her people have developed from a complex history, and this publication has an inclusive approach. A great many GAA members fought in the First World War. More still remained deeply committed to the nationalist parliamentary tradition, and they all served their nation. It is fitting that this book explores all traditions and all human stories. Along with the sometimes forgotten role of women and our camogie clubs in the revolutionary years, the Irish diaspora are not forgotten, and this is to be applauded, as they have been a crucial element in the development of our country and of the GAA.

Le linn 2016 beidh muid mar Éireannaigh ag comóradh céad bliain ón Éirí Amach. Leis an fhoilseachán seo tá muid i gCumann Lúthchleas Gael ag cuidiú le clár comórtha céad bliain. Beidh seimineár staire á reachtáil againn fosta agus beidh clár cuimsitheach le hócaidí chomórtha á reachtáil ag ár Músaem. Tá coiste speisialta bunaithe againn agus beidh siad ag stiúriú ár gclár comórtha. Beidh comórtas do Chorn Domhanda CLG á reachtáil in Éirinn le linn 2016. Tiocfaidh na mílte Éireannaigh abhaile ó ghach áit ar domhan faoi choinne an chomórtais seo agus tiocfaidh méid mór daoine nach Éireannaigh iad ar chor ar bith, ach a bhfuil grá acu dár gcluichí.

I have no doubt that this publication will serve as a catalyst for further local research and study in clubs and counties. The commemoration of the 1916 Rising, and subsequent events, is a significant opportunity for both reflecting on the past and planning for the future. A key element in planning for the future is recognising where we have come from, then setting our sights on where we are going. With the publication of this book, I hope clubs and counties in Ireland and around the world will be motivated to further investigate events and stories in their own communities. The template and topics covered in this book are good models for further local research. It is the individual stories of men and women in our clubs and counties that will add greatly to the jigsaw of our knowledge of this period. I look forward to historical seminars and publications at county and club level. If this occurs, it is arguably the greatest contribution this book will have made to our understanding of this period of upheaval.

I hope this book finds a shelf in every school, every club and county office, and in many homes of Irishmen and Irishwomen. Brave and noble people from all backgrounds devoted their lives to establishing a better Ireland. They shared a vision of an outward-looking nation cherishing everyone equally. They respected all traditions, but held our own heritage, values and culture above others. The generation that formed the Ireland that emerged from the period 1913–23 deserves the focus and recognition this publication provides.

As President of the GAA, I warmly welcome the publication, congratulate the editor and authors, thank our publisher and warmly commend the book to you, the reader. The GAA has remained at the heart of Irish life. We are to be found in every parish in Ireland and a growing number of cities and countries worldwide. Our members are vibrant and engage in positive citizenship everywhere. This historical work, which tells the stories of where we have emerged from, will, I have no doubt, add confidence to the onward march of the GAA and the Irish nation.

Le bród agus gliondar croí, fáiltím roimh an leabhar suimiúl seo agus tá súil agam go mbainfidh sibh uilig lán taitneamh as. Tá áthas orm, mar Uachtarán, go bhfuil Cumann Lúthchleas Gael fós tógtha le scéal na tíre agus dílis fós do scéal na ndaoine a chuir ar an ród chun Náisiúnachais muid.

AOGÁN Ó FEARGHAIL

Uachtarán, Cumann Lúthchleas Gael

CHAPTER 1

Introduction

GEARÓID Ó TUATHAIGH

THE HISTORIOGRAPHY OF THE Irish revolutionary era has been transformed in recent decades. As with the developing historiography of any major historical event or episode, new sources, fresh growth areas of historical enquiry and changing perspectives have been the decisive factors in the transformation. In the case of Ireland, it might also be worth noting the remarkable increase since the 1970s in the number of professional historians conducting research and writing on modern Irish history. To have a sense of the magnitude of the change, one has only to compare what was available in 1966 (on the fiftieth anniversary of the 1916 Rising), in terms of a reading list of serious historical publications, with the daunting bibliography of important work that challenges contemporary students and general readers seeking to stay up to date with recent scholarship. And to scholarly publications one must add the improved access to primary sources facilitated by advancing technology and the growth (in output and public interest) in television documentary history.[1]

Much of the earlier historiography of the turbulent decade 1913–23 had, inevitably, been sharply partisan: oscillating between the valorising and the denunciatory, depending on the 'side' taken by the author. In the case of the nationalist accounts of the struggle for independence, memoirs by several of those who had participated in the events of the decade had their value (first-hand testimony of witnesses), but were frequently self-serving and lacked the documentary support that would have enabled their reliability to be checked. Contradictions, contested accounts and recriminations were predictable outcomes of the publication of some of these accounts of heroic service and famous actions; accounts that focused on the rebels of 1916, the flying columns and daring ambushes of the War of Independence, and the oppression and brutality inflicted on a supportive nationalist population by Crown forces.[2] There were exceptions, works that succeeded in striking a more reflective note, but they were few.[3]

Profiles of the executed leaders of the 1916 Rising (notably the virtual canonisation of Patrick Pearse) and writings on others who had 'died for Ireland', in combat, by execution or on hunger strike were overwhelmingly admiring, as indeed were the popular ballads that celebrated the lives and deeds of those who had 'fought for Irish freedom'. Little was written on the Civil War – certainly it did not feature in the 'official' history taught in schools.[4] However, popular memory was unforgiving in the parts of the country where the division was most poisonous, and the political rivalry between the two main parties in the Irish state was firmly anchored in the split on the Treaty of 1921 and on the Civil War that followed. But for several decades after 1922 there was broad consensus across the political establishment in the Irish state that the 1916 Rising and the War of Independence of 1919–21 constituted a heroic episode in Irish history and was a worthy 'foundation act' for a sovereign national state. The leaders of all the main political parties in the state competed in laying claim to the mantle of the 1916 martyrs: Labour had Connolly, and Cumann na nGaedheal, Sinn Féin and Fianna Fáil had strong personal as well as ideological pedigree on which to proclaim themselves the heirs of the revolutionary generation. There was no great rush, however, to claim the legacy of John Redmond. More remarkably, the massive Irish involvement in the First World War was gradually elided from official public acknowledgment in the independent Irish state, a process later described as an act of national amnesia[5]. It was commemorated by the British Legion, but was increasingly seen as outside – if not incompatible with – the dominant Irish historical narrative of unbroken resistance to British rule, culminating in the final heroic phase of 1916–23.[6] The contrast with the historiography of recent decades could not be greater.

. . .

The nature and extent of the changes that occurred in Ireland in the decade after 1913 have been a preoccupation of scholars for the past twenty or so years. Specifically, there is debate as to whether we are at all justified in speaking of an Irish 'revolution'. Some historians question the appropriateness of the adjective 'revolutionary' to characterise what actually changed in Ireland (and by what means) during the decade. Others contend that only the years after 1916 have valid claims to being described as a revolutionary interlude.[7] On the latter point, it is difficult to see how the 1916 Rising and the political-military conflict that followed it – with the War of Independence, Partition, the Civil War and the establishment of the Irish Free State – can be convincingly divorced from the crisis of constitutionalism and the rise of militias and militancy that accompanied the introduction of the third Home Rule bill (1912), the early mobilisation of the Ulster and later Irish Volunteers, and the establishment of the Irish Citizen Army as part of the intense class conflict in Dublin in 1913.

Nevertheless, one can understand the case made by those who point to the elements of continuity (as distinct from revolutionary 'rupture') between the Ireland awaiting limited Home Rule in 1912 and the Irish national state of the mid-1920s, with its bicameral parliamentary system on the British model (albeit with new nomenclature); its largely undisturbed judicial system (after the innovative Sinn Féin courts had been dropped); its generally cautious economic, financial and fiscal policies; and the continued dominance by established elites of most of the commercial, financial, professional and business heights of Irish society. The abolition of the hated Poor Law system, the introduction of an ambitious Gaelicisation programme in the education system and in branches of state administration, and the decision (after early uncertainty) to establish an unarmed police force, were probably the most radical actions taken by the new government of the Free State to mark the decisive change in character from the old British to the new native Irish state. Indeed, the case has been plausibly made that the thrust of the policies of the first governments of the Irish Free State merits the label 'counter-revolutionary'.[8]

However, perhaps the most radical new direction in recent decades of historical research on the revolutionary period has been the shift of focus from leadership rivalries and elite politics to the rank and file of movements and organisations, and to the wider associational life of the communities in which such organisations operated. This focus on narratives of 'history from below' reflected wider international currents of historical scholarship from the middle of the twentieth century. In the case of Ireland, the establishment of new historical societies and dedicated journals, first in Irish economic and social history and later in Irish labour history, testified to both the burgeoning numbers of professional researchers and to the shifting emphasis towards economic and social history.[9] For the revolutionary period, the 1960s saw the early signs of a changing historiography, with the publication of primary documents and a definite move towards reassessment (and, in various senses, revision) of hitherto dominant accounts and interpretations of, as well as verdicts on, events and key actors of the 'years of struggle'.[10] Some of the revisionist writing was intentionally iconoclastic, and as the conflict in Northern Ireland from the late 1960s raised a host of difficult issues (relating, for example, to the sanction provided by 1916 for the continuing use of force, the issue of majority–minority relations in a divided community, mandates and the rule of law), writings on the revolutionary decade 1913–23 were inevitably inflected by ideological and moral positions on the conflict in the North. Where earlier titles had saluted, without embarrassment, the heroism of the 'glorious years' of the independence struggle (1916–21), a 2012 collection of essays by young researchers gathers its findings, pointedly, under the title *Terror in Ireland.* [11]

But revisionist writings on the revolutionary era were not all driven or coloured by ideological considerations. New sources became available and, combined with new approaches drawing on comparisons with other countries, began to generate an impressive body of publications. In addition to the rich array of written sources, a growing gallery of photographic images of the period, together with contemporary newsreel material, further enhanced the historical record of the events of the revolutionary decade in Ireland and the experience of Irish people involved in the Great War. [12]

A particularly original aspect of the new directions in research emerged in substantial local studies – the forensic examination of the impact of the revolutionary decade on specific areas and local communities. Here the pioneering work was David Fitzpatrick's study (1977) of County Clare. [13] Later studies on other counties have been indebted to Fitzpatrick's industry and example, even where their findings differ from his in explaining how Sinn Féin came to replace the Irish Parliamentary Party (IPP) as the dominant voice of Irish nationalism in the years after 1917, and in their analysis of the relative significance of different groups and organisations (including the Gaelic League [14] and the GAA) in the reconfiguration of Irish nationalist leadership in these years. What is emerging is a more complex picture of the impact of successive phases of the revolutionary interlude of 1916–23 on different localities and communities. Close analysis of issues of social class, age, education, occupational profile, family tradition and strong bonding among cadres of young men has illuminated the importance of local realities and rivalries in determining the variable levels and intensity of political and military activity in different parts of the country and at different times during the years of conflict. [15]

Consistent with the widening of the arc of enquiry beyond the familiar leadership cohort of the revolutionary movements, and reflecting one of the most fruitful new directions in historical scholarship, the role of women in the revolutionary period has been reassessed in the past three decades in an impressive body of scholarly publications. This research constitutes a major act of recovery (in certain areas, discovery) of the experience of women in Ireland in the revolutionary era. This scholarship has investigated not only the leading role of women in the campaigns for such obvious women's issues as suffragism, but also the role of women across the broad spectrum of political and cultural activism – language, health, work and charity issues – in the late Victorian and Edwardian years. There have been studies of dedicated women's organisations (for example, Cumann na mBan) and a clutch of challenging biographies of women activists, as well as writings concerned with the involvement of women in a range of political and cultural movements cresting the revolutionary wave of change in Ireland in these years.[16]

A striking feature of much recent writing on the revolution by younger scholars has been the tendency to de-heroicise and render more complex and problematic the narrative of the military aspects – the violent dimension – of the struggle, notably in the years of the War of Independence and the Civil War. Dark deeds have been excavated and forensically examined, as well as – in some instances more emphatically than – the deeds of heroic sacrifice and resistance to the Goliath of the British military machine that had dominated earlier nationalist narratives. The human cost of the conflict – including the non-combatant, civilian victims – is a central preoccupation, even if, in comparative terms, the actual casualty count (fatalities and injuries) of Ireland's experience of military struggle and violence in the years 1916–23 is relatively low.[17] This new emphasis on the murkier aspects and general human cost of the revolutionary era has not been without controversy. Anxieties have arisen not only from contention and controversy regarding the use of problematic oral evidence from contemporary witnesses with an axe to grind, but also from an unease that the shadow of more recent violence in the Northern Ireland conflict lies too heavily across the moral and ideological positions from which the 1916–23 struggle is being reassessed.

If the recent historiography of the Irish independence struggle has generally darkened the roseate canvas of earlier accounts, the revival of scholarly research and writing, and of general public interest in, Ireland's role in the First World War (1914–18) has been marked, for the most part, by general empathy towards the motivation and idealism of those who joined the colours to fight in Flanders and along the fighting line, and by a strong sense of the tragedy and pathos of the horrific slaughter – death, maiming, an abiding legacy of trauma – as experienced by individual soldiers, their families and their local communities.[18]

Those seeking an understanding of the attitudes of the rank-and-file activists involved in different aspects of the military campaign for independence were dependent for many years on the published accounts and memoirs of a handful of local leaders, on occasional newspaper exchanges and controversies, and on the personal reminiscences transmitted orally – and frequently only to intimates – by veterans. A more concerted effort to collect testimony from veterans, initially in the form of newspaper articles, resulted in a series of 'fighting story' volumes in the late 1940s on the struggle for independence from 1916 to 1921 in counties Limerick, Kerry, Cork and Dublin.[19]

However, the major project for recording the testimony of rank-and-file participants was the setting up of the Bureau of Military History (BMH) in 1947. In the following decade the bureau collected statements from some 1,773 witnesses who were active in various aspects of the struggle for independence from the founding of the Irish Volunteers in November 1913 to the Truce in the Anglo-Irish War in July 1921 (the contentious episode of the Civil War was excluded). Remarkably, this huge body of primary source material (some 36,000 pages of evidence) was then locked away in 1959 and remained closed to researchers until 2003. Access to this invaluable evidence – allowing for the fact that it was committed to paper more than thirty years after the events being recounted – has transformed historical writing on the Irish revolution.[20]

Moreover, a still more abundant harvest is in prospect with the recent opening of the files of the Military Service Pensions Collection, the first tranche of which became accessible to researchers in 2014. This collection – comprising applications, with supporting documentation, made from the 1920s to the 1950s for military pensions relating to claimed active service (or compensation for losses suffered) in the years between 1916 and the end of the Civil War – amounts to almost 300,000 files. Clearly, our understanding of the mind, motivation, attitudes and actions of participants in the independence struggle (even if recounted in retrospect), will be immensely enriched when this new source material becomes fully available.[21] Already, however, the access to the BMH files enjoyed by researchers for more than a decade has had a significant impact on the emerging historiography of the revolutionary period. Virtually all of the more recent research-based publications on this period have made use of these files. New findings have already emerged; for example, Fearghal McGarry's research has revealed that many of the rank-and-file Volunteers who took part in the Rising did not have a precise version or definition of the 'republic' as the form of Irish freedom for which they had taken up arms. [22]

But, of course, those who were militarily active, in any way, during the independence struggle were a minority within their local communities: indeed, apart from the act of voting, those actively involved in political organisation were likewise a minority. What the majority thought of these stirring historical events, how their everyday lives were affected by them: these are questions that must also concern historians and that require attention to different areas of life and different kinds of evidence. The closer study in recent years of the plenitude of social, cultural and political varieties of civic activism in this period has revealed how porous were the boundaries between different national movements and projects, how miscellaneous and promiscuous were the enthusiasms of a wide range of people and groups of cultural evangelists. Of course, different enthusiasts were more fervent about certain projects than about others, and the surviving evidence is more abundant for some than for others. Vigorous debate and argument, and competing opinions relating to history and identity, language, literature and artistic standards, were the order of the day in the surge of late Victorian and Edwardian Irish revivalism. [23]

Political differences did not operate as impregnable barriers between participants in this broad movement of cultural and civic revivalism. In certain projects of social and political progress (the cooperative movement, arts and crafts, the women's rights movement), 'constructive' Irish unionists worked closely with nationalists of various stripes. Certainly, within the broad church of Irish nationalist sentiment, there were no impregnable barriers between separatists and Home Rulers, constitutionalists and physical-force nationalists, when it came to giving general support to such cultural causes as the Gaelic League. It is undeniable that the breach between the Redmondite mainstream and the clandestine republican separatists of the Irish Republican Brotherhood (IRB), on the issue of the participation of the Irish Volunteers in the Great War, was ultimately decisive in sharply dividing nationalist opinion in late summer 1914. And the later Rising of 1916 would further polarise political opinions in ways that affected a wide spectrum of cultural nationalist organisations and activities – including the Gaelic League. But, for all that, there remained a broad constituency of Irish nationalists, active in different areas of Irish national life, that resisted for as long as possible being driven into 'splits' or exclusive camps.

The GAA was, par excellence, the major national organisation that refused to split during the years of division and increased political polarisation after 1914. This was a more considerable achievement, perhaps, than is commonly recognised; it is also an achievement that requires some qualification. The various bans adopted by the GAA – against members playing foreign games, excluding from membership those serving the Crown in uniform, in the army and police – were inherently divisive, even if understandable in the circumstances of the time. However fervent the leadership cadre of the Association may have been in defending and implementing these bans, they were not universally approved of within the broad nationalist community. Indeed, even as the independence struggle intensified after the establishment of the Dáil and the outbreak of military action from January 1919, the extension of a ban on civil servants taking an oath of allegiance to the Crown as a condition of their employment caused division and difficulty within the GAA, as Mike Cronin's chapter in this volume indicates.

Furthermore, in so far as the eclipse of the Redmondite movement by the separatist Sinn Féin popular front after 1917 had a recognisable social-class dimension, this was also shadowed in sporting allegiances. The Catholic upper bourgeoisie, to a considerable extent, would continue to cleave to elite Catholic schools whose sporting traditions and ethos gave preference to the games of empire and in which Gaelic games would rarely become the main sports. Sporting allegiances of the urban working class would, likewise, be influenced by the legacy of the bans and the exclusivist strategy that underpinned them. Yet, even as the GAA generally moved into closer alignment with the strengthening separatist front of Sinn Féin after 1916, the Association was never 'captured' by any one political group and never sought to repel or expel more moderate nationalists of the Home Rule variety. Undeniably, in the aftermath of the 1916 Rising the GAA increasingly came to be classified and treated – by the British government and by others – as belonging to the camp of the subversive collectivity of Irish separatism advancing under the banner of Sinn Féin. If the GAA could not marshal the support of the entire national community in the promotion of its games, it remained committed to being a broad church. Remarkably, in the multiple schisms that opened up in Ireland in the decade after 1913 – notably in the face of Partition and a bitter Civil War – the GAA did not experience a split.

The continuing deployment of new evidence (diaries, letters, newly released official documentation) has contributed enormously to our awareness and understanding of the totality of the Irish experience of conflict, whether in the trenches and battlefields of the Great War or in the valleys, villages and streets of Ireland during the Anglo-Irish War and the Civil War. However, the interpretative framework within which new evidence is evaluated and deployed also demands attention. For example, it is understandable that there should be a strong public interest in exploring how the shift in the political mood in Ireland (from a predominantly Redmondite Home Rule disposition to a more assertively Sinn Féin disposition) or, more dramatically, how the actual fighting (attacks, ambushes, assassinations, arrests, curfews and reprisals) affected ordinary people going about their daily lives. In this context, there is particular value in considering, where the evidence allows, how those in uniform (policemen, soldiers, IRA Volunteers and Ulster loyalist militia groups) related to or were perceived by their local communities as the decade of revolution unfolded.[24] Close examination of key domains of social life – the routines and rituals of daily life – may facilitate such consideration: people's participation in religious worship, children's school attendance, adults doing their shopping at the local shops and, of course, people's participation in sports and leisure pursuits. Indeed, a major aspect of the associational culture of any community is the world of sport and leisure.

· · ·

Scholarly research and writing on sport has been a particularly rich seam of the new social history that has achieved a strong presence in the historiography of modern Irish history during the past thirty years. The growing interest of professional historians in the importance of sport in Ireland owed much to the advances in academic interest in Britain and in other countries in sport in the Victorian and Edwardian periods. The emergence of organised sport (with rules, regulations, clubs, competitions and discipline) was assessed in the context of key social and cultural structures and patterns of collective behaviour, with scholars increasingly concerned with issues of geography, social class and, more recently, gender, as determinants of participation (actively or as spectators) in various sports and leisure pursuits. The ideological dimensions of sport as character formation were scrutinised in the context of late-Victorian imperialism.[25]

Many of the questions and insights generated by this flowering of historical research in Britain had a relevance to Ireland that would engage the interest of a rising cohort of scholars. However, the particular circumstances of Ireland were inevitably reflected in the historiography of sport as an emerging branch of Irish social and cultural history. Thus in Ireland the establishment of organised sport and dedicated sports organisations in the late-nineteenth century was linked at key junctions with political developments, notably with the strong currents of political nationalism and with various strands of a cultural nationalist movement driven by anti-colonialist and nativist impulses. The new wave of sports history would engage these specific Irish themes within the wider framework of considering sport as part of the social history of a particular period and people. The role and influence of the GAA in Irish society would inevitably be a central concern of this emerging social history, which encompassed historical sociology and cultural geography as well as conventional documentary history.[26]

Earlier writings on the GAA and its activities had leaned heavily on compilations or on vividly evocative accounts of specific clubs, competitions, games and the heroic exploits of 'legends' of the games. These accounts – often undertaken as a labour of love by local journalists, teachers, priests and dedicated club officials – have an undeniable charm; many are indispensible repositories of information, and the best have an enduring value.[27] The new research-based publications – in many instances by scholars who combined rigorous research with a passionate interest in the games – began to become more prominent from the 1980s. There had been precursors: Ó Maolfabhail's examination of the origins of hurling appeared in 1973.[28] Marcus de Búrca's commissioned history of the GAA, published in 1980, was measured and reflected careful research.[29] Liam Ó Caithnia's richly documented and compendious accounts of the origins and pre-organisation history of hurling and football in Ireland did not receive the acknowledgment that the author's immense scholarship merited.[30] W. F. Mandle's challenging 1987 study examined the interplay between the GAA and the political currents of Irish nationalism.[31] As with the new wave of political history, respectful but well researched biographies of leading founders of the GAA aimed at setting a new standard. [32]

The emergence of a cohort of younger researchers soon began to register in academic writings on sport in Ireland in general and in specific studies of Gaelic games and the GAA. The Sports History Ireland Society, founded after an inaugural conference in Dublin in spring 2005, was a significant new departure. It promised from the outset that 'The new Society … will provide an ongoing forum for the discussion, encouragement and promotion of sports history in Ireland' and further declared that 'A key ambition of the Society is to establish a network of local historians across Ireland who are interested in working in sports history'. The Society has held annual conferences since its inception and interest in its work has grown steadily. Moreover, the penetration of sports history into established domains of social history is evident in the appearance of research findings and articles on Irish sports history in such academic journals as *Irish Economic and Social History*, as well as in international journals dedicated to publications in sports history.[33]

New sources – including the meticulous mining of local newspapers – and sharply focused local studies gradually began to fill out the history of sport in Ireland in a much more complex and multilayered narrative than had been previously available.[34] Research-based studies of a range of sporting codes and organisations became more numerous and permitted informed comparison and a confident overview of the place of sport in the wider narrative of Irish social and political history.[35] In the case of the GAA, the fruits of the new approaches being adopted and the advances being made were well represented in the 2009 collections of essays *The Gaelic Athletic Association 1884–2009*,[36] as well as in a growing body of monographs and articles, many by the authors of the chapters of this volume. Inevitably, the bar of scholarship set by the leading researchers has inspired the wider community of non-academic researchers in sports history to raise their game. The attention to preserving records and to general archival care has also improved. Here the GAA has adopted an enlightened approach, with Croke Park itself, through its Museum and Archive facility, setting the good example.

• • •

Commemorations, official or otherwise, may take many forms. They sometimes arouse controversy, usually because of the 'meaning' that is being attached to the event or episode being commemorated by those doing the commemorating. Because commemorations invariably meet the needs of the living rather than those of the dead (whose needs are past our knowing), they are frequently contentious. This is especially the case where the government of a state takes the leading role in shaping and staging a major historical commemoration. How the commemoration of key historical events can be safely aligned with the dominant state ideology, and how significant may be the dissenting voices challenging such alignment, are recurring aspects of such contention. This has been the case, to a greater or lesser extent, with certain key commemorations in Ireland: for example, the annual commemoration of the 'Twelfth', the bicentenary of the 1798 rebellion and the sesquicentenary of the Great Famine.[37] The anniversaries of the 1916 Rising and the public events commemorating that Rising have been the subject of intense scholarly reassessment in recent years.[38] Likewise, the manner in which the impact of the Great War on Ireland was commemorated (and for periods officially neglected) in independent Ireland has come in for reassessment as part of the events and publications marking the centenary of that war.[39]

While historians are not immune to the hazard of present-centred views of the past, their professional training requires and prompts them to subordinate these views to the surviving evidence about past events and to seek to explain historical events in terms of the ideas, attitudes and expectations of those who lived through these events, in so far as that surviving evidence allows us to do so. In short, what we owe to the past, more than anything else, is the obligation to study it with an open mind and to seek to understand the actors of earlier times in the context of their own time and with a scruple for the evidence that has survived.

It is this spirit that informs this volume. Its purpose is to contribute to an understanding of the decade of revolution in Ireland from 1913 to 1923, by viewing the events of that decade through the prism, as it were, of an organisation central to the associational culture of Ireland at the time. Three principal strands bind the collection: what was the role of the GAA (its leaders, players and units of organisation) in the main events of the revolutionary decade; what impact these seminal events had on the activities, organisation and operational effectiveness of the GAA as a sporting organisation; and what the 'internal' story of the GAA itself was during this fateful decade. It is hoped that the exploration of these themes by the authors will lead readers to an enhanced understanding of how a major voluntary body in Irish national life functioned in a decade of extraordinary disruption and conflict, and how even the most heightened ideological and political consciousness and commitment had to come to terms with the complex realities of everyday life and the needs of ordinary people. There is no single conclusion that can encapsulate the findings of these individual chapters. But the abiding sense of the collection as a whole is of the extraordinary high value that the national 'community' of the GAA – players, administrators and spectators – attached to the Gaelic games themselves. At a time of prolonged and divisive conflict in Ireland, with a rebellion against the established state (and security apparatus), the eclipse of a long-established nationalist Home Rule elite by a rising Sinn Féin collective, a guerrilla war followed by a bitter civil war, and the partition of the island of Ireland, the GAA did not split. It took the strain and trauma of the years of disruption, and it held together. Shrewd leadership played its part in this achievement. But the value that ordinary people attached to the games – as spectacle, as affirmation of local identity, as social event – is the key to understanding why the GAA held firm in a time of trial.

CHAPTER 2

The Triumph of Play

PAUL ROUSE

The 1903 All-Ireland football final between Kerry and London.

I N THE YEARS BEFORE 1916, Gaelic games enjoyed a period of spectacular growth at local and national level. This growth was rooted in the development of the GAA as a modern sporting organisation. In the organisation of its games, in the manner in which preparation for those games was conducted and in the playing of games, the GAA was at every level dedicated in the first instance – and usually in the last, also – to meeting the imperatives of modern sport. The story of Gaelic games in the years immediately before the 1916 Rising is, ultimately, the story of the triumph of play.

• • •

The impact of a new generation of GAA officials – men who rebuilt the Association in the first decade of the twentieth century after its almost fatal collapse in the 1890s – was profound. These men were nationalists; they believed in an independent Ireland, believed that the GAA should support the idea of Irish independence and introduced a series of rules that sought to promote an 'Irish Ireland'. Barriers were erected between the 'native games' of the GAA and 'foreign games' such as rugby and cricket. Between 1901 and 1905 the GAA at national level introduced a set of rules decreeing that anyone who played, promoted or attended foreign games (the listed foreign games were cricket, hockey, rugby and soccer) could not participate in the GAA. Later, it was added that any-one who was a member of the police or the British Army was prohibited from membership of the GAA. Further, no GAA club was allowed to organise any entertainment at which 'foreign dances' were permitted, and any GAA member who attended dances run by either the British security forces, or by foreign-games clubs, was liable to a suspension of two years.

A devotion to nationalism, though, is just one aspect of the story – an aspect that colours the history of these years, but that cannot be considered to define it. Alongside their avowed nationalism, this new generation of GAA officials was also entirely modern in how it conceived of sport. Almost to a man, they were young enough not to have known a time when sporting clubs and sporting organisations did not provide the framework for people to play sport. In terms of the GAA, this framework rested on the championships in both hurling and in Gaelic football run from 1887. The championships were open to all affiliated clubs, which would first compete in county-based competitions run by local county

The 1903 All-Ireland football final between Kerry and London in progress. The points posts, as seen, were removed in 1910 as part of a series of rules changes that helped popularise Gaelic games by 1913.

committees. The winners of each county championship then proceeded to represent that county in the All-Ireland championships. These two basic ideas – county championships between local clubs and national competition between competing counties – provided the structure that allowed for the GAA's long-term development. From the very first All-Ireland championships in 1887, a trend developed whereby the champion clubs of each county selected a number of players from other clubs to assist them in inter-county matches. Over time, more and more players were brought in to supplement the county champions. By the revolutionary decade, the idea of a county being represented by the best players from any club within its boundaries, rather than merely the champion club, was firmly established. It was a development that added greatly to the popular appeal of Gaelic games and by the revolutionary decade the GAA was established in every county in Ireland in a substantial way.

Gathering popularity was also rooted in improvements in the standards of play. During the 1890s and the early 1900s rule changes were introduced that opened out the play. Hurling and Gaelic football retained a devotion to physical combat, but became more accommodating of the idea of skilful play. This, in turn, drew larger crowds to matches. By 1915, Croke Park in Dublin was the established venue for the All-Ireland finals. This had only recently been confirmed. More than half of the first twenty years of finals were played outside Dublin. Some matches were held on

The 1903 All-Ireland football final between Kerry and London in progress.

private grounds; the 1901 and 1904 All-Ireland hurling finals were staged in a field on the farm of Maurice Davin, the first President of the GAA, in Carrick-on-Suir, County Tipperary. As the GAA grew in the early years of the twentieth century, it sought to develop its own ground and this led, eventually, to the purchase of Croke Park. This relatively small piece of land on Jones' Road on the north side of Dublin had been used for horse racing, athletics and soccer in the late nineteenth century. The GAA used it intermittently in the 1890s, but following the purchase of the land in 1908 by Frank Dinneen, journalist and former President of the GAA, it became synonymous with Gaelic games. Dinneen renovated both the sporting and spectating facilities at Jones' Road. The ground was purchased by the GAA in December 1913 as its national headquarters and renamed 'Croke Memorial Park'.[1] The growth of hurling and Gaelic football as major spectator sports by 1915 was confirmed by the development of Croke Park. As W. F. Mandle has noted, 'by 1912 crowds of between 12,000 and 20,000 were commonplace at finals.'[2] This emergence of a culture of attending events on a regular basis and in vast numbers transformed sport in the late nineteenth and early twentieth centuries.

The sustained growth of the GAA was mirrored by that of its great rivals, soccer and rugby. Take, for example, the manner in which the surge in crowds attending GAA matches was replicated at other sporting events. When Ireland played England in a rugby international in Cork in 1904, the attendance reached 12,000. The Irish Rugby Football Union (IRFU)

The 1903 All-Ireland football final in progress.

developed Lansdowne Road as a venue for international rugby, and regularly drew crowds of more than 10,000 to matches. Crowds attending soccer matches were also increasing during this period. In 1904 a crowd of 6,000 attended the Leinster Cup Final in Dublin. Attendances at soccer games in Dublin were much lower than those in Belfast, where up to 20,000 people were estimated to have attended a match between city rivals Linfield and Belfast Celtic. By the eve of the First World War, 21,000 people were attending the annual Irish Cup Final.[3]

Viewed in a particular light, the sustained, multilayered growth of the GAA appeared to offer a tremendous opportunity for nationalists within the Association. This was the case not least because the young men who togged out in ditches or took bicycles and trains to win matches were precisely the material of which revolutions are traditionally made. Could not this expansion of interest in Gaelic games be channelled to lend momentum to the cause of Irish nationalism? Certainly, the most outspoken of the new generation of GAA officials were zealous in their belief in the transformative power of the GAA and saw the Association as primarily engaged in a project of national liberation. In their mind, the GAA would sit beside the Gaelic League in an attempt to define a peculiar Irish identity. In certain clubs and counties, the zeal for radical nationalism revealed itself more clearly than in others. In Wexford, for example, men such as Seán Etchingham (who was a columnist on GAA matters for the *Enniscorthy Echo*), Seán O'Kennedy (an outstanding footballer for the New Ross Geraldines) and Enniscorthy men Pádraig Doyle and Frank Boggan attempted to push the GAA in Wexford towards a more radical nationalist position. They promoted not just Gaelic games, but also language revival through the Gaelic League and temperance through the County Wexford Temperance Council. At a meeting of the Enniscorthy-district GAA clubs in November 1912, for example, Frank Boggan and Pádraig Kehoe (for several years the leading official of the Red Rapparees club in Enniscorthy) argued passionately against the practice of GAA teams togging out in licensed premises. Boggan argued that 'no true Gael should touch intoxicating drink nor make a dressing room of a licensed premises.'[4] A local priest, Fr Murphy, told the members of the Gaelic League in Enniscorthy that they should be involved with Gaelic games and not with 'the games of the foreigner' and their 'athletic souperism'.[5] In an attempt to confront such 'souperism' on every front, the Enniscorthy Gaelic Athletic Tennis Club was established in 1914, and was a huge success in its first year. Although not officially a part of the GAA, members of the Association were its leading lights, including Michael de Lacey, a schoolteacher who fought in the 1916 Rising.[6]

The problem for those who wished the GAA to be more than a mere sporting organisation was that there were many members whose involvement was rooted in a love of sport and who conceived of the GAA only in terms of sporting engagement. The pragmatism involved in running a broad-based organisation ensured that the ambition of drawing a line between 'Irish Ireland' and 'West Britain' was no straightforward task. In 1912, for example, across the fields from Enniscorthy in Bunclody, the GAA club passed a vote of thanks to Robert Hall-Dare, the huntsman and British Army officer, for the use of a field for Gaelic games.[7] Across Ireland, there was a willingness to do business with those whom the GAA was supposed to oppose. As historian Tom Hunt has noted, the Castlepollard Hurling Club presented a special hurley to the Countess of Longford in 1906 'in consideration of her ladyship's thoughtfulness to the hurling club in erecting seats for their accommodation as well as leaving a field for their disposal all the year round.'[8]

Implementation of the ban rules was contentious. After all, their introduction did not enjoy unanimous support within the Association and there were almost annual attempts to have them weakened or removed. Policing such rules was difficult – if not impossible – and, in Enniscorthy, the foundation of the rugby club in November 1912 placed one more temptation in the path of Gaels. It was not one that could always be resisted. At least eight men from the Enniscorthy Volunteers GAA Club attended a rugby match in 1913 and were suspended. Indeed, the number of GAA men attending rugby matches was acknowledged to be large at the Annual Convention of the Wexford GAA. Such men were condemned for giving moral and financial support to foreign games.[9]

Even the clubs run by idealistic officials became tangled up in ban-related controversy, leaving the lingering suspicion that even apparent ideologues were prepared to sacrifice 'Irish Ireland' in order to win a match. Pádraig Kehoe's club was several times accused of transgressing the ban rules. The Bunclody team Slaney Rangers objected to the Red Rapparees' victory in the 1909 county final on the grounds that two of the team's players were members of the British Army.[10] Then, in 1912, after another Bunclody team, the Insurgents, had lost to the Red Rapparees in a junior football final, the Insurgents objected that a member of the winning team, James Quinn, was a British soldier. At a meeting to discuss the objection, Frank Boggan, as chairman, said that Quinn had been discharged from the army as he had joined when he was fifteen or sixteen years old and had now been bought out. The objection was defeated, yet Quinn's census return shows him as a reservist in the British Army.[11]

Worse was to follow when one of the star players of the Enniscorthy teams, which had won hurling and football championships since 1900, Aidan Connolly, turned to rugby. Connolly had won seven senior football championships, including captaining the Red Rapparees to victory in 1913. He had also won a senior hurling championship. Then, on St Stephen's Day 1913, Aidan Connolly played in the centre for Enniscorthy Rugby Club in a match against Lansdowne.[12] He was suspended from the GAA for 1914. When he sought readmittance, he was castigated by Seán Etchingham, and the two men had a vicious exchange in the newspapers. Connolly accused Etchingham of being a fraud, and was accused, in turn, of forsaking the GAA for rugby because he had been overlooked for the Wexford county team. Etchingham quoted to him the lines: 'He acted so oddly, we doubted his sanity. Till we discovered the cause was his vanity.'[13] Interestingly, Pádraig Kehoe, often so zealous in his promotion of the ban rules, had proposed the motion that Connolly should be readmitted. The fact that Connolly was vital to the success of the Red Rapparees club of which Kehoe was a leading administrator no doubt explained his actions.

The greatest testament to the triumph of play during the revolutionary years is the overwhelmingly banal nature of the minute books of the institutions that organised Gaelic games. Clubs, county committees, provincial councils and the GAA's Central Council worked to ensure that matches took place, that those matches took place in good order and that as many people as possible were able to spectate. This is not to suggest that the politics of war and revolution did not repeatedly impinge on the playing of the games. As other chapters in this book make clear, the operations of the GAA were shaped by the context of global and national conflict. Throughout these years, however, there lies evidence that the GAA was dominated by the imperative of organising sport and not by the impulses of those of its members who wished it to free Ireland.

This is evident in the fact that while many GAA members may have sympathised with the Volunteer movement after its establishment, others voiced their opposition to any formal link between it and the Association. A letter to *The Clare Champion* read: 'allow no politics in, our Association is in existence alone to foster Irish pastimes.'[14] GAA officials in Limerick refused applications by the Volunteers for pitches to use for drilling purposes, as it would be 'wiser to keep clear as an athletics body of the Volunteer controversy'.[15] Indeed, within a month of the Volunteers being founded the GAA had decided against any formal link, against officially advising members to join and against allowing the use of Croke Park for drilling purposes, as it would cut up the pitch.[16] And there is also widespread evidence that the activities of the GAA actually impeded those of the Volunteers. The *Limerick Leader* reported in April 1914 that 'the usual drill of the Limerick Corps of the Irish Volunteers will not take place on Sunday next owing to the fact that the 1st Round of the Thomond Feis Shield Hurling Tournament will be played that day'.[17] Emphasising the need to avoid overstating the relationship between the GAA and the Volunteer movement, William Murphy has written: 'there were countless ordinary members of the GAA, who chose the hurley rather than the rifle.'[18] Indeed, prominent Volunteer J. J. O'Connell later remarked: 'When a match conflicted with a parade or a field day, too often the parade or field day was put into the background … It was a fact that the Volunteers did not receive from the GAA the help they expected – nay to which later on they might fairly be considered entitled.'[19]

In essence, the GAA was consumed with sporting matters at every level. Examples of this abound: look, for instance, at the meetings of the Leinster Council in February, March and April 1915. The minutes reveal hours spent arranging fixtures, appointing referees, hearing appeals, reviewing objections, organising trains, paying expenses, passing motions of sympathy and settling border disagreements. The conduct of these meetings demonstrates a commitment to play that underlines precisely why the GAA proved so successful. There was also a commitment to integrity: a Wexford footballer who took a ball after a match in Waterford was declared suspended until he returned it to its rightful owner.[20]

The priorities of the GAA were fully revealed during 1916. Firstly, its response to the 1916 Rising was to deny involvement flatly. It issued a statement saying that all allegations 'that the Gaelic Athletic Association had been used in furtherance of the objectives of the Irish Volunteers are as untrue as they are unjust'.[21] Then, in the second half of 1916, the GAA sought to engage with the British authorities to safeguard the organisation's sporting operations. The first episode concerned the attempts of the British government to enforce an Entertainment Tax on sporting and other recreational bodies throughout the United Kingdom. As the relevant bill was being moved through the House of Commons, an amendment was introduced exempting any organisation founded 'with the object of reviving national pastimes'.[22] This amendment was introduced specifically in response to GAA efforts, through John O'Connor MP, to avoid payment of the tax.[23] Yet, as the legislation was passing onto the statute books, there were angry exchanges, with claims that special favour was being given to 'an organisation whose membership is open to men who are in open rebellion against this country and closed to all men who join His Majesty's Forces'.[24] The accusation was denied by the Chancellor, who intimated that it would be a matter for the Inland Revenue to decide if indeed the GAA warranted exemption.

While awaiting this decision, the Central Council of the GAA took the initiative and sent a deputation to General Sir John Maxwell in an attempt to secure GAA exclusion from taxation and to arrange for the provision of special trains to GAA matches. It speaks volumes for the priorities of the GAA that it should attend a meeting with Maxwell. After all, it was Maxwell who on Holy Thursday had been appointed Commander-in-Chief of the British Army in Ireland. Using extensive martial-law powers, he crushed the 1916 Rising. In its immediate aftermath, he was the chief architect of government policy and oversaw a series of courts martial that saw 171 prisoners tried and 90 death sentences imposed. Fifteen of those death sentences were carried out over ten days in May 1916. It was also Maxwell who had presided over the internment of more than 2,000 of the 3,500 men and women arrested after the Rising. Most of this number had no connection with the Rising and included hundreds of GAA members. And yet, the Central Council of the GAA was prepared to meet him – it is the ultimate proof of the triumph of play.

• • •

If, in its organisation of play, the GAA was in most respects a mirror of its rival associations, a similar claim can be made of its modernisation in terms of preparing for matches, which brought dramatic change to how players prepared for games. Training regimes stressed the importance of physical fitness, skill-based drills and practice games. The dramatic transformation in how teams prepared for matches was clearly influenced by professional sports, notably soccer. It was also made possible by an extraordinary financing operation, without which the new approach to preparing for matches could not have been undertaken. In essence, the preparations of successful inter-county teams as war raged in Europe and as Ireland moved towards rebellion confirmed the priorities of officials and of players.

When Clare won the 1914 All-Ireland hurling championship, they were reputed to have prepared better than any team in history. This revolution in preparation was rooted in past failure. In July 1914, the Clare county board issued an appeal for funds to help its team be 'properly trained and equipped', because 'we now find ourselves occupying a very insignificant position'.[25] The ambition was to ape what successful counties 'like Kilkenny, Kerry and others had done'.[26] As a means of fundraising, Clare chairman J. Shearin suggested organising some concerts throughout the county: 'Then they could get the players to Ennis to train.'[27] The Clare training fund – like the training funds in many counties – was well subscribed, with the GAA clubs, the general public and businesses all contributing.[28] As Clare progressed to the 1914 All-Ireland hurling final, they headed for a week's training in Lahinch and in Lisdoonvarna before all their championship matches, with Clare County Council, a local National Insurance inspector and a local doctor, Dr McDonagh, all giving use of their cars to convey the team.[29] Throughout the week before the 1914 All-Ireland final they stayed in the Temperance Hotel in Lisdoonvarna,[30] and among the exercises they undertook were running, walking, hurling and gymnastics, as well as receiving massages.[31] Each man was up at 7 a.m. for a 5-mile walk and was usually in bed by 10:30 p.m. to rest and recuperate.[32] The training was overseen by the trainer for the team, Jim O'Hehir[33] (father of the renowned Gaelic games commentator Mícheál Ó hEithir); he instructed that no drinking or smoking should take place, for even 'smoking of any kind is almost as harmful as drinking'.[34] There were strong rumours, however, that some members of the team had occasionally indulged in 'certain spa water brewed on the banks of the Laney'.[35] There were other distractions, too, as a letter writer to *The Clare Champion* wrote: 'Our boys being so good looking, and of course such heroes in the eyes of the fair sex, attract quite a number of fair ladies to the vicinity of their training quarters every evening and as a result we have some "tripping in the light fantastic toe" which is all very well in its own way, taken in moderation … but it should not come off every night and on no account be prolonged after ten.'[36]

Collective training was looked upon in disgust by some. Kerry's Dick Fitzgerald, the great star of Gaelic games in that era, lamented the increased emphasis towards professionalism, arguing that players were being 'unfairly forced to go into special training'.[37] *The Clare Champion* reported that some people in Clare were unhappy with the approach being taken by their players and were 'linking this as professionalism and are reluctant to donate'.[38] Most usually, however, the attitude was that adopted by a letter writer to *The Clare Champion*: 'If we want to win we have to go through with it.'[39] And win they did: Clare hammered Laois in the 1914 All-Ireland hurling final by a scoreline of 5–1 to 1–0.[40]

Before Laois lost the 1914 All-Ireland final to Clare, an anonymous letter had been sent to the secretary of the Laois county committee which implored the players to 'leave off work and train. If ye do not, ye will be not only beaten, but disgraced.'[41] As it was, the Laois team had actually trained together for the 1914 final every day for three weeks at the county ground in Maryborough, using money raised by the county committee. The Annual Convention of the Laois county committee had agreed that 'a fund be established to defray the expenses of training the Senior inter-county teams' and that that fund would be administered by a specially elected committee.[42] A circular was issued by this Training Fund Sub-Committee in August 1914:

> The preparation of the team for the Leinster Championship was carried out at the personal expense of the members of the team. This

has involved a serious drain on the means of the men, who, in many cases, had to provide substitutes to fill their places of employment during frequent special practices.

It would be too much to expect them to bear the expenses of the extra special course of training which it will be necessary for them to undergo for the playing of the All-Ireland Final. The team is mainly composed of working men to whom the loss of a day's wages is a serious matter, and they have, as stated, already sacrificed a considerable sum in this way.[43]

Contributions were received from GAA clubs across Queen's County, from the Tullamore club in neighbouring King's County (as Offaly was then called), from local businesses and from natives of Queen's County who were living across Ireland, particularly in Dublin.[44] To raise money, the committee had printed collecting cards where people could write in their subscriptions; receipt cards were printed for those who subscribed.[45] Some who were solicited for money wrote back in apology that they could not raise more. M. Collier wrote from 22 Árd Righ Road, Arbour Hill, Dublin that he had thought he would 'do better, but things are so upset with the war it's hard to get money'. Others were unable to raise any money. The GAA club in Monadrehid, Queen's County, wrote that they could raise nothing because they 'had to pay one of our players 10s a week last month that got hurt'.[46] The generosity of other donors was rooted in self-interest, for instance a donation from the management of Wynn's Hotel on Lower Abbey Street in Dublin, which was already established as a venue for GAA players and supporters. It was in Wynn's Hotel that the Laois players ate breakfast and dinner on the day of big matches in Dublin.[47]

The amount of money required was made clear in a letter from the captain of the Laois team, Bob O'Keeffe, a schoolteacher based in Borris-in-Ossory.[48] In a letter to John J. Higgins, secretary of the Laois county committee, O'Keeffe stressed the need to pay for substitute workers for members of the hurling team who would miss work. O'Keeffe wrote: 'We will have to pay a man to take Jim Hyland's place also. He is a coach-builder. He is working at home but they are a very large family and they could not very well afford to have Jim away so long.' The money raised by the training fund covered not just the cost of providing employers with substitutes for the hurlers, but also the cost of train fares and meals for

Gaelic Athletic Association.

——(o)——

Leix and Ossory Training Fund.

——(o)——

MARYBOROUGH,

AUGUST 29, 1914.

DEAR SIR,—

As you are, no doubt, aware, the Senior Hurling Team representing our County have, by their recent victory over the County Kilkeeny Team (All-Ireland Champions) become Champions of Leinster for 1914. They are accordingly in the All-Ireland Final.

It is, therefore, of the utmost importance that our men should be thoroughly trained for the All-Ireland contest, and to ensure this it has been decided by the County Committee of the G.A.A. to appeal to all lovers of our great National game for contributions in aid of a Training Fund.

The preparation of the team for the Leinster Championship was carried out at the personal expense of the members of the team. This has involved a serious drain on the means of the men, who, in many cases, had to provide substitutes to fill their places of employment during frequent special practices.

It would be too much to expect them to bear the expenses of the extra special course of training which it will be necessary for them to undergo for the playing of the All-Ireland Final. The team is mainly composed of working men to whom the loss of a day's wages is a serious matter, and they have, as stated, already sacrificed a considerable sum in this way.

Now that they are setting themselves out to win for our County the much-coveted honour of the Championship of All-Ireland, the County Committee appeal with confidence to the Gaels of Leix and Ossory and to all friends of the Gaelic Athletic movement to contribute to the Training Fund.

Subscriptions will be received by the undersigned, or by the Secretary of your local Gaelic Athletic Club, and, as our men will go into training about the 10th September, 1914, Subscribers would greatly help matters by handing in Subscriptions before that date. **UP LEIX !**

Yours faithfully,

Rev. J. J. KEARNEY, C.C., Maryborough, President.

JAMES MILLER, Mountrath, Trustee.

JOHN J. HIGGINS, Maryboro', and M. J. SHERIDAN, Maryboro', Hon. Secs. to Training Fund.

Funding appeal launched by the Laois county board to pay the wages of the hurling team who would be absent from work due to the extra training involved in preparing for the 1914 All-Ireland hurling final.

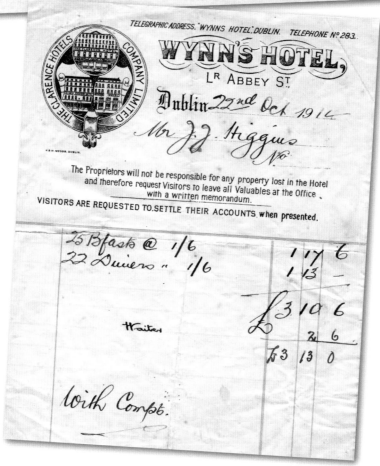

GAELIC ATHLETIC ASSOCIATION.

LEIX AND OSSORY TRAINING FUND.

Maryborough,
September 1914.

The Training Fund Sub-Committee beg to acknowledge
with thanks, subscription amounting to £ : :
received from .... on September
.... 1914.

} Hon. Secs.

TELEGRAPHIC ADDRESS, 'WYNNS HOTEL, DUBLIN. TELEPHONE Nº 283.

WYNN'S HOTEL,
Lʀ ABBEY Sᵀ.

Dublin 22ⁿᵈ Oct 1914

Mr J. J. Higgins
Nº

The Proprietors will not be responsible for any property lost in the Hotel
and therefore request Visitors to leave all Valuables at the Office
with a written memorandum.
VISITORS ARE REQUESTED TO SETTLE THEIR ACCOUNTS when presented.

25 Bfasts @ 1/6   1 17 6
22 Dinners " 1/6   1 13 -
                     £3 10 6
Waiters   2 6
                     £3 13 0

With Compⁱˢ.

TOP: Leix and Ossory Training Fund receipt card.

BELOW: Invoice from Wynn's Hotel for the 1914 Laois hurling team. Wynn's Hotel
had earlier contributed to the Laois and Ossory Training Fund.

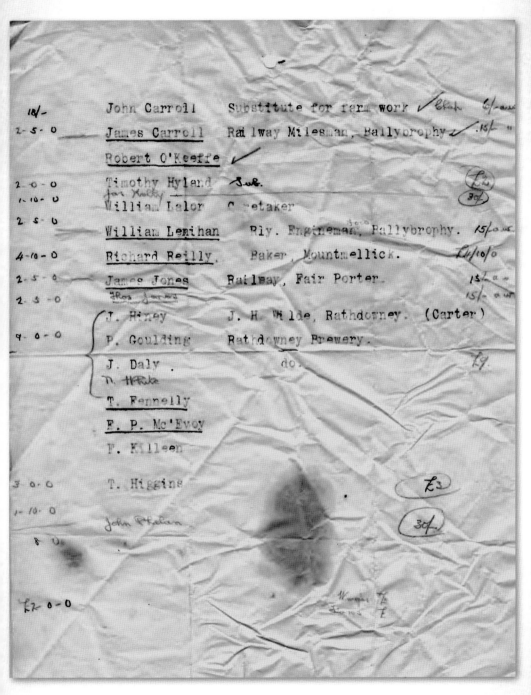

18/-	John Carroll	Substitute for farm work
2-5-0	James Carroll	Railway Milesman, Ballybrophy
	Robert O'Keeffe	
2-0-0	Timothy Hyland	Sub.
1-10-0	for Nally William Lalor	Caretaker
2-5-0	William Lenihan	Rly. Engineman, Ballybrophy. 15/-
4-10-0	Richard Reilly	Baker, Mountmellick. £4/10/0
2-5-0	James Jones	Railway, Fair Porter. 15/-
2-3-0	Thos Jones	15/-
	J. Hiney	J. H. Wilde, Rathdowney. (Carter)
4-0-0	P. Goulding	Rathdowney Brewery.
	J. Daly	do. £9
	D. HPRike	
	T. Fennelly	
	F. P. Mc'Evoy	
	F. Killeen	
3-0-0	T. Higgins	£3
1-10-0	John Phelan	3d.
8-0		
£2-0-0		

Team sheet listing the occupations of some of the 1914 Laois hurling team.

the players. O'Keeffe mentioned the costs of covering the expenses of the players, and understood that 'this will involve a big sum of money and it will go near the £80 that I had in my head all along. I would like, if at all possible to have every man free of any loss whatever.'[49] Replacing E. P. McEvoy, a farmer's son, cost 10s per week for three weeks for a substitute worker and 1s 3d per day for sixteen days to cover the cost of his train fare from Abbeyleix to Maryborough.[50] Laois was fortunate to be a crossing point for trains and, indeed, several of the hurlers were employed on the railways. Others worked as bakers, brewers and caretakers, in addition to a strong farming contingent.[51] The team had many other ancillary expenses. A dozen sliotars (hurling balls) were bought from Quigley's of Barrow Street in Dublin. They were 'made of the best Irish hide' and cost a total of 30s.[52] Another dozen sliotars were bought from James Lalor of Three Castles in Kilkenny, while his brother, Martin Lalor, was asked to make hurleys for the players, at a cost of 3s 6d apiece.[53]

All the efforts of Laois in 1914 had ended in defeat, but 1915 offered a new opportunity. At that point the club that won a county's internal championship had the right to pick the captain of the county team, and that captain had the deciding say on who should constitute the team. Across the GAA, picking a county team was a delicate balance between avoiding alienating the members of your own club and picking the best players from the other clubs in the county. Indeed, it was a consistent challenge to get the best players from all the clubs to represent the county. This was partly because of the tensions that emerged between clubs that competed against each other in the local championship.[54] In Laois there was a new and intense rivalry between Ballygeeghan and Kilcotton.[55] There were also problems between other clubs. After one club match, O'Keeffe had written that 'when we have cleared up [doctors'] fees for the battle with Clonaslee we may go bankrupt'.[56] For 1915, Ballygeeghan – the new Laois champions – nominated their best player, John Finlay, to captain Laois. Finlay (possibly under advice or pressure from the county committee) determined on picking the best hurlers in the county, and the eventual team that represented Laois contained just six Ballygeeghan players.[57]

Finlay was also progressive in his approach to training. He believed that the team's preparations for the 1914 final had actually been hindered by the fact that they had trained too hard and that 'some of the players on the team were not able to stand the training they went through'.[58] Early in 1915 he wrote to his players advising that they do their utmost to win the Laois championship and then the All-Ireland: 'This we can do by acquiring the staying powers and speed necessary for a player to do his best for the whole of an hour's hard play.' He advised that players initially go on long, slow runs, reaching a distance of 3 miles. They should then start to build sprints of up to 50 yards into these runs.[59]

It should be noted that players in this era were also expected to train on their own. One of the stars of the Cork team was Larry Flaherty, who had won an All-Ireland as far back as 1903. Flaherty had learned hurling ('as many') by playing the game as a boy, using a sycamore branch and a can. As an adult, he developed a training regime that saw him train on a hill behind his house in Douglas, commencing at 5:30 a.m. He followed a regime of jumps, as well as tying a 6-lb weight to his hurley before working on his swing. (Flaherty lived into his nineties and later commented on watching hurling on television in the 1970s: 'To be honest, I don't like watching fellows doing things which I sometimes feel I could still do better myself.')[60]

After Laois duly beat Kilkenny and then Dublin to retain the Leinster championship by the end of August 1915, preparations to win the All-Ireland final were properly put in train. Money was raised through renewed appeals to supporters, and was used to fund a refined training regime, with elaborate drills for the players to follow during practice. Copies survive of practice drills for catching, dribbling, striking, sideline pucks, free pucks and fighting for possession. In the drill that worked on fighting for possession, it was proposed to send a ball a short distance ahead of two players who would then fight for it 'somewhat like two dogs for a hare'.[61] In the two weeks before the final, the Laois players came together to train three times a week, for two hours on each occasion. To do this, some had to secure permission from their employers to leave work at 2 p.m. in order to be in Maryborough to train before the light faded.[62]

A significant input into the training was made by Fr J. J. Kearney, chairman of the Laois county committee and President of the Maryborough Hurling Club. In the weeks before the final he wrote to the players stressing the importance of speed and intensity: 'There will be no time for fancy play or raising the ball in an All-Ireland final. Men should practise striking ground balls when running at top speed.'[63] Kearney – in tandem with other members of the county committee – believed that the team needed external expertise if it was to win an All-Ireland.[64] They approached the great Kilkenny hurler Dick 'Drug' Walsh to take charge.

The 1915 Laois hurling team, winners of the All-Ireland hurling final.

Walsh knew all about winning championships. He had recently retired, having won seven All-Ireland medals, three of them as captain.

Walsh was approached and duly agreed. He did some work with the team, including bringing Kilkenny hurlers in sidecars to Maryborough to play practice matches on three successive Sundays.[65] Illness then prevented Walsh from attending training for several days, though he was

ELAND CHAMPIONS 1915.

in Croke Park for match day.[66] By then, the players had been given a type-written document: 'Notes for players previous to match'. This reiterated all the work that had been done in training, and stressed the importance of moving the ball quickly and playing unselfishly. It concluded: 'The team possessing the greater SPEED AND DASH will win.'[67] And win is what Laois did: by 6–2 to 4–1. The revolution in preparation had worked, and it was now clear to all that winning an All-Ireland championship required a level of training that had not previously been contemplated.

. . .

Refined preparation changed the nature of matches. By 1912, Gaelic football and hurling matches were more open and more skilful than had previously been the case. In the 1880s, the first matches played by the hurlers and footballers of the GAA were raw and often fierce. Style, skill and open play drew favourable comment, but what enthralled most was – as Michael Cusack called it – 'men lovingly at war'. Teams drove at each other as they sought to get the ball along the ground towards the opposition goal. A glue of players, with arms and legs stuck in every direction, rumbled around the field. Along the fringes, the weaker and quicker players waited for the ball to come close to them. Scores were a rarity, but this was not necessarily a cause of lament amidst the blood and thunder of battle.[68]

The initial rules for hurling and football had been framed by Maurice Davin, the GAA's first president, and for the most part, were somewhat vague, amounting to little more than guiding principles of play. This suited players who relished physical battle. It says much for the intense nature of the play that, when Callan played a team from Kilkenny city in the first ever game of Gaelic football in February 1885, the match ended in a scoreless draw.[69] Controversy also surrounded the GAA's first rules for hurling. Turning age-old pastimes into modern sport involved distilling tradition and a certain element of compromise. When the men of Meelick, County Galway, saw the new rules of hurling, they were not impressed. One of their number – who signed his name as 'Old Hurler' – wrote to the *Western News* in Ballinasloe saying that this new game was only 'a slight improvement on those effeminate games, croquet and lawn tennis'. The 'Old Hurler' concluded by defending the traditional hurling rules of east Galway, saying that 'nothing vicious or unchristian is tolerated amongst them'.[70]

Within the framework of local and national championship, GAA teams who aspired to success refined the way the games were played. 'Kick and rush' became 'catch and kick', and a series of rule changes – in particular, reducing team sizes from twenty-one players to seventeen and then to fifteen, standardising the size of the ball, allowing substitutes, introducing linesmen and revising the scoring system – helped to enhance the games. It became easier to move the ball faster into open spaces and the quality of games improved. Gaelic sport retained its devotion to physical combat, but became more accommodating of the idea of skilful play. This was confirmed in 1914 by Dick Fitzgerald, captain of the Kerry team, who published a book called *How to Play Gaelic Football*. This book stressed that Gaelic football needed to be seen as 'scientific' and skills-based.[71] Fitzgerald was clear that no other football game could match Gaelic football. The fact that there were no offside or knock-on rules, he wrote, left it free of the 'artificiality' of soccer or rugby.[72] The great 'genius' of the game, however, was its ability to prize combination team play and still leave room for displays of individual brilliance.[73]

The GAA's propagandists repeatedly stressed the courage and discipline of the men in its ranks. P. J. Devlin – writing as 'Celt' in his book *Our Native Games* – acknowledged that early matches had been more than a little tempestuous, but that all was now well: 'There was a bitterness in early championship contests that arose from traditional encounters, and too often bad-blood was aroused and lamentable incidents occurred. Familiarity with competition helped to obliterate these unhappy tendencies, and the sprit of mutual emulation which the Gaelic Athletic Association has come to promote soon effected a wonderful change for the better.'[74] His words echoed those of Fr James B. Dollard, who wrote in 1907 of the manner in which 'brawls and fights' had disappeared from the GAA: 'it is understood that common sense and moderation are to be practised.'[75] There was more than a minor element of wishful thinking in this. The capacity of GAA matches to descend into a certain anarchy may have been diminished, but it was nonetheless real. This was true for club matches, but also for inter-county ones. When Cork played Limerick in the semi-final of the Munster senior hurling championship in July 1915, *The Freeman's Journal* was moved to lament the 'regrettable incidents at Thurles'.[76] Some 14,000 people had come to Thurles for what promised to be a tremendous contest. Within four minutes of the throw-in, however, two players – as the referee put it in his match report – 'came to blows. Excited by the fight, some spectators ran in from the sideline and the endlines. Peace came relatively quickly and stewards were clearing the field, when a player and a spectator renewed combat. More joined in and all attempts to clear the pitch proved futile.' The referee, ultimately, decided to declare the match abandoned.[77] The GAA had modernised, its players trained as never before, the organisation of matches was entirely in keeping with the modes of the era, but primal passions are not easily dispelled.

Ultimately, the very expansion of the GAA in the years before 1916 had left it *less* likely to adopt a radical nationalist position. Too many of its members were interested in the Association only (or almost only) for its sports and not for its wider cultural or political ambitions for things to be otherwise. Even the adoption of a radical nationalist position by some within its leadership cadre could never be translated into action across the broad membership of an Association where winning and watching matches was what inspired most. Within the leadership itself, the demands of running a thriving sporting organisation saw officials consumed with arranging fixtures, booking trains, appointing referees, responding to appeals and objections, managing finances, and all the unforeseen issues that arise whenever people attempt to organise anything together.

CHAPTER 3

Croke Park

PÁRAIC DUFFY and GEARÓID Ó TUATHAIGH

Éamon de Valera throwing in the ball to start the 6 April 1919 Gaelic football match between Wexford and Tipperary in Croke Park, in aid of the Irish Republican Prisoners' Dependants Fund.

I N THE HISTORY OF the Croke Park stadium, the decade 1913–23 is of pivotal importance. The decisions that led to the GAA acquiring the ground upon which today's world-class facility stands all date from this period, as do the circumstances in which the stadium acquired its name, and the horrific event that would lead to the naming of the Hogan Stand. This chapter will consider, in the wider historical context of Ireland itself, the immediate circumstances and the key decisions, personalities and events which justify our identifying the decade 1913–23 as a vital period in the history of the GAA's (and Ireland's) principal stadium.

• • •

Dublin in 1913 was a city of conflict. The bitter labour dispute between Larkin's trade union and the Dublin employers, led by the formidable Catholic businessman William Martin Murphy, had divided the city. The labour dispute (whatever the immediate causes, or the role of strong, forceful personalities in prolonging it) reflected deeper, underlying social problems, notably those of housing, health and poverty, which afflicted the poor who lived within the old core areas – lying between the canals – of Dublin city.[1]

Former aristocratic districts such as Gardiner Street and Summerhill had become abandoned by the urban elites, while the better-off middle classes increasingly moved out to salubrious suburbs, such as Pembroke and Rathmines and, in time (by the later nineteenth century), to Clontarf. As one commentator has concluded, 'From here the better-off were spared the smells and dirt of the old city, the sight of its beggars and homeless, the dangers of contagion, but could still travel in by tram or train to avail themselves fully of all that the city offered in terms of commerce and culture.'[2]

As the upper classes and more prosperous middle classes moved out from the old large mansions in the city, these once elegant houses had increasingly become congested, poorly maintained and chronically sub-divided tenements, frequently run by exploitative or indifferent landlords. These slums – heavily concentrated in the inner city and the old squares on both sides of the river – were notorious, occupying an unenviable position near the top of the European table for urban deprivation and squalor. At the turn of the century, the death rate for the Dublin city area was 33.6

per 1,000 people; in London, it was under 20 per 1,000. The principal cause of this shocking death rate was the prevalence of consumption (tuberculosis), especially among young adults, and was inextricably linked to the congestion and inferior housing of the poor. By the first decade of the new century, it was acknowledged by all informed commentators that any serious strategy for reducing or eliminating the scourge of the disease would have to be linked to slum clearance and the provision of healthy housing for the working classes and the unemployed poor.

So great was the scandal of poor housing that in 1913 the Local Government Board launched a comprehensive investigation into housing conditions in Dublin. The report, completed in 1914, confirmed that the squalor in which thousands were living (especially but not exclusively in single-room accommodation in tenements) was the cause of multiple health hazards. The photographic record that accompanied the report shocked and shamed many who had not up to then been forced to confront the issue.[3]

It would be misleading, however, to reduce the story of life in Dublin of this period to the experience of the poor who lived in the dire conditions of the inner-city tenements. Citizens of all social classes had leisure interests. Those who could afford to do so could travel by train and tram – and, increasingly from the early twentieth century, by bicycle – to and from the fashionable shopping streets, or to attend the growing number of cinemas in the city area. And the middle classes (for the most part) could afford the fees to join sports and leisure clubs. In addition, certain trades or firms provided some facilities for their own members.

There was also an array of outdoor leisure pursuits that attracted, as participants or spectators, a much wider public. These included athletic contests and varieties of football that had become increasingly organised and better administered by the late nineteenth century. At the centre of Dublin's outdoor leisure and sporting life were the games of the GAA.

The GAA had suffered serious disruption, indeed decline, in the early 1890s, for which political factionalism in the wake of the Parnell split provides only part of the explanation. An unsettled period of administrative direction, at both central and local levels, combined with the indifferent application of rules and discipline, were also contributory factors.[4] However, by the close of the decade there were signs of recovery, and in the first decade of the new century there was unmistakable evidence of growth and expansion in all major areas of the Association's activities.

The main factors contributing to this revival and expansion are by now well understood. They included the emergence of a new cohort of gifted players and effective referees and officials; a long period of stable, confident and coherent administration from 1901, coinciding with the election of James Nowlan as President and of Luke O'Toole as Secretary; a close alignment of the Association (and its leadership at national and local levels) with a more assertive and broad-based nationalist sentiment, in both cultural and political life; better and more representative attendance at Annual Conventions; the establishment of Provincial Councils;[5] the promotion of the main games in schools; the inauguration of inter-varsity competitions in hurling and football; and the establishment of a special new game for women – *camógaíocht.*[6]

A feature of this recovery and expansion was the emerging importance of Dublin to the administration and vitality of the Association. From 1904 the Association had its administrative headquarters on O'Connell Street in Dublin; from 1909 the Annual Convention was held in Dublin; and a reduced (but more efficient) Central Council met regularly in Dublin. Most significant, however, was the evidence that, for major games, large crowds could be attracted to a Dublin venue. In late 1912 the All-Ireland football final between Antrim and Louth attracted 18,000 to Dublin, while, a few weeks later, 20,000 attended the hurling final. This evidence of growing support for the games left the Association's finances in a healthy state by 1913.[7] But, for O'Toole and the Central Council, it lent urgency to the quest to find a suitable ground for the Association in Dublin, a need that the Central Council had identified from as early as 1906.

By the early twentieth century Dublin GAA clubs were using about a dozen grounds around the city. But from the late 1890s many major games were played at Maurice Butterly's City and Suburban Racecourse on Jones' Road, just beyond the North Circular Road. The value of a ground accessible by transport coming to the city from around the country was demonstrated in the summer of 1913 when the long-awaited football final of the Croke Memorial Tournament between Kerry and Louth drew 25,000 spectators to a drawn game and 35,000 to the replay. It is estimated that 20,000 people travelled to Dublin in special-excursion trains, and temporary stands were erected in the stadium. Clearly, the time had come for the GAA in Dublin to address the issue of a suitable headquarter ground.[8] O'Toole and the Central Council were presented with an offer by a dedicated GAA man, whose name is little known today, even to GAA people – Frank Brazil Dinneen.

. . .

Frank Brazil Dinneen, from whom the GAA purchased the City and Suburban Racecourse on Jones' Road in 1913.

Limerick native Frank Brazil Dinneen (1863–1916) was a noted athlete in his youth.[9] His participation in the early athletics competitions of the GAA was the prelude to a life-long commitment to the Association. A period as a leading official in his native Limerick was followed by his active membership of the Central Council, even as he continued to administer competitions and act as handicapper for athletic contests under the Association's auspices. Dinneen was elected Vice-President of the GAA in 1892, President of the GAA three years later in 1895 and in 1898 became, for a short period, Secretary of the GAA. His terms of office in these various positions were marked by some impressive administrative and financial advances.

But Dinneen also aroused controversy. His strong republican political leanings, together with claims that his own business interests were not always sufficiently distinguished from the financial affairs of the Association, caused disquiet and drew strong criticism from certain quarters. Dinneen resigned as Secretary in 1901, to be followed by the long tenure as Secretary of Luke O'Toole – generally acknowledged as the first 'full-time' administrator of the Association. However, Dinneen continued to assist the Association in different capacities (notably in athletics and in negotiations with the government), as well as being an active journalist covering GAA activities, up until his sudden death in April 1916.

Arguably the most crucial legacy left by Dinneen to the GAA originated in his 1908 purchase from the Butterly family, for £3,250, of the City and Suburban Racecourse on Jones' Road, Dublin. The ground had been used for a variety of sporting activities since the 1870s, but had become seriously run-down in the interval between Maurice Butterly's death in 1905 and Dinneen's purchase of the ground from the family three years later.[10] While it is generally accepted that Dinneen had the interests of the GAA in mind in taking his initiative, the purchase was a commercial transaction, and Dinneen naturally required a return, not least as he spent further money in improving the venue by adding terracing and improving the playing surface. The GAA regularly availed of the ground, paying a fee of £10 per event. However, financial pressures obliged Dinneen to sell about 4 acres of the original 14-acre site to Belvedere College (for £1,090). Even after this transaction, the financial demands of running the ground continued to present difficulties for Dinneen.

Fate decreed that, in 1913, two priorities of the GAA converged. The Association had committed itself to commemorating its founding patron, Archbishop of Cashel, Dr Thomas Croke, in a suitable manner. Following a decision at the Annual Convention of 1911, a Croke Memorial Tournament was organised, with the bulk of the proceeds destined for the Croke Memorial Fund. Matches were held during the next two years. A dedicated group in Tipperary was active in offering advice on the form of the proposed memorial. At the same time, the Central Council, seeing a strong decade-long growth in attendances at major games, and now with a more active fixtures list, keenly felt the need for a suitable ground of its own in the country's capital.

At the Quarterly Meeting of the Central Council on 6 July 1913 there was a discussion on the form that the memorial to Dr Croke might take. It was proposed that '… a ground be purchased out of the funds of the Croke Memorial, the ground to be known as Croke Park'.[11] The proposal was not voted on, but a subcommittee was established to consult with the Tipperary people on the issue. At a Special Meeting of the Central Council on 27 July 1913, the Association's Secretary, Luke O'Toole, reported that he had consulted with the Tipperary group and that they (particularly the priests) favoured a statue of Croke in Thurles. There was a further

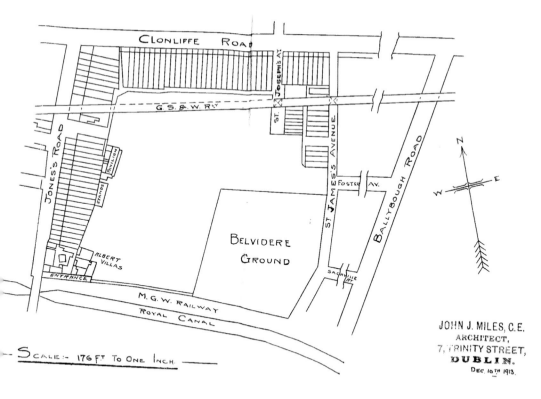

Map of the land purchased by the GAA in 1913.

suggestion that a portion of the fund also be used for a community hall in Thurles, on condition that it be known as Dr Croke Hall. Crucially, however, the meeting adopted a proposal that '... the remainder of the fund be devoted to the purchasing of a ground in Dublin to be called Croke Memorial Park Ground [sic]'.[12]

Luke O'Toole moved quickly on the issue of the acquisition of a suitable ground. At a Special Meeting of the Central Council on 17 August 1913, 'The secretary reported that Mssrs Hogan, Crowe and himself had visited several grounds around Dublin as directed at the last meeting, but they could only recommend two sites as suitable, Jones's Road and Elm Park, Merrion.' The Jones' Road site comprised 9¼ acres and included two houses (Albert Villas). It was decided that all members of the Central Council should visit Elm Park to assess that ground as an option before any final decision was reached.[13] Discussions had commenced with Dinneen on terms for the acquisition of the Jones' Road site, and on 7 September a further Special Meeting of the Central Council heard that Dinneen was seeking £3,625 for the ground. Support for the Elm Park option was not lacking – Dinneen was not universally popular.[14] But, finally, at the Quarterly Meeting of the Central Council on 4 October 1913, it was agreed (on a tight vote of eight to seven) to make Dinneen an offer of £3,500 for the Jones' Road ground. It would prove a historic decision.[15] The transaction was completed before the end of the year.

The purchase of the Jones' Road ground – and its renaming as Croke Park – marked the beginning of an evolution in which the newly acquired national venue for the Association's major games became incrementally the headquarters for its administration. Indeed, as early as 1 November 1913, a note appended to the minutes of a Special Meeting of the Central Council registered the appointment of Luke O'Toole as 'Secretary to Central Council and Manager of Croke Park at £75 per annum'.[16] In early January 1914 it was agreed that one of the two houses on the site acquired from Dinneen should 'be given to the Secretary at a nominal rent'.[17] It was also agreed that rooms attached to the pavilion be fitted out for meetings and that a Grounds Sub-Committee be established for dealing with Croke Park. A dedicated company was incorporated with responsibility for running Croke Park.

Thereafter, the management and development of the ground became an important aspect of the administration of the Association as a whole. (The issue of the Croke Memorial in Tipperary, notably its funding and precise location, would continue to demand attention, and it would be 1920 before the statue was finally erected.)[18] As early as June 1914, funds were deployed in erecting an enhanced wall along part of the perimeter of the ground.[19] The greater significance of the stadium in the affairs of the Association is evident in the increasing use of the office at Croke Park for meetings and in the fact that, by 1916, the 'Croke Park accounts were given separately' to the Annual Convention held in City Hall in Dublin.[20]

The naming of the new stadium was significant. In honouring a revered name from the foundation of the Association, the title disarmed some of the criticism from those who had wanted the Central Council's disbursement of the funds from the Croke Memorial Tournament to be directed exclusively to the Tipperary memorial. The Association's foresight in purchasing the Jones' Road ground was rewarded, as the acquisition of a national stadium had immediate benefits for the GAA: Croke Park at once consolidated, and became a visible symbol of, its growing

The Archbishop Croke memorial statue in Thurles, County Tipperary.

significance as a national institution in the general associational culture of early-twentieth-century Ireland. The advantageous location and ease of accessibility of Croke Park had been clear for some time. The further advantages (operational and, over time, financial) of having the administrative headquarters of the GAA housed on the site of the new national stadium were also grasped from the outset, as the arrangements for O'Toole's residence and the refurbishment of meeting rooms indicate. The medium- and long-term development potential of the Jones' Road site, so close to the city centre, was also promising.

The prestige of a central venue in Dublin for a national organisation growing in popularity had, already in 1913, been acknowledged by mainstream nationalist political leaders: both John Redmond and John Dillon (neither previously known as informed or enthusiastic followers of Gaelic games) had turned up at major games in Jones' Road in that year.[21] Political leaders of nationalist Ireland deemed it appropriate – even advantageous – to be present at major GAA games; by 1914 'Croke Park' was a venue that confirmed and enhanced the profile of leading political figures. The Nowlan-O'Toole leadership – though their own political leanings were towards more advanced nationalism – was careful to keep Croke Park 'open' for the broad swathe of nationalist Ireland prepared to support the Association's aims and games.

From the outbreak of the Great War through to the end of the Civil War, all aspects of Irish social life, including sport and leisure, suffered ongoing and, sometimes, severe disruption. The GAA was not immune to the turmoil; from the end of 1913 the lure of volunteering drew attention away from participation in sports. The outbreak of war in the summer of 1914 was followed by the autumn split in the Irish Volunteers (between the majority who stayed loyal to Redmond and the minority who rejected his advice to join the army and fight in Flanders), the first of a succession of splits within nationalist Ireland that posed challenges for the avowedly 'inclusive' GAA. The determination to stay 'open' and to avoid taking sides was evident in the decision not to allow Croke Park to be used for the drilling of volunteers. The officials of the Association – including O'Toole and Nowlan – were personally in the Sinn Féin/Irish Volunteers camp, but the Association would strive not to take a divisive position. Even when the GAA was condemned in the British denunciation of nationalist organisations blamed for the 1916 Rising, the Association reiterated its non-political and non-sectarian character.[22]

However, in the aftermath of the Rising, as British government measures – the imposition of the Entertainment Tax; the curtailment of public assembly without a licence; the curtailment of rail travel, which seriously affected excursions to games in Croke Park – harassed nationalist Ireland and polarised public opinion, the GAA moved away from the Irish Parliamentary Party and closer to the emerging Sinn Féin popular front. This reflected the shift in political sentiment within the wider nationalist community. While there was a police presence outside the main entrance to Croke Park on 4 August 1918 – 'Gaelic Sunday', the day on which the GAA organised Gaelic matches across the country in defiance of the laws forbidding them – the scheduled games went ahead, before 'a very large gathering of spectators' and with 'no interference whatever with the progress of the contests'.[23] Electioneering in late 1918 seriously disrupted fixtures, but games resumed and attendances returned during 1919, with benefit matches for the Irish Republican Prisoners' Dependants Fund (IRPDF) attracting crowds, including the new political leaders of Dáil Éireann.[24]

Practical concerns were often as pressing as matters of high policy. At the Annual Convention in 1916 the following motion was passed: 'That no trotting competitions be permitted in Croke Park for at least a week before inter-provincial ties and that no horses be allowed at any time on the playing pitch'.[25] In subsequent years pitch maintenance remained a priority. Thus, in early January 1920, a meeting of the Grounds Sub-Committee sanctioned a sum of £130 for the re-sodding of the playing pitch during the month of February (during which all matches would be suspended), and a later meeting added 'levelling' to the pitch improvements to be undertaken.[26]

Financial constraints were a constant pressure, forcing temporary interruptions of labour employed on the ground during spring 1917.[27] Nevertheless, despite the disruption to fixtures and finances caused by the turbulence of the war and the aftermath of the 1916 Rising, the ambitions to develop the stadium were never abandoned. A Special Meeting of the Central Council on 11 October 1919 heard a report from the Grounds Sub-Committee 'regarding the contemplated improvements at Croke Park'. The report was adopted unanimously and action was determined on specific recommendations, including a decision that 'Belvedere College be approached with the view of purchasing of a small piece of their enclosure adjoining the grounds so as to increase and continue the high bank for the full distance running alongside the playing pitch'.[28] The Belvedere College land would feature in successive plans for the further development of Croke Park for many years.

Despite the many demands on the Association's funds, the Central Council had the foresight to set aside money for development works and repairs at Croke Park. In October 1919, for example, it was agreed that a sum of £3,000 be earmarked and lodged in the bank 'under the name of Croke Park Repairs Committee'.[29] Before the end of that year the Grounds Sub-Committee had met again to discuss the selection of architects and contractors for the proposed developments at Croke Park.[30] The confidence in the future role of the stadium was further reflected in the decision of the Annual Convention in 1920 that all future All-Ireland finals be played in Croke Park.

Inevitably, the disruptions caused by the War of Independence and the Civil War would lead to delays and difficulties in embarking on large-scale developments. As the War of Independence became more intense, games came to a virtual standstill in the period from spring to autumn 1920. It was an attempt to kick-start games after these disruptions that led to one of the darkest episodes in the history of the Association and of Croke Park – Bloody Sunday.[31]

A challenge game between Tipperary and Dublin was fixed for Croke Park for Sunday, 21 November 1920. On the morning of that day, a counter-espionage unit under the direction of Michael Collins had ruthlessly executed fourteen suspected British intelligence officers in various locations in Dublin. As news of the killings spread, senior officers of the GAA had anxieties about proceeding with the game before eventually deciding that it should go ahead. A crowd just short of 10,000 turned up. In his history of the Association, Marcus de Búrca recounted the details of the grim afternoon:

Around 3 p.m. … a British plane flew over and emitted a red signal-flare. Immediately Black-and-Tans began to climb over the walls at each end of the ground, some using ladders. At once a withering fire was directed straight into the crowd, first from small arms and then from machine-guns hastily set on the ground just inside the main entrance. After about ten minutes an RIC officer advanced across the pitch, announcing a proposed search of spectators. An initial stampede resulted; most of the crowd was detained and it was some hours before the search was concluded. After the shooting and subsequent stampede, thirteen people lay dead around the ground; close on 100 were injured.[32]

Among the dead were the Tipperary player Michael Hogan and three young Dublin boys, aged ten, eleven and fourteen.

Remembrance of this terrible act of reprisal would find tangible form in Croke Park itself: Michael Hogan is honoured to this day in the name of one of the main stands in the stadium. The horrific event strengthened the bond between the GAA and the government of Dáil Éireann, an attachment that went beyond mere sentiment and sympathy, as the Dáil moved to assist the GAA in the financial difficulties with which it was beset. These stemmed from the loss of revenue due to cancellation of fixtures, but were exacerbated by the fact that the development works sanctioned in 1919 (now well advanced) were not yet paid for. In January 1921 the Dáil sanctioned a loan to the GAA on favourable terms, and also cleared its debt, which represented a major relief, not least for those awaiting payment for works carried out in Croke Park.[33]

Continuing disruption to games occurred in the first half of 1921, though activity was maintained in Dublin and parts of Leinster. Understandably, there was anxiety among the public about attending games in Croke Park, for fear it would again suffer the wrath of the Crown forces. However, with the Truce in July 1921, a kind of normality returned: fixtures and attendances increased and Croke Park had a particularly busy schedule of games.[34] It was to be a brief recovery, as the outbreak of the Civil War brought a halt to games in the summer of 1922.

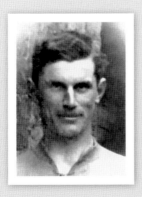

Tipperary player Michael Hogan, who was killed on Bloody Sunday, Croke Park, 21 November 1920.

Croke Park the day after Bloody Sunday.

Discussions between the GAA and the government of *Saorstát Éireann* on the refurbishment of the stadium, in preparation for the revival of the Tailteann Games being contemplated by the government, had encouraged the GAA to embark on further major improvements (and expenditure). But the government grant fell short of what was required, and by the end of 1922, with games at a virtual standstill and gate revenue drying up, the contractors had to agree to be paid by instalments. Though the end of the Civil War was followed by a resumption of games, the overhang of debt presented difficulties for a number of years thereafter.

Yet, it is striking that, notwithstanding the huge disruptions of the years of the War of Independence and the Civil War, the Central Council, at O'Toole's prompting, never lost sight of the need to continue to develop Croke Park. Thus, in July 1922, contractors were finally agreed for the works sanctioned. The award and the execution of these contracts were sensitive matters at a time of heightened political consciousness, as the new Irish state struggled to establish itself. For example, the desirability of using Irish raw materials in the upcoming works on Croke Park was actively debated; it was 'decided that in the absence of Irish cement to have the best Portland cement used'. Moreover, when the issue of the use of a cement mixer was discussed, there was a preference expressed for the use of direct labour (in the interests, one assumes, of providing employment).[35] In late 1922 (as noted above), the Central Council sought the best possible terms for spreading out the payments to the contractors involved in constructing 'the new stands'.[36]

The constant attention to the playing surface and the ambitious development plans indicate that the spectacle of the games at Croke Park was being considered in terms of both the playing conditions and the spectator facilities. Practical issues were sometimes deeply sensitive, especially during the Civil War. For example, the Central Council, responding to complaints from some patrons, decided in March 1923 that allowing collections (for various causes) within the ground was an intrusion on the comfort of spectators and that it should no longer be permitted.[37] It is not difficult to appreciate the political sensitivity of seemingly practical decisions of this kind.

By the summer of 1923, with the ending of the Civil War, a long period of political and social upheaval in Ireland marked by conflict and disruption in the ordinary lives of citizens had been brought to a close. The disruptive impact of this upheaval was more keenly felt in some parts of the country than in others, but the countrywide organisation that the GAA had become by 1923 could not but feel the impact of the conflict. Dublin, certainly, in the previous ten turbulent years, had experienced more than its quota of conflict, casualties, destruction of property and dislocation of social life.

But the GAA had emerged from the upheaval with its organisational structure intact, and, in the aftermath of the Civil War, its clubs, games and competitions would prove vital sites of bonding and healing in communities that had been riven by civil strife. Croke Park was undergoing major redevelopment and would be a worthy site for the Tailteann Games of 1924, the ambitious sporting gathering to which the new *Saorstát* looked to offer an appropriate expression of a renewal of the nation's ancient prowess. The Jones' Road ground – acquired fortunately, one might say, through the happy coincidence of Luke O'Toole's opportunism and ambition for a major GAA ground in Dublin and Frank Brazil Dinneen's foresight, financial stresses and lifelong commitment to the GAA – had become a national stadium.

• • •

In the second decade of the twenty-first century, the GAA is an indispensable forum for the expression of Irish national life, and Croke Park is a national stadium of international distinction. One may claim justifiably that the revolutionary decade of 1913 to 1923 can be considered a seminal decade in laying the foundations for this rise to eminence. The place that Croke Park came to occupy in the imagination and affections of Irish people in the century after 1913 is truly remarkable. The colloquial references to 'Croker' are revealing. Running out onto the pitch on All-Ireland final day is the ambition of players in every county and becomes the treasured memory of those fortunate enough to realise that ambition. In the decades after partition in 1920, visits to Croke Park had a special significance for teams and supporters from the counties in Northern Ireland, who otherwise felt cut off from the life of the national community. In more recent years Croke Park has been the site of multiple acts of historical reconciliation, in ways that go beyond its primary role as a world-class stadium. Any attempt to understand or explain the exceptional role of this stadium as a unique historical reference in modern Ireland must inevitably return to the events of the decade of revolution.

CHAPTER 4

Luke O'Toole:
Servant of the GAA

CORMAC MOORE

Luke O'Toole, Secretary
of the GAA, 1901–29.

LUKE O'TOOLE'S TIME AS Secretary of the GAA, between 1901 and 1929, witnessed sweeping changes for the Association and for the country as a whole. Ireland transformed fundamentally in this period, with the GAA and some of its key personnel involved in many of those seismic shifts. Married with the political changes affecting Ireland were the changes within the GAA, many of them spearheaded by O'Toole – the first person to hold the role of Secretary on a full-time basis. O'Toole was a deeply committed Irish nationalist, but a servant to the GAA first. Throughout his time as Secretary, particularly during the revolutionary years from 1913 to 1923, O'Toole played a delicate juggling act of safeguarding the progress of the GAA while remaining committed to Ireland's march towards independence. This chapter will explore how O'Toole, aided by others on the GAA's Central Council, managed to achieve this. Sometimes he was forced to choose one cause over the other – with the GAA invariably the cause to which he demonstrated the greatest commitment.

Luke O'Toole was born in Ballycumber, Tinahely, County Wicklow in 1873. Having attended the local national school, he went to a secondary school in Dublin. In his early twenties O'Toole joined the Benburb Gaelic Football Club in Donnybrook. He earned his living through the ownership of two newspaper shops near his residence at Mount Pleasant Square, but he became immersed in the administration of the GAA almost from the moment he settled in Dublin. He became club delegate to the Dublin county committee in 1899, and quickly became identified with the younger 'reformers' within the Association. He advanced rapidly, and at the Annual Convention in Thurles in 1901 he was elected Secretary of the GAA. Clearly, there was a mood for reform and renewal.[1]

∙ ∙ ∙

The Annual Convention of 1901 proved to be one of the most eventful meetings of the GAA, with the election of James Nowlan as President and Luke O'Toole as Secretary. At that meeting it was also agreed to clear all debts and to revise the constitution of the Association – an Association that was almost defunct at the time.[2] O'Toole defeated GAA founder and first Secretary, Michael Cusack, by nineteen votes to seventeen. Writing fifteen years later, Thomas F. O'Sullivan, a key participant in the GAA at that time, commented on the importance of the meeting:

> The foundation of the Association as we know it today – a well-officered, intelligently-governed, and wisely directed national organisation with large resources at its command – was laid in 1901 … there was a large accession of young men to the governing bodies of the organisation, and their ability, earnestness, enthusiasm, and patriotism raised the whole character of the movement within a few short years.[3]

Not only would the new officers bring renewed energy and vigour to the GAA, they also moved it towards a more nationalistic path. Nowlan had served on the Supreme Council of the IRB, an outlawed organisation committed to the removal of British rule by forceful means.[4] The Royal Irish Constabulary (RIC) believed O'Toole was also in the IRB; it was claimed he attended IRB meetings with Nowlan in 1901.[5] It was also reported that O'Toole was Ireland's representative for Clan na Gael, the Irish-American organisation also committed to armed resistance to British rule in Ireland. W. F. Mandle remarked that O'Toole, at the 1902 Annual Convention (held in January 1903),

> reported on the Clan na Gael's plans for the GAA. The Americans wanted 'Every Gael in Ireland ready for the fray' and to that end proposed to the full convention what had apparently been discussed at a secret IRB meeting the previous day, namely the re-organisation of the leaders of the GAA in each county in circles of six, a structure that would have duplicated that of the IRB itself.[6]

A clear manifestation of the GAA's commitment to separatist nationalism in the early 1900s was the reintroduction of the lapsed bans on foreign games and the policing and military forces of Britain. On the same day Nowlan and O'Toole were elected in 1901, the ban on foreign games was reintroduced, and was made binding in 1905. Vigilant committees were sanctioned in 1902 to monitor GAA members' adherence to the ban rules. RIC and other military personnel were banned in 1906. Jail wardens were added to the list in 1909 and in 1911 GAA members were prohibited from attending dances or other forms of entertainment organised by the

RIC or British soldiers.[7] O'Toole was a keen advocate of the ban rules. Commenting in 1921 on Irishmen playing rugby, he remarked, 'it was only the Seonín spirit that tried to ape everything English that could ever draw any man of Irish blood to the games of the foreigner'.[8]

Once elected Secretary, O'Toole, as the chief administrator of the Association, tasked himself with the rejuvenation of the GAA, particularly in areas where it was weak and disorganised. Along with people like well-known Limerick-born referee, Michael Crowe, he visited many parts of the country looking to revive the Association.[9] He oversaw the setting up of the Ulster Provincial Council, the last provincial council to be established, in 1903 and he was the key instigator in inaugurating Gaelic games competitions abroad.[10] Reminiscing in 1914 on the progress the GAA made under O'Toole and Nowlan, Crowe remarked:

> I propose to show the legacies they were left in the shape of several hundreds of pounds on the wrong side; Championships in arrears by many years, and credit exhausted – gone, to all appearances, and never to return … they have honestly laboured for the betterment of the Association, quietly, without hope of reward, and with black despair staring them in the face. Few Gaels of the present day have ever heard that at the commencement of the period to which I am referring a motion was actually tabled to wind up the Association … It is sufficient for us of the present to know that the patriotism and indomitable spirit of a small number of men saved the situation.[11]

The first ten years of O'Toole's term were impressive. The GAA procured an office for the first time in 1904, at 68 Upper O'Connell Street, Dublin. The Association's finances improved considerably in that period, too. The GAA had been in debt by £800 in 1901, but by 1910 it was a profitable body.[12] O'Toole also pushed for an official newspaper of the Association, overseeing the publication of *The Gaelic Athletic Annual and County Directory* in 1907, followed by *The Gaelic Athlete* in 1912.[13] Placing the GAA on a solid footing would prove vital as Ireland plunged from one political crisis to another from 1912 onwards, affecting every Irish person and organisation in the process.

• • •

At the 1911 Annual Convention a motion from Dublin county board was passed moving the Association further away from politics by the prohibition of the naming of clubs after living people. Clubs and members of the Association were also disallowed from speaking at political meetings or demonstrations with their connection to the GAA being highlighted by the press.[14] The following years would see this rule breached regularly, including by O'Toole, who spoke at the inaugural meeting of the Irish Volunteers in November 1913.

The year 1913 was a momentous one for the GAA and O'Toole, with the purchase of Croke Park and with it the appointment of O'Toole as ground manager of the stadium on a salary of £75 per annum.[15] The GAA was able to afford Croke Park due to the holding of the Croke Memorial Tournament in honour of the founding patron of the Association, Archbishop of Cashel, Dr Thomas Croke, which made a profit of over £1,872.[16] It did lead to an acrimonious dispute with the Tipperary county board, which wanted all of the profits from the tournament devoted solely to a memorial in Croke's honour in Tipperary, with the county board at one point threatening legal action.[17] O'Toole also came in for criticism from many quarters for receiving a bonus of £100 for organising the tournament, which was seen as extravagant by many. One commentator lamented the anomaly of the amateur status of the players being 'so strictly insisted upon' while 'certain officials can get paid nice fat sums from time to time'.[18] O'Toole countered that he was entitled to a 10 per cent commission on all gates – a commission he did not accept for the Croke Memorial Tournament and that would have entitled him to close to £300.[19] He had even offered to buy gold medals out of his own funds earlier in the year for the winning teams of the tournament, a gesture seen as too generous by the Central Council.[20]

O'Toole was not impervious to reproach from others for delays in replying to letters from different county boards.[21] J. J. Walsh, chairman of the Cork county board and regular critic of the Central Council, put down a motion to have O'Toole's salary reduced by 25 per cent in 1912 for 'dilatory methods of answering correspondence', claiming the Cork county board had to write several times to him before receiving a reply, a claim vehemently refuted by O'Toole.[22] O'Toole was rebuked the same year by Sinn Féin for inviting the Lord Mayor of Dublin, Lorcan Sherlock – a member of the Irish Parliamentary Party (IPP) – to the All-Ireland finals.[23] Although a Sinn Féin sympathiser, O'Toole, with the support of the Central Council, refused to alter his policy, believing in the importance of the support of leading parliamentary figures to promote the GAA.[24] Invitations to Sherlock were stopped the following year, however, after the Lord Mayor accepted the honorary presidency of a soccer body, the Leinster Football Association.[25]

O'Toole did publicly support a body that initially did not have the backing of the IPP and its leader John Redmond – namely, the Irish Volunteers.[26] The Irish Volunteers, established in late 1913 at the prompting of Eoin MacNeill, was Irish nationalism's response to the Ulster Volunteers. Speakers at the inaugural meeting held at the Rotunda Ice Rink in Dublin on 25 November included MacNeill, Patrick Pearse, Tom Kettle (who had previously played on the same Gaelic football team as O'Toole and would die on the battlefront in the First World War[27]), Peadar Macken, Michael Davitt (son of the Land League founder), Tom Kelly and O'Toole, who, in a brief statement, 'appealed to all Irishmen to join the organisation'.[28] Nowlan, the GAA President, followed up by saying GAA members should join and 'learn to shoot straight'.[29] However, when the fledgling organisation asked for the GAA's permission to use Croke Park for drilling purposes a month later, the request was turned down. At the same meeting it was agreed that GAA members wishing to join the Volunteers 'were quite free to follow their own inclinations in the matter, and it was not for the Council to advise them for or against'.[30]

Although no official support was forthcoming from the GAA, many county boards were instrumental in setting up branches of the Irish Volunteers in their areas[31] and Robert Page, a member of the provisional committee of the Irish Volunteers, was allowed to give a promotional speech at the GAA Annual Convention of 1914.[32] Many of the GAA's decisions over the coming ten years would mirror its approach in its involvement with the Irish Volunteers – cautious support for political events as long as the GAA would not suffer any major consequences. Up until 1914, the GAA actively supported most strands of Irish nationalism, including bodies such as the IPP, the Gaelic League, the Ancient Order of Hibernians, the IRB and trade unionists.[33] It was rarely forced to choose one strand over the other. It did receive some criticism for its failure to act on its commitment to hold a tournament in aid of the Wolfe Tone Committee, an IRB front. Although the tournament was approved in September 1913,[34] O'Toole delayed in seeing it realised. It took the Leinster Council, not the Central Council, to see it finally commence in the early part of 1915.[35]

GAELIC ATHLETIC ASSOCIATION, LIMITED.

NOTICE is hereby given, that an Extraordinary General Meeting of the Gaelic Athletic Association, Limited, will be held at Wynn's Hotel, Lower Abbey Street, Dublin, on Saturday, the 19th day of December, 1914, at 8 o'clock p.m., when the subjoined resolutions will be proposed as extraordinary resolutions :—

RESOLUTIONS.

1. That, in pursuance of the objects stated in the Memorandum of Association, the property, assets, debts, liabilities, and undertaking of the Gaelic Athletic Association and the Trustees thereof be acquired and taken over by the Gaelic Athletic Association, Limited, and that the said Gaelic Athletic Association, Limited, shall indemnify and keep indemnified the said Gaelic Athletic Association and the Trustees or any of them against said debts and liabilities.

2. That the Central Council of the Association are hereby instructed to execute and do all deeds and things necessary to carry the foregoing resolution into effect.

3. That the existing Rules of the Gaelic Athletic Association shall continue to apply, as far as applicable, to the Gaelic Athletic Association, Limited, until the Annual General Meeting, to be held in the year 1915.

" That, as the Gaelic Athletic Association is the largest and best organised body of its kind in the world, and as its constitution is National in the truest sense, and as we consider the present situation to be of the greatest concern to the Irish Nation, we, the Kerry County Committee, request the Central Council to summon immediately a Convention of the Association for the purpose (1) of amending the conditions of the Association so as to allow of the affiliation of Rifle Clubs in the same manner as Hurling and Football Clubs as now affiliated and (2) of promoting Inter-Club, Inter-County, Inter-Provincial and All-Ireland Championships in Rifle Shooting. And that copies of this Resolution be forwarded to the Secretary of the Association and the Secretaries of each Provincial Council and County Committee."

Proposed by Michael Griffin, Seconded by J. M. Collins.

JAMES McDONNELL, Hon. Secretary, Kerry County Committee.

AND NOTICE is hereby given that at said Meeting the subjoined Resolution will be proposed as an extraordinary Resolution.

AND NOTICE is hereby also given that a further Extraordinary General Meeting of the Company will be held on the 16th day of January, 1915, at the same time and place, for the purpose of receiving a Report of the proceedings at the above-mentioned Meeting, and of confirming (if thought fit) as a Special Resolution the subjoined resolution.

RESOLUTION.

1. The following words shall be added to Article 5 at the end thereof :—" The members of the Central Council and the Athletic Council for the time being and one delegate from each Province, as determined by the Association, to be elected by the registered Athletes and Cyclists of said Province, shall also be members of the Association." The following words shall be inserted in Article 7 after the end of the first sentence :—" The delegates from Provinces as provided in Article 5 shall also be elected before the Annual General Meeting, and remain members for a period of twelve months, unless re-elected. The members of the Central Council and Athletic Council shall be members of the Association from the termination of an Annual General Meeting to the termination of the next Annual General Meeting."

By Order,
LUKE J. O'TOOLE,
Secretary.

Croke Park, Jones' Road,
December, 1914.

Agenda for the 19 December 1914 meeting of the GAA, at which the Kerry county board proposed allowing the affiliation of rifle clubs, in the same manner as hurling and football clubs.

Prior to the First World War, membership of the GAA and the Irish Volunteers was not seen as a commitment to radical separatism.[36] The split in the Irish Volunteers in 1914 – with the many who answered John Redmond's call to help the British Army on the front forming the National Volunteers – also saw a split in the GAA ranks.[37] Laois county board even proposed the following motion for the 1915 Annual Convention: 'That volunteering in the army for the present European War shall not entail any disqualification from playing under the Gaelic Athletic association'.[38] The motion was withdrawn as it was seen as illegal to hold two opinions on the war under the Defence of the Realm Act, something that would become quite apparent if a debate took place at the Annual Convention.[39] Kerry county board's proposal to inaugurate rifle clubs under GAA auspices[40] had to be shelved as it could lead to an escalation of the split in the Volunteers.[41] It was even mooted to host a conference 'under the impartial supervision of GAA county organisations' to help heal the split.[42] O'Toole himself was an advocate of the GAA adopting a neutral stance between the National Volunteers and Irish Volunteers.[43]

The start of the First World War caused additional problems for O'Toole and other GAA administrators, with the British military occasionally using GAA grounds for manoeuvres. A ground in Limerick, used as a cavalry encampment, was 'so cut up as to be more adaptable for the "plough" of a cross-country championship than for a hurling encounter'.[44] The overall disruption to the GAA at the outbreak of war in 1914 was minimal, however, with its programme of matches hardly affected that year.

As the war progressed, the GAA's neutral stance faltered, with more and more counties – in 1915, Kerry, Kildare and Roscommon; in 1916, Cavan, Down, Kilkenny, Meath and Limerick – choosing to support the Irish Volunteers over the National Volunteers. The British authorities held the view that the GAA, 'although nominally non-political was in reality strongly Sinn Fein'.[45] Many nationalists saw people like O'Toole, Nowlan and others in the Central Council as 'pro-German'[46] and Sinn Féin sympathisers. The Ancient Order of Hibernians, through its organ Board of Erin, called on the supporters of Redmond, John Dillon and Joe Devlin to seek their place on the Central Council of the GAA.[47]

⋯

The Annual Convention of 1916 was held on Easter Sunday, 23 April. It was a very short affair and was over by early afternoon.[48] Harry Boland, along with others, stayed at Luke O'Toole's house at Croke Park that night.[49] The Easter Rising commenced the next day. Many prominent GAA members were arrested, including the President, James Nowlan.[50] Nowlan's arrest was queried in the House of Commons. It was stated that he would be detained and that until 'no hostile association detrimental to the public safety and the defence of the realm is apparent the military authorities will order release'.[51] O'Toole managed to avoid capture and took sanctuary at his birthplace in Ballycumber, Tinahely, County Wicklow.[52] Remaining in Wicklow for three weeks, O'Toole contemplated managing GAA affairs almost singlehandedly, with so many other officials imprisoned.[53]

He finally returned to Dublin in the second week of May and convened a Central Council meeting for 28 May. At that meeting the main topic of discussion was not the Rising, but an Entertainment Tax proposed by the British government.[54] O'Toole had been part of a delegation sent to London earlier in the year. They met with Redmond and other MPs, who introduced them to the Chancellor of the Exchequer, in an effort to receive exemption from the tax.[55] The GAA was advised it would receive exemption on the condition it removed its bans on foreign games and forces,[56] something the GAA refused to do.[57] The meeting of 28 May did discuss a report from the Royal Commission on the Rebellion in Ireland, in which Sir Matthew Nathan, the Under-Secretary for Ireland, implicated the GAA in the preparations for the Rising.[58] The GAA issued a rebuttal denying its involvement, saying that it was non-political, that it had never opposed the British Prime Minister's visit to Dublin in 1914, that many GAA members were of different political persuasions, and that policemen and soldiers were not denied entry to GAA events.[59] This was a clear effort to disassociate the GAA from the Rising (which was not an uncommon stance at that time, but very different from that of Mayo MP John Dillon, who fought a lone battle in the House of Commons on behalf of the insurgents[60]). With Nowlan still incarcerated, O'Toole must shoulder a great deal of responsibility for this decision. It was a typical one for him – putting the GAA's survival over his own personal political beliefs.

With the mood of the country swinging decisively towards the insurgents, the GAA followed suit at the end of 1916. It was decided in November to send delegates to a conference with the objective of forming a political prisoners' amnesty association, which according to Nowlan was 'not to be considered as related to politics'. At the same meeting it was decided to organise a tournament for the Irish National Aid and Volunteer Dependents Fund. O'Toole was chosen to be centrally involved in both initiatives.[61] The GAA also agreed to grant Croke Park as the venue for the first Irish Volunteers meeting since the Rising.[62]

O'Toole called a meeting of the Central Council later that month as the British authorities, as part of their measures to curtail excursion travel, had refused to allow special trains for the All-Ireland finals.[63] He mentioned the particulars of an interview he had with General Sir John Maxwell, Commander-in-Chief of the British Military in Ireland[64] – a meeting he would later deny attending at the 1918 Annual Convention.[65] For this he was called a liar, with it being claimed that he had in fact described Maxwell as 'a fine manly fellow'.[66] Regardless of O'Toole's views on Maxwell, no compromise was agreed upon. It was decided that a deputation be sent to London again to meet with Redmond and other MPs to lobby for special trains.[67] O'Toole also sent circulars to county boards asking them to lobby their local MPs, a request snubbed by Cork county board, an indication that the IPP was losing support from the public.[68] The lobbying was to no avail, and the All-Ireland finals had to be rescheduled by O'Toole.[69] The cancelling of special trains saw a severe disruption to GAA matches,[70] which was most keenly felt by O'Toole. It inspired some innovative ways to transport fans to All-Ireland finals. Deprived of special trains, in 1919 the Cork county board commissioned a steamer to bring their fans to Dublin for the All-Ireland hurling final against Dublin.[71]

The GAA refused to pay the Entertainment Tax. This led to the conviction of Jim Ryan, secretary of the Limerick county board, for refusing entry to a police officer into the Gaelic Grounds in Limerick to see if people were being charged for the levy. Ryan was imprisoned for six months.[72] The Central Council was also summonsed to court for refusing to pay the Entertainment Tax at a match held in Croke Park on 7 January 1917. In the court case, O'Toole claimed 'the Dublin Committee were responsible, and not the GAA',[73] another example of O'Toole working within the remits of the law and not being openly defiant. The judge agreed, and in subsequent proceedings, Andrew Harty, acting chairman of the Dublin county board, was convicted instead and fined £12 10s – a fine the GAA refused to pay.[74] These Limerick and Dublin cases would be the only instances where action was taken by the authorities for the GAA's refusal to pay the Entertainment Tax.[75]

The actions of the Central Council in dealing with the British authorities in 1916 on the Entertainment Tax and special-trains issues led to a motion of censure from Harry Boland and Jack Shouldice, secretary of the Leinster Council, at the 1918 Annual Convention. The motion was passed by twenty-seven votes to twenty-five. Boland described the Central Council's position as 'scandalous' in going to the Commander-in-Chief of the British Forces 'to ask permission to run their games'.[76] Yet Boland himself had requested at the Leinster Annual Convention in April 1916 that GAA councils and county boards protest to Major-General Friend and Dublin MPs for the military and police raid of *The Gaelic Athlete*'s office the previous month,[77] a similar stance conveniently ignored by him. Although censured, Nowlan and O'Toole were re-elected. J. J. Walsh, always quick to criticise, 'alleged that the Central Council, particularly the officers, had neglected their duty to the Gaels of the Country', an allegation with which the majority of delegates did not agree.[78] Walsh was very much drawn to the physical-force camp, realising, as he would later recount:

> the potentialities of the GAA as a training ground for Physical Force. Its national ideals were of the highest. Contamination with the alien and all his works were taboo. With a struggle for world domination in the offing, I was satisfied that we had the nucleus of the material that might one day strike a blow at the ancient foe.[79]

• • •

By 1918 people like Harry Boland and J. J. Walsh were coming to the fore, manoeuvring the GAA towards more extreme measures, convincing the GAA to embark on a showdown with Dublin Castle.[80] The most spectacular example of open defiance occurred on 4 August 1918, now known as Gaelic Sunday. Luke O'Toole's involvement was paramount to the success of the day. O'Toole called a meeting of the Central Council on 20 July after he had been interviewed at Dublin Castle, where he was informed no hurling or Gaelic football match would be allowed to take place in future without a permit.[81] It was agreed that 'no permit be asked for under any conditions' and anyone who sought a permit would be immediately suspended from the Association.[82] It was further agreed 'to arrange for Sunday August 4th at 3pm … a series of matches throughout each county to be localised as much as possible'.[83] O'Toole issued an order to the press calling on '54,000 Gaels' to 'actively participate in our native pastimes all over Ireland' on 4 August.[84]

O'Toole, it appears, underestimated the numbers willing to participate, it being believed that more than 100,000 people took part in over 1,800 matches held that day.[85] 'Although it may well be that the victory took place over an enemy that had decided not to take part in the battle', it was

still a decisive victory for the GAA and entered the 'mythology of Irish nationalist defiance'.[86] It is also worth noting, as remarked by William Murphy, 'that the occasion on which the association acted with greatest vigour and unity to oppose the British state occurred when that state threatened the very business of the association – its games'.[87] It stopped the authorities from interfering with GAA matches and O'Toole could start arranging fixtures without disturbance for the first time since 1916. He was hampered, however, by the outbreak of the 'Spanish flu' epidemic, which engulfed the world at the end of 1918[88] and claimed the lives of

(L–r): Michael Collins, Luke O'Toole and Harry Boland at Croke Park for the 11 September 1921 Leinster hurling final.

many Irish people, including GAA players.

Further evidence of the GAA's embrace of a more extreme stance against British rule came with a decision of the Central Council to ban civil servants from taking the Oath of Allegiance to the British Crown. Even though Nowlan preferred each county to make its own ruling on the matter, his suggestion was not agreed to, with the majority believing the Central Council should take a lead.[89] This decision was ratified at the Annual Convention of 1919 after an acrimonious debate, with many opposed to the move.[90] O'Toole, in his Secretary's Report, supported the ban on civil servants taking the oath, claiming it was more serious to take the oath than to attend a rugby match. He pointed out that many civil servants who were GAA members had refused to take the oath and had subsequently lost their jobs, concluding by saying, 'We retract nothing, neither do we apologise'.[91] In a more vocal hardening of his views, he also condemned the British authorities for subjecting the GAA to a 'reign of terror', in reference to the arrests of many prominent GAA figures after the War of Independence commenced months earlier.[92]

Although not actively involved in the hostilities, O'Toole was a friend of many of the key participants of the War of Independence, often convening card games or providing sanctuary in his house for men on the run from the law. Visitors to his house in Croke Park included Michael Collins, Harry Boland, Dan Breen, Seán Treacy and Eoin O'Duffy.[93]

It was O'Toole, in his house, who introduced O'Duffy to Collins. Collins convinced O'Duffy to join the Irish Volunteers within an hour, described by O'Duffy as 'the happiest day of my life'.[94] With O'Toole's blessing to use Croke Park, 'Harry [Boland] and Mick [Collins] had the whole playing pitch on which to exercise with the camán', helping them to keep fit while on the run.[95] Collins and Boland would appear in public together at Croke Park in September 1921, after the Truce of the previous July, alongside their friend O'Toole, on the occasion of the Leinster hurling final. Collins threw in the sliotar at the start of the match.[96] Both men would be shot dead a year later on opposing sides of the Civil War.

• • •

O'Toole saw the fortunes of the GAA severely hampered by the War of Independence, with fixtures coming to a standstill across the country, particularly in Munster and Connacht. With matches being banned and many players unavailable due to revolutionary commitments, the GAA saw very few inter-county fixtures realised in 1920.[97] The Tipperary football team challenged Dublin to a friendly match in late 1920, concluding by asking, 'Mr. O'Toole, could you oblige with a date?'[98] Dublin publicly accepted the challenge through the press. The date chosen was 21 November 1920, with Croke Park as the venue.

The match that day was preceded by the IRA killing of key personnel within the British secret service stationed in Ireland.[99] News of the killings reached O'Toole early in the morning and he conferred with Nowlan, Jack Shouldice, Dan McCarthy and Andy Harty from Dublin on whether to go ahead with the match or not.[100] He had been informed 'through reliable private sources that [they] were likely to have a visit from the Auxiliaries. Some form of raid', according to his honorary assistant at the time, Stanley J. Clarke, writing in 1963.[101] It was believed that if the match was called off 'the GAA would appear to be identified with what happened the previous night',[102] and it was agreed to continue with the match as planned. Just before the match was due to start, at 2:30 p.m., O'Toole was approached by three IRA men, Harry Colley, Seán Russell and Tom Kilcoyne, who advised him that a force of Auxiliaries and military was being mobilised for Croke Park, and to call off the game.[103] Fearing that 'an announcement to clear the stadium would lead to a panic-induced exodus … and that a crush would develop at the turnstiles',[104] O'Toole believed the best course of action was to go ahead with the match. Seven minutes after the match started, the military and police opened fire on the crowd. In the ensuing panic, many took refuge in O'Toole's house and made their exit from there.[105] The British forces later realised the house was being used as an escape route, and it was surrounded, with one old man shot at the back entrance. He crawled through the gate into the yard of the residence, where he died.[106]

In total, fourteen civilians were killed in the incident, including the Tipperary footballer Michael Hogan, with hundreds more injured.[107] Many high-ranking British military officers visited O'Toole during the following few days, threatening to 'commandeer and close the grounds for at least six months' unless the GAA made an official statement.[108] O'Toole's residence was also raided and searched the following May.[109] He was one of four spectators who gave evidence at the subsequent Court of Enquiry.[110] Of all the events in which O'Toole had been involved, Bloody Sunday 1920 must have been the most harrowing for him. He was the one who sanctioned the match to go ahead, despite protestations. His house, the scene of some of the atrocities that day, would serve as a constant reminder of what had happened.

The immediate aftermath of Bloody Sunday saw the fortunes of the GAA plummet further, with all fixtures suspended until further notice, to avoid the risk of another atrocity.[111] Just twenty-seven people were in attendance at the Annual Convention of 1921, held in O'Toole's office in Croke Park.[112] Nowlan, who had been elected President the same day that O'Toole was elected Secretary, stood down after twenty years as President, and was replaced by Dan McCarthy. The Central Council had a liability of almost £13,000 by the end of September; it needed fixtures to take place to recover some of its debts.[113] It was believed, 'owing to the altered circumstances of the political situation'[114] after the Truce of July that year, that matches could again take place, and the GAA could claw back some of its fixture backlog – in particular, to see the cancelled All-Ireland championships spanning back to 1920 finally completed. In February 1922, it was arranged for the 1920 hurling and Gaelic football championships to be completed by May.[115] It was hoped that the 1921 All-Ireland championships could be completed by the end of 1922.[116]

Civil War intervened, however, leading to a further delay in the completion of the delayed All-Ireland contests. The province most affected was Munster. O'Toole sent circulars to the Munster Council on

MANAGER OF CROKE PARK LUKE O' TOOLE

16

10th Witness,

having been duly sworn is examined by the Court and states:-

I am the manager of Croke Park, Football Ground. On November 21st at about 3.15.p.m. a Football Match was started at Croke Park. I was watching the match from the commencement. I was on the Grandstand on the Jones' Road side of the ground. About 10 minutes after the start of the game an aeroplane flew over the ground and returned on a second occasion and then went in the direction of Phoenix Park. A moment or two after that a man came across the ground to where I was sitting and told me that an armoured car was at the front gate. I got up from where I was sitting and went to the entrance gate leading into the side-line seats. I left the gate open after me and went on to the high bank facing and just inside of the main gate. I was looking at the armoured car for a space of four or five seconds, when firing commenced at the canal end of the ground. I saw the driver of the car. He was sitting in the car. As far as I remember I could see his head and shoulders. I don't remember how he was dressed. From what I saw of the car I am not prepared to say whether it was an armoured car or not. I went immediately I heard the firing and took cover under the wall by the entrance gate. When I first heard the shots I could not see anybody firing. Firing continued, and I remained lying on the ground. I saw police come into the ground through the main gate. They were not firing. After this the people were collected together and the police fired some shots up in

the air. The people were being searched at the
time and it seemed to me that the police fired to
prevent a rush towards the gate. I saw no one
killed or injured on that part of the ground. All
the people including myself, were searched as we
left the ground. I went outside the ground and
remained outside for about half an hour. I then
returned and informed one of the police outside that
I resided on the ground. He told me that I would
have to see the officers on the gate. I then went
to the officer and told him that I had been searched
and that I wanted to get back to the ground, as I
lived there. He told me that if I had been searched
I could pass on, and the men inside passed me into
the house. My house is just inside the canal
entrance gate. I saw one body lying on the ground,
in the North East Corner of the ground. Most of
the casualties appeared to have occurred on the East
and South sides of the ground.

The Court then inspect Croke Park Football Ground,
a rough sketch of which is attached to the proceedings
marked "G"

FACING PAGE AND ABOVE: Eyewitness statement given by Luke O'Toole to the Court of Enquiry established after Bloody Sunday. THE NATIONAL ARCHIVES, KEW

a regular basis asking for fixtures to take place in order for the All-Ireland programmes to be completed.[117] O'Toole, along with the rest of the Central Council, wisely remained neutral throughout the Civil War. The Central Council was approached by the Cork county board in December 1922 asking for its intervention by calling for an All-Ireland conference for the 'purposes of considering ways and means towards peace'.[118] The Cork county board's suggestion came soon after the assassination of Seán Hales, pro-Treaty Cork TD, and the subsequent retaliatory executions of four republicans, including Dick Barrett, former inter-county footballer and hurler from Cork.[119] Although not hopeful of 'getting a representative congress together at present', the Central Council, 'though non-political, would work with any body or Committee likely to bring about peace and unity'.[120] A deputation was appointed by the Central Council 'to ascertain the views of prominent members of the association on both sides as to peace' and report back to the Central Council with a view to calling a special All-Ireland Convention for 4 February 1923.[121] As was the case with most other major initiatives of the GAA, O'Toole was a member of the deputation. After deliberations, however, the deputation ruled it would be unwise to hold a special conference 'under present conditions', and the GAA's efforts to mediate in the Civil War were abandoned.[122]

· · ·

Once the Civil War ended in 1923, O'Toole was assigned the near-impossible task of bringing the championships up to date. He also oversaw the huge expansion and upgrade of Croke Park to a capacity of 66,000, sanctioned in 1920 to prepare it as the centrepiece stadium for the new state's showpiece international cultural event, the Tailteann Games, first held in 1924.[123] O'Toole, with extraordinary vigour and energy, set about reorganising the GAA after the tumultuous revolutionary years. With the unexpected death of his wife, Bridget, in 1925, he also had to rear eight children alone.[124] The heavy toll proved too much, and he died on 17 July 1929 – fittingly, at his desk in Croke Park, drawing up an agenda for an upcoming Central Council meeting. He worked for the GAA right up to the end.[125]

O'Toole's successor as Secretary, Pádraig Ó Caoimh, is considered by many as the 'Architect of the Modern GAA'.[126] O'Toole should be accorded the title 'Architect of the GAA'. Without his energy and his often prudent judgement, there may have been no GAA for Pádraig Ó Caoimh to inherit. Through his efforts, the GAA survived and expanded to be in a healthy position by 1929.[127] O'Toole's achievements are all the more impressive considering the political events that dominated his time in office – events that severely affected his ability to carry out his role. O'Toole's involvement, as well as Nowlan's, in political decisions has been criticised as too little by some, too much by others. It is clear, however, that the one objective that permeated every decision O'Toole made was the survival of the Association to which he had devoted so much energy. O'Toole, although a deeply committed nationalist, was first and foremost a servant to the GAA.

CHAPTER 5

The GAA and the Irish Parliamentary Party, 1913–18

JAMES McCONNEL

Laurence Ginnell TD (centre) at Croke Park in 1919.

WRITING IN 1919 OF THE ELECTORAL DEFEAT of the Irish Parliamentary Party (IPP) at the hands of *Sinn Féin* the previous year, Stephen Gwynn noted that the GAA had 'always [been] antagonistic to the parliamentary movement', though he conceded that, in turn, IPP's 'rank and file had [shown] little sympathy with the new movements which were manifesting themselves' in the early twentieth century.[1] There is no doubt that the Association had experienced Fenian entryism from its inception in 1884; that secret IRB members held senior positions in the GAA in the Edwardian period; that prominent GAA members welcomed the advent of the Irish Volunteers (when the IPP initially did not) and expressed support for the MacNeillite wing after the acrimonious split of September 1914; that a considerable number of those who were 'out' in 1916 were also Gaelic athletes; or that the organisation raised funds for the families of those killed or imprisoned as a result of the Rising. But whether any of this really amounted to the antagonism retrospectively claimed by Gwynn is open to question. After all, since the 1990s, historians have – as part of a broader questioning of the emphasis on politics in the historiography of the GAA's early years – tended to throw cold water on some of the Association's grander claims about its separatist credentials.[2] Alvin Jackson, for one, has argued that there was a 'significant Redmondite wing' within the GAA before 1916 and that IRB members within the Association tended typically to be 'cautious strategists', wary of taking the organisation in too radical a direction.[3]

As for Gwynn's other claim, about the IPP's stance towards the GAA – this also needs to be handled with some care. Rather than a lack of sympathy, the truth is that the IPP's attitude towards the GAA (whether at national, provincial or county level) was characterised, in fact, by a benign, if unfocused, goodwill in the period to 1918. This was, in large part, because the IPP saw the Association as a very different kind of organisation to the Gaelic League. While IRB penetration of the Edwardian GAA may well have been more thoroughgoing than in the case of the Gaelic League, the Association possessed no high-profile Fenian Gaelicists of the type so prominently associated with the language movement, it had no official mouthpiece (like *An Claidheamh Soluis*) that consistently criticised the IPP, it never jettisoned its ostensibly neutral political stance (as the Gaelic League did in 1915), and it was not banned by the British after 1916 for its subversive activities. This is not to deny that the GAA harboured radical elements within its ranks in these years, but it is to argue that the activities of the GAA as a whole seem never to have seriously troubled the IPP.

• • •

The Edwardian IPP numbered within its ranks various MPs with links to the GAA, with many of these connections dating back to the earliest decades of the Association's history. Timothy Harrington MP (who died in harness in 1910) was one of several members who allowed his name to be used on the circular that announced the first meeting of the new organisation, held in Thurles on 1 November 1884.[4] Though no MPs actually attended the inaugural meeting, the Parnellite press warmly welcomed the new organisation.[5] In his capacity as editor of *The Irishman*, James O'Connor (elected MP for Wicklow in 1892) was particularly supportive. More importantly, Parnell, who 'had long displayed antipathy towards Gaelic pastimes', accepted – though not with quite as much enthusiasm as Archbishop Croke – the meeting's invitation to become one of the three patrons of the new association.[6] Almost immediately, he set out to gain control of the organisation; at a meeting in Cork six weeks later, John O'Connor (formerly a Fenian and shortly to become a Parnellite MP for Tipperary) sought to annex the new organisation to the National League. Another future MP, J. P. Farrell, founded the GAA in County Longford in the 1880s.[7] As a consequence, in Leinster and Munster, the National League took over the nascent association for a time (though in some areas – such as Kerry – relations soon broke down).[8] Evidence of these early links is to be found in the fact that as well as the clubs named after separatist heroes like Robert Emmet and Charles Kickham, there were clubs named after prominent Home Rulers: the Killerin John Dillons, the Corofin Colonel Nolans, the William O'Briens of Monagea, County Limerick, and the Gladstonians of Balbriggan, County Dublin.[9]

Other Edwardian MPs had first-hand experience of the IRB's entryist tactics with regard to the early GAA.[10] The future Mid-Tipperary MP John Cullinan proposed the ban on foreign games in 1886, though Michael Joyce – later MP for Limerick City – was, by contrast, a lonely dissenting vote against the exclusion of rugby players from the Association.[11] In 1887, the IRB's work of 'packing' that year's GAA convention was carried out in Queen's County by a future MP for one of its divisions, P. A. Meehan, while in the fallout from the controversial convention itself, Kendal O'Brien (later an MP for Tipperary) was vocal in his support for the new Fenian-dominated executive.[12] Even after the grass-roots backlash reconstituted the executive following the 1888 convention, some Fenians – like the future Sligo MP P. A. McHugh – still managed to secure election as county representatives.[13]

If, after the Parnell split, the Association was never again 'quite the creature of the IRB' that it had been before 1891, it remained the 'scene of interplay between … contending forces' within Irish republicanism until 1899, and it was not until 1901 that a new generation of IRB figures began rebuilding the Association on sounder organisational lines.[14] Even before this, the Dublin MP William Field (who served as Treasurer of the GAA in the early 1890s) had been a prominent advocate of the Association's adoption of a more non-political stance.[15] Senior figures associated with the Association in the Edwardian era may have had reservations about the new United Irish League and 'parliamentary tactics', but they recognised after 1900 that it would be sensible to avoid antagonising the reunited IPP.[16]

In the new century, only one of these Fenian MPs continued to be involved with the GAA. William Duffy (who had been among the IRB men Michael Cusack originally consulted when he first campaigned for the revival of Gaelic games) had served as county secretary for Galway until the Parnell split. He retained close links with the local Association and he was praised by the Galway county board in 1903 as having 'always zealously rendered powerful assistance to the cause of the Gael'.[17] The same year, he told his constituents that he had come 'to unfurl … the rebel flag of green in old Galway and to do a man's part to kill English games among the people'.[18]

But, otherwise, the number of MPs with close links to the GAA after 1900 was relatively small. The MP for South Leitrim, T. F. Smyth, was chairman of his county's Association between 1905 and 1907, while the Limerick MP Tom Lundon (who described himself as having been 'connected from infancy' with the Association) was a member of the GAA's Limerick county board and was elected as its vice-president in 1904.[19] In 1914 he acted on behalf of the Association in opposing the Weekly Rest Day Bill, which would have prohibited the playing of Gaelic games on Sundays.[20] Even the presence within the IPP of such an ardent Gael as Eugene O'Sullivan only serves to underline this wider point. He had

Charles Stewart Parnell, leader of the Irish Parliamentary Party and patron of the GAA

captained the team that won the Kerry senior football championship in 1901, and in 1903 became chairman of the Kerry county board. Elected as an independent nationalist in the January 1910 general election, he was admitted to the IPP, but lost his seat as a result of an election petition shortly afterwards.[21] His admission was, then, essentially an accident, rather than a deliberate effort to appeal to the Gaels of the GAA. While the IPP felt that persuading Douglas Hyde to become an MP would have real benefits for its sometimes fraught relationship with the Gaelic League, no such proposals ever seem to be have been entertained in the case of the GAA.[22]

This is not to say that the Edwardian IPP was indifferent to the GAA before 1914. Attendance at games by MPs, such as agrarian radical and later Sinn Féin TD Laurence Ginnell, demonstrated interest and support. At a local level, 'the GAA was well integrated into the fabric of local nationalist life', and numerous backbench MPs interacted with the Association on this basis.[23] Thus, Tom O'Donnell attended the Kerry county board's Annual Convention in 1902, while J. P. Nannetti attended a GAA meeting in Sandymount the same year.[24] In 1903, 1906 and 1910, Willie Redmond donated presentational silverware to County Clare's GAA.[25] As he observed in 1906, 'I am sure the GAA is doing much to make the young men healthy and manly, and brave and good-humoured'.[26] Eight years later he enthusiastically identified himself with Clare's victory over Laois in the All-Ireland hurling final.[27] Other MPs interacted with Gaelic sportsmen from their constituencies in similar ways.[28] William McKillop donated a cup in 1907 to the Armagh county board (which remained a feature of Armagh football for decades afterwards). In 1908, A. J. C. Donelan donated medals to the Midleton GAA club, while in 1910 J. P. Hayden presented a set of medals for the Roscommon hurling championship.[29] Other members represented their local associations in parliament.[30] While this engagement was certainly opportunistic, it was not nearly as cynical as one modern authority has claimed.[31] After all, as in one case in Mayo, such presentations seem often to have been at the direct request of local Gaelic sportsmen.[32]

The highlighting of such connections between the IPP and the GAA is not to deny that in the years before the First World War local GAA teams in some counties were front organisations for separatists. Nor should it be assumed that the IPP was ignorant of all of these connections,[33] but it needs to be remembered that the significance of such connections was always constrained by the small size of these movements nationally.[34] In some areas, IPP bosses were also keen Gaels. In the midland counties examined by Michael Wheatley, '[m]any Irish party figures' were involved in the local GAA and there was a 'significant local overlap between Irish party activists and those prominent in local Gaelic sports'.[35]

As for IPP involvement at a national level, there is considerable evidence of periodic – rather than sustained – interaction. John Redmond attended the Croke Memorial Tournament football final in 1913 and was introduced to the captains of the two teams before the game started. He apparently gave such a 'glowing account' of it to John Dillon that Dillon attended the All-Ireland football final between Kerry and Wexford in December of the same year. 'It is so long since I attended a match,' Dillon remarked, 'that I didn't know how the game was to be started. I was delighted with the play and the magnificent skill displayed by the two teams.'[36] The Kerry MP Michael Flavin was also in the audience watching (having 'travelled up with the Kerry players').[37]

One authority has described this pre-war interest as representing a 'final effort to exploit the GAA's popularity'.[38] This is true, but only up to a point. The GAA was probably very happy to receive the attention of Home-Rule Ireland's presumptive prime minister and his deputy (who reportedly received a 'very hearty reception' from the assembled spectators).[39] This was, after all, at a time when Irish self-government seemed imminent and when the Association was as keen as any other Irish organisation to ensure that it had a good relationship with the new regime.[40] Indeed, though the GAA's Central Council was not (in 1911) willing to prevent local clubs from adopting names with separatist associations, when it was called on the following year by Sinn Féin to account for its invitation to Dublin's pro-Home Rule Lord Mayor to attend the All-Ireland finals, the implicit censure was unanimously rebuffed.[41]

Given that Home Rule was on the immediate horizon, this was sensible politics for the GAA. Indeed, elements within and without the Association were, like many others in the period between 1912 and 1913, busy 'picturing in the near-future a self-governing Ireland' and what their place would be in it.[42] In 1912 it was reported that the Association was 'already considering the probable effects … that will take place in their own workings when the country is governed by Irishmen'. It was anticipated that the ban on soldiers and prison wardens joining the GAA would be repealed, and that the Association would coordinate the Irish

Olympic team in the near future.[43] As *The Gaelic Athlete* (customarily more radical than the mainstream of the GAA) observed in March 1912, 'we are solid on the policy of Gaelicising the new regime'.[44]

In this context, there is little evidence to suggest any deep-seated mutual hostility. As *The Freeman's Journal* explained in mid-1913, the GAA was 'another branch of the national movement, the movement that encourages Irish games and pastimes and teaches healthy, brawny young Irishmen to play them and to be proud of them'.[45] In turn, whatever the personal sympathies of members of the Central Council, '[t]he vast majority of GAA members, like the Irish public at large, continued to support the IPP'.[46]

· · ·

As MP for West Clare, Willie Redmond identified himself closely with the county team that won the All-Ireland hurling final in October 1914. So much so, in fact, that after the game he drove with the team to a nearby hotel and entertained them as his personal guests.[47] That the outbreak of the First World War a little over two months earlier had prompted his brother to endorse Irish enlistment in the British Army did not apparently trouble Clare's winning players, or at least not enough for them to reject Redmond's hospitality. Others may, of course, have taken a different view; after all, *The Gaelic Athlete* had warned in August 1914 that there was a real risk of Irishmen 'wander[ing] unthinkingly on the side of imperialism'.[48]

In the months following the outbreak of the war, the IPP retained the support of the great majority of ordinary nationalists, as evidenced by the result of the split in the ranks of the Irish Volunteers. Certain GAA historians have been at some pains to explain why such a radical organisation as the GAA – 'almost unbelievably' – did not likewise splinter in September 1914 along the same fault line as the Volunteers.[49] True, the Secretary of the GAA Central Council, Luke O'Toole, had spoken at the inaugural meeting of the Irish Volunteers in November 1913, but then at least one Home-Rule MP had also attended the founding meeting, while three more initially welcomed the formation of the Volunteers (including the aforementioned J. P. Farrell, who helped found the GAA in County Longford).[50] The 'passive hostility' of the IPP leadership quickly silenced these MPs, but it also had a considerable cooling effect on the Central Council of the GAA. In the absence of Redmond's endorsement of the Volunteers, the Central Council adopted the 'prudent course' of remaining officially neutral.[51] Accordingly, the GAA leadership refused to recognise the Volunteers formally (as the latter had hoped it would) and did not permit the organisation to use Croke Park for the purposes of drilling.

In advance of the IPP's belated recognition of the Volunteers in May 1914, members of the Central Council made various conciliatory gestures towards the paramilitary organisation (as when a member of its executive addressed the GAA's Annual Convention in 1914). Such efforts may have been judged necessary because the Volunteers appear to have been somewhat disgruntled by their treatment at the hands the Association.[52] The IPP's reservations about the Volunteers were, of course, less of a dampener on GAA activity at grass-roots level, and in some areas county boards as well as rank-and-file members strongly supported the new organisation.[53] Still, as Fearghal McGarry has suggested, in other areas where the Volunteers were established, 'Ninety per cent of the GAA was just GAA.'[54]

Notwithstanding the early support of elements within the GAA for the Volunteers, when the split occurred in September 1914, the overwhelming majority of GAA members and supporters did not side with the MacNeillite faction. Instead, as in County Kerry, '[m]embers ... acted much like their non-Gael brethren', in that they sided with the IPP.[55] As for the Central Council, it continued its policy of passive support for the IPP. Indeed, while the Gaelic League's growing politicisation attracted criticism from Redmondites, the 'deference' of the Central Council was all too evident when the GAA's 1915 Annual Convention was deliberately scheduled in order to allow delegates the opportunity to attend the Redmondite National Volunteer parade being held on the same day.[56]

That the Irish National Volunteers platform at this event included the veteran GAA and IRB member Frank Dinneen has prompted one historian to 'marvel' at the 'reconciliation of [such] a lifelong separatist [with such] ... pro-imperialist[s]'.[57] But then as far back as the 1901 Galway by-election, Dinneen had supported the Redmondite candidate against John MacBride (despite instructions to the contrary from the IRB), and in 1907 he had privately corresponded with John Redmond about the political threat posed by a nascent Sinn Féin.[58] Dinneen's 'reconciliation' is arguably indicative of the complex relationships, developed over decades, between senior GAA and IPP figures, which problematise the notion that the Association and the IPP were irreconcilably hostile to one another.

Indeed, when Dinneen died shortly before the Easter Rising, the IPP was 'specially represented' at his funeral by four MPs (including William Field and William Duffy), while John Dillon also attended and John Redmond sent a message of condolence to the family.[59]

Several other funerals at this time reinforce the close connections between the IPP and the GAA. In December 1915, the MP for North Louth, Augustine Roche, died. Among those attending his funeral were the current president, honorary treasurer, and secretary of the Cork county board.[60] Earlier the same year Roche – who had 'always taken a keen interest in Gaelic pastimes' – had presented a 'valuable solid silver cup' to a new Gaelic football club founded by students at the Cork School of Art.[61] That he publicly supported the war effort did not put off these Cork Gaels.[62] Likewise, the funeral of the veteran MP (and erstwhile Fenian) J. J. O'Kelly in December 1916 saw among the mourners the GAA's Secretary Luke O'Toole.[63] Like Roche, O'Kelly supported the Allies in the war (owing to his long sympathy with France).[64]

That these networks were still important before (and, indeed, after) the Easter Rising is indicated by the GAA's approach to the Entertainment Tax in 1916. The new tax was to apply to all entertainments, excepting those held for educational or charitable purposes. In a parliamentary debate on the tax on 12 April 1916, the IPP put up two MPs with long GAA associations – John O'Connor and William Duffy – to argue the case for the specific exclusion of the Association from its application.[65] As their appeal was rejected, the GAA sent over a deputation (consisting of its President, Secretary and Frank Dinneen) the following day and it subsequently met with John Redmond, O'Connor, Duffy and the chief whip, Pat O'Brien, in the House of Commons.[66] On 15 April, Redmond and his colleagues accompanied the GAA deputation to a meeting with the Chancellor of the Exchequer, Reginald McKenna, at the Treasury.[67] The GAA reportedly found the interview 'very satisfactory', since the following day McKenna introduced an amendment to exempt non-profit-making organisations that existed to revive national pastimes.[68]

In stark contrast to the response of *The Times* (which commented that 'if the Sinn Féiners want to have their hurling free of tax they can go into the trenches and hurl – bombs'), the IPP evidently worked hard to assist the GAA with the Entertainment Tax.[69] In turn, the GAA clearly saw the IPP as a vital medium in its petitioning of the government.[70] Despite these combined efforts, however, a parliamentary question subsequently revealed that the GAA would still need to 'satisfy the Commissioners of Customs and Excise ... that they come within the exemption clause'.[71]

The Easter Rising, which broke out less than a week later, delayed but did not halt the GAA's efforts to be exempted from the new tax. Despite official suspicions about the Association in the aftermath of the Rising (voiced publicly by the Under-Secretary for Ireland, Sir Matthew Nathan), moderates on the Central Council sought to distance the GAA from the rebels and tried to resume 'business as usual'.[72] At its first post-Rising meeting at the end of May, the Central Council immediately returned to the question of the Entertainment Tax and resolved to ask John O'Connor to approach the government again to '[a]scertain ... if the Association were exempt'.[73] In November, O'Connor reported back to the GAA that exemption from the tax would be contingent on the GAA altering its constitution banning soldiers, policemen and civil servants from being members. This was the same message communicated to the Association by Sir John Maxwell.[74] The Association resolved to refuse this demand and decided to refrain from paying the tax.[75]

This combination of 'pliability and resilience' (which one authority has argued characterised the GAA in the wake of the Easter Rising[76]) is also evident in another episode that brought the Central Council and IPP together: excursion trains. Although the GAA was not proscribed after the Easter Rising, it faced a variety of practical obstacles in the running of inter-county and inter-provincial competitions. At a Special Meeting at the end of November 1916, the Central Council considered the most serious of these obstacles: the curtailment of special and excursion trains imposed by the British military. This was, in fact, an old problem in a new form (since the GAA's pre-war relationship with the main railway companies had periodically been difficult).[77] Following an unsuccessful interview with Maxwell in November, the Central Council turned once again to the IPP and resolved to appoint a 'deputation ... to wait on Mr Redmond and other Irish members with the view of seeking their influence towards approaching the Chief Sec[retar]y to obtain facilities in the matter of special trains.'[78] The GAA deputation travelled to Westminster, where they found the IPP 'generally ... in sympathy with the view of the deputation', but the Chief Secretary continued to insist that the ban on excursion traffic covered the United Kingdom as a whole and so could not be varied for the GAA alone.[79] John Dillon, however, persevered and successfully persuaded the government to allow special trains to operate for the 1916 All-Ireland semi-finals at least.[80]

Whether there was, as has been claimed, 'a decisive turning point' in IPP-GAA relations after this point is questionable. Clearly, though, by the time of the Association's Annual Convention in March 1918, there were signs that the moderation of the immediate post-Rising period was being challenged internally. At the Convention (held in private session), Harry Boland narrowly carried a motion censuring those members of the GAA who had formed the various delegations that had waited on Maxwell and Redmond in the autumn of 1916 concerning taxation and the provision of excursion trains.[81] Still, about one-third of the delegates abstained and the majority ultimately endorsed – 'on the whole' – the conduct of the Central Council.[82]

Meanwhile, the picture at a local level in the years after the rebellion was messier than is sometimes claimed.[83] In Clare, Sinn Féin's growth after the Rising owed more to the support of 'zestful' grass-roots Gaels than the Association's officers, while in Cork the correlation between GAA membership and Sinn Féin membership diminished as the new party grew.[84] In east Galway, 27 per cent of Sinn Féin officers had been associated with the GAA before 1916, while the radicalisation of the Association in Tyrone 'squeezed' out local constitutionalists.[85] This process did not go unnoticed by the parliamentary movement. Even before the Rising, some elements – notably the Ancient Order of Hibernians – had been critical of the GAA's politicisation.[86] But it was not until 1917 that a number of nationalist MPs openly drew attention to what they saw as the 'extreme element of the Sinn Féiners … [carrying] their views into the GAA'.[87] Even then, there was never any unilateral policy of hostility towards the Association. After the government resolved that no further sporting events could be held without a permit, the Central Council responded by organising a day of resistance – on 'Gaelic Sunday' (4 August 1918), Gaelic games were played across the country without permits. Nationalist MPs supported this protest. In July 1918, J. T. Donovan MP intervened in parliament to protest at the interference by the police with football and hurling matches, while in August John Dillon strongly criticised the system of requiring permits to be secured for the holding of public events (including GAA games).[88] Joe Devlin also criticised the government for the way it was waging its 'militarist war … upon every section and every element in the country', including Gaelic sports.[89] Even if, in making these speeches, MPs implicitly distinguished between Gaelic games and the GAA, that they refrained from openly criticising the Association is nonetheless significant.

• • •

Seven years after the final defeat of the IPP, the former nationalist MP Matthew Keating recalled that sometimes when at Westminster 'I wondered if the views of some of my [cultural nationalist] friends were sounder than those of the [parliamentary] school to which I belonged. Intellectual men were saying … that the turning point in the revival of nationality was caused by the Gaelic League and the GAA'.[90] It is impossible to know how many of his parliamentary colleagues harboured similar doubts or concerns. What is clear is that though Keating was a native Irish speaker, he was no more prominent in the IPP's engagements with the GAA or the Gaelic League than the bulk of his fellow Edwardian nationalist MPs. David Fitzpatrick has written of the GAA that '[w]hat … [it] offer[ed] the politicians [was] … offered indiscriminately to Sinn Féiners and Redmondites alike: zest for Ireland, tangible rather than rhetorical reminders of Irish nationality … aggressively un-English games'.[91] But, in turn, what the IPP offered the GAA (influence, profile and patronage) it also offered to a range of Irish associations and clubs across Ireland. In this sense, during much of the first two decades of the twentieth century, the GAA was little different from the host of other Irish organisations that jostled for position and attention.

CHAPTER 6

The GAA and the First World War, 1914–18

ROSS O'CARROLL

The Kerry and Wexford teams parading before
the 1913 All-Ireland senior football final.

I N THE 130 YEARS OF THE GAA's EXISTENCE, the subject of the Association and the First World War is one that has never been formally discussed, or at least documented at large. There are a small number of impressive local histories, but as part of the general GAA history, it remains undocumented.[1] This may be due to a desire to edit the Association's official history down to solely a part of the Irish nationalist movement, and to ignore quietly the role thousands of GAA men played in a foreign war, or it may simply be the daunting challenge facing historians in gathering evidence on the topic. Nonetheless, this gap in GAA history needs to be examined. While the consequences of the war on the day-to-day running of the Association are relatively straightforward to extract, the extent to which GAA members went to fight in Flanders Fields is difficult to quantify. There is a dearth of source material, which prevents a forensic exploration of the theme. However, local and national newspapers as well as individual accounts help to provide some clues as to the degree of GAA participation in the trenches.

This chapter aims to partly fill the gap in the Association's history on the subject of the First World War. The first part of the chapter examines the practical implications the war presented for the Association and how the organisation, and particularly its administrators, responded to the changed landscape. The latter half of the chapter investigates a number of different themes: the extent of GAA members' involvement in the war; the impact the war had on the Association locally; the dichotomy of attitudes among the GAA community towards the war; and the reasons why GAA members enlisted.

By the beginning of 1914, the GAA was thriving. The year 1913 was recorded as one of the most successful in its history. The Ulster GAA Provincial Council reported a year of 'unparalleled success, with great progress in every direction'.[2] This was most evident in Derry, traditionally a soccer stronghold, and was acknowledged by Luke O'Toole, Secretary of the GAA, who awarded the county board £30.[3] In Leinster, the continued increase in the number of clubs affiliated to the Association was a sign of its growing appeal to the wider public.[4] In Munster, the chairman of the Limerick county board, John Kelly, proudly stated that the Association 'was never in a more flourishing condition in the county'.[5] Finally, in Connacht, the secretary of the Galway county board argued that 1913 had been 'a record one for the GAA and although we may not have kept pace with other parts of Ireland in the wonderful rate of progress ... there is every prospect that in a few years' time we will be able to take our place in the front ranks of the GAA'.[6]

The Freeman's Journal confirmed the scale of the GAA's national progress, remarking that the fiscal success of 1913 was down to the 'unprecedented interest taken by the public all over the country in the series of matches played'.[7] Against the backdrop of such success, the voice of the GAA, *The Gaelic Athlete*, noted that the Association's 'bearing upon modern Irish life is too pronounced to permit of the subject being lightly dismissed any longer'.[8]

All told, it was apparent that the GAA had made considerable advances since its foundation in November 1884. However, this progress was not to continue uninterrupted. The outbreak of war in Europe affected the fortunes of every sporting organisation in Ireland between 1914 and 1918. The GAA was also influenced by the political nature of Association members, many of whom upheld a strong nationalist ideology. Famously, the GAA was no mere sporting organisation. The challenge for the Association was to ensure a successful marriage between fostering sporting development and pursuing a political ideology. Against that backdrop, there was little doubt that the First World War would prove to be a complex hurdle to overcome.

· · ·

The immediate effects of the Great War upon Irish society were severe, with many facets of daily life affected. Sport was no exception. Soccer matches, race meetings and athletic sports fixtures all suffered, as transport facilities were limited and many men decided to answer the call to enlist and go to the front.[9]

For some sporting organisations, events on the continent were em-braced with enthusiasm. F. H. Browning, President of the IRFU, urged the young professional men of Dublin rugby clubs 'to do their bit' and join the war effort.[10] Shortly thereafter, the Irish Rugby Union Corps was established.[11] The GAA was not immune to the impact of the war either. While the Association made a concerted effort to continue its programme, many of its games, including some high-profile matches, were postponed.

Once Britain entered the war, recruiting drives began and many young men were swept up by the fervour to fight against 'the Hun'. As a result of the subsequent mass mobilisation of troops and equipment throughout the country, the main railway company, Great Southern and Western Railway, was forced to curtail its normal passenger services. It was no surprise, then, that countless sporting fixtures and events were cancelled. One horse-race meeting was abandoned because 'it [was] highly probable that horses could not reach the course'.[12] The illustrious Royal Dublin Society horse show, cricket fixtures[13] and tennis competitions all suffered similar fates.[14]

The IRFU adopted a rather pro-war position. The *Sunday Independent* wrote that 'the attitude of the various rugby unions and their clubs is splendid ... The Irish players have banded themselves together to fight for their country'.[15] In a kind gesture, the Leinster Branch of the IRFU held a meeting to raise funds for 'players disabled in the war'.[16] Shortly after the war began, the union abandoned all its fixtures, save for schoolboy, charity or war-relief matches.[17] So taxing was its involvement, Edmund Van Esbeck argues, that it was 'not until the season of 1919–20 that club competitions and a full international programme were once again restored'.[18]

Soccer also suffered. The North of Ireland Football Club cancelled its fixtures for the season.[19] Reduced gate receipts inevitably led to questions about the sustainability of 'pro' clubs.[20] Neal Garnham has written that the war led to a huge scaling down of soccer activity in Ireland, and a renaissance only occurred at the end of the 1916–17 season, possibly due to a slowdown in recruitment.[21]

In February 1915, the *Irish Independent* provided a frank assessment of how the war was impacting on sport. It discussed how various sports championships had been abandoned, which was, in its view, a very wise decision, considering many of the best performers were serving in the colours.[22] It also added that the daily lists of the sportsmen at the front afforded ample evidence of the serious drain the war was having on clubs of every description, including soccer, hockey, cricket, swimming and polo.[23] In slight contrast, the report predicted that Gaelic meetings were not as likely to be affected, although it remarked that 'even here the competitors must necessarily be fewer than usual'.[24]

However, the lack of proper transport facilities played havoc early on with the GAA's schedule. In August 1914, the inter-provincial hurling and football championships between Munster and Connacht were postponed 'owing to no special trains being available due to military demands', while a similar decision was made regarding the Munster hurling semi-final between Clare and Limerick.[25] Accordingly, the often polemical *Gaelic Athlete* ran with the headline 'Bang Bang', as fixtures billed for Maryborough and Limerick were also shot down. These developments provoked the newspaper to assert that 'the crisis had penetrated through GAA lines'.[26]

A similar fate befell athletics, which was also controlled by the GAA. Several of its meetings were postponed, including the Munster inter-county athletics and cycling championships.[27] Naturally, the GAA in rural Ireland was hardest hit.[28] Upon the suggestion that he take up the position of secretary of the Mayo county board, Thomas Ruane, fearing the war's continuation, responded that he could not, 'as it would be impossible to reach meetings owing to inadequate train facilities'.[29]

Lack of transport was not the only cause of postponements. The Limerick senior hurling championship final was postponed on more than one occasion as the Markets Field was being used by the military authorities.[30] Interestingly, after the final was eventually played, the *Limerick Leader* applauded the state of the surface, 'considering military horses did an amount of damage'.[31] The prestigious Cork senior hurling final between Midleton and Blackrock was also deferred due to military horses occupying the Cork Athletic Grounds.[32]

In an era when team training and regular squad-bonding sessions were increasingly common, some counties found their preparations seriously hindered by financial constraints caused by the war.[33] Following the postponement of Clare's game with Limerick, *The Clare Champion* explained how the war meant that insufficient funds were available for a team-training camp in Lahinch for the rearranged match. Lamenting this, the writer argued that, had the team travelled, they might have been in 'a thoroughly fit state'.[34] Meanwhile, in Laois, a letter, in response to an appeal by Laois officials to gather funds for training the senior hurling team, stated: 'I thought I could do better, but things are so upset with the war its [*sic*] hard to get money'.[35]

October 1914 letter from M. Collier to the Laois and Ossory Training Fund Appeal stating that 'things are so upset with the war its [*sic*] hard to get money'.

In its assessment of the war's impact on the Association, *The Gaelic Athlete* printed a rather amusing and pessimistic editorial about the 1914 championships. 'Where do we stand now? Nowadays no secretary can guarantee when a match will be brought off ... who knows but the Gael of the future may yet be confronted by an inscription over the tombstone of the 1914 championships: "German invasion"!!'[36] The Kilkenny journalist 'Vigilant' concurred, pointing out that 'the possibilities of bringing off the All-Ireland final in September are looking somewhat remote'.[37] In fact, the All-Ireland junior championships and the Croke Cup football competition were not completed within the year.[38] Unsurprisingly, however, the Association remained intent on continuing with its schedule. For the GAA, itself a vehicle for cultural nationalism, not to proceed with its games would have been inconceivable, and its commitment to these ideals was reflected in its determination to continue its activities.

To some extent it was successful. Local and national reports of games are available during the early weeks of August and later.[39] The *Sunday Independent* even congratulated the Leinster Council for fulfilling the Leinster football final fixture.[40] The *Cork Examiner* also noted that 'owing to the war, it is not possible to give the usual space to the matches', something which may explain the lack of media coverage.[41]

GAA revenue inevitably suffered. The Kerry county board recorded 1914 as a remarkably bad year, leaving it in a very weak position, and in urgent need to fundraise.[42] The Munster GAA Council suffered disproportionately more than its provincial counterparts, as the Limerick and Cork sports fields were both commandeered.[43] Down over 40 per cent on 1913,[44] the Munster Council secretary remarked that the financial results were 'due to the war, and not to any fault of the Council'.[45]

Antrim GAA suffered too, in part, the secretary explained, due to the war.[46] It was also a difficult financial year for Kilkenny, although the chairman tempered this when he said that 'last year was a year of war, we have done fairly well'.[47] Galway county board also reported that gate receipts were down considerably, 'principally due to the postponements of matches through lack of railway facilities'.[48]

In spite of these facts, the GAA's Secretary, Luke O'Toole – possibly in a bid to project a positive spin – remarked in his annual report that 1914 had been a year of continued growth and prosperity.[49] While never guilty of impartiality, 'Vigilant' commented that, despite the drawbacks encountered, the Association was 'in every way a flourishing and more widespread institution than ever before'.[50] To this end, it must be considered that the Association did not suffer significantly from the war, and while some games may have been sacrificed, and finances may have taken a hit, 1914 was not altogether unsuccessful in a broader context.

The Gaelic Athlete, in its yearly appraisal, brilliantly illustrated why people such as O'Toole and 'Vigilant' were so sanguine. Far from being misguided, there was an air of pragmatism to how they felt. The appraisal talked of a country denuded of a considerable share of its male population and suffering from mass unemployment and serious travel restrictions – and yet 30,000 people had flocked to Croke Park to see an All-Ireland final.[51] This was indicative of the strength of the GAA and the hold it had on people, as well as being a testament to its professionalism and courage, to go on with its games at a time when other associations in Ireland and England had seen their games draw to a standstill, by choice or otherwise.

The Association's decision to continue with its games helped it avoid any of the long-term consequences other sporting organisations encountered. In fact, the vacuum created in the Irish sporting sphere by the war may actually have benefited the GAA. By the end of 1915, the Association was in a far healthier position – the inaugural Wolfe Tone Memorial Tournament had proved successful, big crowds had been drawn to games and morale in general was high.[52] However, while the Association rose to the challenges presented by the war, and maintained its vibrancy throughout the country, the impact of, and the attitudes towards, the war differed from county to county and, indeed, from member to member.

• • •

From its inception, the GAA was associated with Irish nationalism. Garnham writes that this association provided a fundamental starting point, and one which it was impossible to ignore.[53] Writing in 1916, GAA official and IRB man T. F. O'Sullivan contended that by the beginning of the twentieth century the GAA was a sporting organisation imbued with a distinctly nationalist ethos. O'Sullivan argued that the GAA had helped save thousands of young Irishmen 'from becoming mere West Britons'.[54]

Early histories of the Association helped to engineer the impression of a sporting body that had entered the political arena from its beginning. Consequently, when faced with the outbreak of the Great War in 1914,

how would the GAA and its members react? Would O'Sullivan's rhetoric counter John Redmond's call for all young men to enlist in the Crown forces, as 'the interests of Ireland, are at stake in this war'?[55] Would the fate of Catholic Belgium engender support from the shores of Ireland, or would the GAA and its members, seeking an opportunity to assert their own national identity and culture, react unfavourably to any calls to join the colours?

During the war's first year, it appears that many members had taken heed of Redmond's call. The *National Volunteer* reported that a large contingent of GAA men had joined the colours.[56] Indeed, in early 1915, the British Under-Secretary of State for War was asked if he was aware that the 'majority of Reserve Men and recruits who have joined in Ireland have been members of the Association'?[57]

The Kerry and Wexford teams parading before the 1913 All-Ireland senior football final. James Rossiter, who played in this final, fought with the Irish Guards and once wrote home that he felt more nervous before an All-Ireland final than before an Irish Guard attack on the Germans.

Some reports attest to this. Gunner Daniel Desmond of the Royal Garrison Artillery, killed in France, was a 'prominent member of the old Dunmanway F.B.C. which won the county championship in Gaelic football in 1897, and competed for All-Ireland honours subsequently at Jones's Road against the Kickhams'.[58] A renowned athlete and former captain of the Cork junior team, Rifleman Harry Burgess was also killed in France.[59] Private John McGeough was reportedly missing at the front. He was involved in the Irish Guards machine-gun section, and in his pre-army days was 'keenly interested in Gaelic pastimes'.[60] Bombardier D. T. O'Sullivan died in France. He was the brother of Michael J. O'Sullivan, the 'well known Cardiff-Irish hurler, who was serving with the Irish Guards'.[61]

Some GAA members played a major role in the war. Corporal John Cunningham was a well-known Thurles man, and a leading member of the local GAA club, who in pre-war days had played for the Leinster footballers. Part of the Leinster Regiment, he was awarded a Victoria Cross for an act of heroism and superb courage that caused his death. His obituary cited his 'most conspicuous bravery and devotion to duty ... there is little doubt that the superb courage of this NCO cleared up a most critical situation'.[62]

One of the most famous GAA players to have fought in the war was Wexford's James Rossiter. Private Rossiter of the Irish Guards played in the All-Ireland football finals of 1913 and 1914, narrowly missing out on All-Ireland glory. One GAA pundit described him as 'small in stature' but 'never slow to dash in and secure his ball' and 'seldom inaccurate'.[63] In one letter home from the front, he wrote how he felt more nervous before playing an All-Ireland final than in an Irish Guard attack on the Germans. Rossiter's brother also volunteered and was accepted into the Royal Garrison Artillery.[64]

Reports are also available documenting Connacht GAA men involved in the war. In 1915, *The Mayo News* reported that 'the members of the GAA in Mayo, who knew him well, will regret to learn of the death of Mr Martin Quigley ... in France ... before joining the Connaught Rangers, he was an esteemed member of the Junior Stephenite football club'.[65] According to his medal card, Quigley arrived in France on 8 October 1914, and his death is recorded on 12 February 1915.[66] The same newspaper also reported the death of Private Patrick Feeney, of the Connaught Rangers, who was a prominent footballer for the Mitchels Club.[67] Sligo county footballer Joseph O'Dowd also died in France.[68]

Clare GAA seems to have been badly affected. Seán Kierse cites a report in *The Clare Champion* in January 1916, which stated that 'unhappily the ranks of the Killaloe GAA have been sadly depleted owing to the war'.[69] Another report a month later suggests that the situation had further deteriorated; it remarked that 'recruiters are very busy in Killaloe, with renowned local athletes among the men recruited'.[70]

Following Clare's exit from the 1915 hurling championship, it was remarked in *The Gaelic Athlete* that the team's decline was 'probably accounted for by the loss of players they have sustained'.[71] A report in *The Clare Champion* in January 1916 suggests that some famous Clare players enlisted. It comments that 'the Gaels of the Banner county will be glad to hear that Sergeant George Fitzpatrick, Connaught Rangers, who was seriously injured in the Dardanelles is now recovered, and it is the famous

The 1914 Clare team, which included John Fox who, in 1915, enlisted in the Irish Guards and joined the Munster Fusiliers. Fox was injured in the Battle of the Somme in 1916, rescued by another serving Clare man and brought home to Ireland.

"Muff's" fervent desire that the war may soon be over in order that he may once again don the Green and Gold'.[72] The piece also mentions other prominent players serving with the 16th Division, reporting 'it is their foremost wish that the team would be kept going till they return'.[73]

In late 1914, the GAA section of *The Clare Champion* reported, 'we will be glad to hear that Kelly who played against Bealaha at Carrigaholt is alive and a prisoner of war in Germany'.[74] In the same paper in November 1914, an observer, writing facetiously on the recent poor state of football in the county, questioned why 'from Kilkee we hear nothing' and wondered if Sam Longford, Lanky Bill and all the boys had volunteered for the front.[75]

One famous Clare player who did enlist was John Fox. Born and raised in Newmarket-on-Fergus, Fox played wing back in the county's maiden All-Ireland win in 1914. One report on the 1914 Munster final noted

The Antrim football team that contested the 1912 All-Ireland senior football final.
William Manning was in this team, but later perished in France fighting for the
Royal Dublin Fusiliers.

 -Ireland Finalists

Fox's fitness. It is little wonder such a superb local athlete would be sought after by the British.[76] This may be one reason why his recruitment was reportedly seen as a minor propaganda coup for them.[77] In July 1915, Fox enlisted into the Irish Guards and joined the Munster Fusiliers. Growing up in the heartland of prominent Home Rule MP Willie Redmond, it is no surprise that Redmond was a major influence in his joining the colours.[78] Fox was injured in the Battle of the Somme in 1916. With shrapnel in the head, he was rescued by another serving Clare man, local itinerant Martin Faulkner. He was brought back to Dublin for treatment, but doctors advised against surgery and the remnants of the Great War remained embedded in his head until his death in 1967.[79] According to Fox's grand-nephew, Fox and Faulkner were initially captured, only to be later released by a German priest; Fox maintained that his Irish blood saved his life.[80]

Upon his return to Ireland, Fox was officially prohibited under Rule 21 from playing hurling, due to his involvement with the British Army. Yet he still remained involved in the GAA, featuring for Newmarket-on-Fergus on a few of occasions, although the former Clare great was saddened when jeered at matches for taking 'John Bull's soup'.[81]

The Cork GAA scene suffered too. Commenting that it was unnecessary to ask why, *The Southern Star* reported in September 1915 that 'for the moment the GAA in this part of the country seems to be in a state of hibernation', and it proceeded to call on a 'few of the best Gaels in each Parish to come together and resurrect the Association'.[82] An earlier report in April 1915 had suggested that, while the GAA in Skibbereen was suffering from the pressures of the war, GAA members of the local club had made the correct decision to enlist. At a meeting of Skibbereen Gaels, the chairman pronounced that 'for some time past, we had not a meeting of our branch of the GAA … that did not arise out through apathy … during our usual periods of practice a great movement sprung up, a war has been forced upon us … but Ireland has given her answer, this is a non-sectarian organisation'.[83]

The GAA in Ulster was not immune to the exigencies of the war either. In the 'Belfast Notes' of *The Gaelic Athlete*, it was written that 'the European crisis has been responsible for many of our most prominent teams "going weak"', with the Saint Peter's club having lost 'no less than nine of their best players'.[84] By May 1915, this figure had increased to twenty players, causing the disbandment of the team.[85] Seven members of the O'Neill Crowley's Gaelic Athletic Club, Belfast, had also died in action by July 1917.[86]

Dónal McAnallen has unearthed the names of several prominent Ulster GAA men who fought in the war.[87] Lance Sergeant William Manning of the Royal Dublin Fusiliers, who played for Antrim in the 1912 All-Ireland football final, perished in France in May 1918.[88] GAA officials in Ulster also enlisted. Patrick Holland, Dungannon, secretary of Tyrone GAA, and John Mooney, secretary of the Craobh Ruadh Gaelic Athletic Club, volunteered for service in the Royal Flying Corps.[89]

Ironically, one GAA man who did not enlist suffered at the hands of the Germans. The prominent hurler for Redmonds GAA Club Florence Buckley was a fireman on board the cargo ship SS *Iniscarra*, which was torpedoed by a German submarine. He had played on the Cork team in the 1915 All-Ireland hurling final against Laois.[90] The Cork county board passed a vote of condolence on his death.[91] Interestingly, the journalist 'Carbery', an 'unrepentant nationalist' according to one GAA historian,[92] wrote a piece on Buckley. He praised him for sacrificing his life 'in order that those at home may be provided with the necessaries of life'. He continued by reflecting that the names of men such as Buckley 'may not figure on the roll of honour, but their heroism will not be questioned'.[93]

Whether the same sentiment would have been expressed had he died in Flanders is worth considering, for attitudes of GAA members, in particular officials, towards the war were complex. In July 1915, the honorary secretary of the Galway county board, Stephen Jordan, was charged with having made statements considered prejudicial to recruiting.[94] At the 1914 Convention of the Cork county board, the acting chairman spoke bullishly on the aforementioned debacle of the county final (which was postponed due to military horses occupying the Cork Athletic Grounds). He said that Cork GAA had 'given our enemies an opportunity of belittling our Association' and it was up to all concerned to 'confute our enemies and lift the credit of the Association to the proud position it has all along held.'[95] At the time of the postponement, the chairman, devout nationalist J. J. Walsh, replied with certain insincerity to remarks that the ground was of bad sod as a result of the military horses' occupation, saying 'well we must make a sacrifice for the Empire … I am sure the grounds can be quickly put in order'.[96]

Within the Association the dichotomy of views towards the war was illustrated at one Galway county board meeting. The chairman affirmed the British as the 'most uncivilised nation in the world bar none' as a discussion proceeded on the motion of the GAA's Central Council to remove from the Association civil servants who took the Oath of Allegiance.[97] One delegate asked if there was any difference between these men and those who travelled to fight for the British Army on the 'misguided advice of leaders'.[98] The chairman replied that there was a big difference in favour of the civil servants as far as he could see. However, some support was expressed towards ex-British Army men; one delegate exclaimed that 'when on pension they did not belong to the Crown forces'.[99]

The attitude of GAA officials in Wexford seems to have been particularly critical of the war effort. Seán Etchingham, president of the Wexford county board, was a staunch critic of any man who had visions of joining the colours. A GAA columnist for the *Enniscorthy Echo*,[100] he invariably sought to demonise members who had thoughts of enlisting, and wrote that no honourable man would ever support recruitment into the British Army.[101]

Etchingham argued that 'never before was it so absolutely necessary for the Gaels of Ireland to realise their responsibilities and to strictly adhere to the national principles guiding the Association ... let the Gael stand firm and true to God and Ireland'.[102] The most dramatic example of Etchinghm's anti-war crusade came during a meeting of the Wexford county board in February 1915, when he argued that monies granted to a Mr J. Quinn, received for injuries sustained in a football match, be rescinded as he had since enlisted.[103] Indeed, a level of organised resistance towards the war seems to have existed in Wexford. Following the Volunteer schism, it was reported that members of the GAA, led by Wexford county board member Seán O'Kennedy, were 'all among the dissentients'.[104]

In many respects, the attitudes of the GAA hierarchy towards the war effort are demonstrated in a motion by the Laois county board in 1915, which sought to permit volunteering for the army during the war without the possibility of exclusion from the Association. The Laois chairman had argued that, with the increasing growth in the National Volunteers, it was due time that a move should be made to delete the rule prohibiting ex-British Army men from competing.[105]

The Gaelic Athlete expressed its annoyance that such a motion should be put forward and pleaded with Laois to withdraw it immediately, for 'there are many Gaels who will totally disagree with it ... the only course they can adopt consistent with their duty to their fellow Gaels, is to with-draw'.[106] Following its late withdrawal, *The Gaelic Athlete's* editorial spoke with delight at the outcome, for it would only have entailed 'playing into the hands of parties who have never been distinguished by an inordinate display of affection for the GAA'.[107] However, the fact that Laois GAA countenanced the idea at all indicates not only that large numbers of GAA members were involved in the war effort, but that not all high-ranking officials took such a hard-line position on the war.

Was it that the GAA in Laois feared for its survival upon the return of the suspended war veterans, or was it simply a case that Laois GAA felt it was the duty of all Irishmen to aid in the quest for European freedom? The more likely scenario seems to have been the former – given the scale of Irish involvement in the war, the crossover between GAA members and those in support of the war effort is unsurprising. A healthy relationship between the two parties certainly existed in Borrisokane, County Tipperary. On one occasion, the large number of GAA members on its roll book may have caused the local National Volunteers company, which supported Redmond's call to join the war effort, to postpone a planned march in November 1914, 'owing to the final of the hurling championship in Ardcroney'.[108]

General goodwill towards the war effort also emanated from across the GAA spectrum. When Michael O'Leary, the son of well-known hurler and footballer Dan O'Leary, was awarded a Victoria Cross for 'conspicu-ous bravery at Cuinchy',[109] his father was unequivocal in his assessment of his son's achievement – 'I knew he could do something good if the chance came his way.'[110] At the 1915 Annual Convention of the South Wales GAA board, secretary W. J. Fogarty was reportedly given a positive send-off to join the Irish Brigade.[111] The West Wicklow GAA board president, Reverend J. Clinton C. C., received a similar send-off from clubs as he left to take up duty as an army chaplain.[112] Finally, in Carrigaline Hurling Club, County Cork, members passed a resolution extending their deepest sympathies to John Barry, 'occasioned by the death of his brother Michael in France on the second day of the great battle'.[113]

In 1931, Phil O'Neill wrote that despite the Association generally standing firm to its 'old ideals and to the principles of its founders … it is sad to relate that a few one-time prominent members of the GAA turned recruiting sergeants for England and made a special appeal to the hurlers and footballers of Munster'.[114] Maybe O'Neill was referring to former

Limerick GAA county chairman and Munster Council member, Lawrence Roche, who 'led the royal Munster Fusiliers in the capture of Guillemont, a feat unequalled for bravery in the whole history of the War'.[115] He was granted a commission and proposed to establish an athletes' section in the Irish Brigade, issuing a special appeal for volunteers from among his former GAA colleagues and others.[116]

There are also reports in some newspapers of funds for wounded soldiers being raised at an athletic sports meeting at Glasson, 'under the auspices of the Gaelic Athletic Association'.[117] James McGuinn has written that a fund was also set up in Sligo in 1914, to which 'members of the golf club, soccer club … and Gaelic football club all subscribed generously'.[118]

References to the war were still evident throughout 1918. One observer in *The Mayo News* asked 'what has come of the Kiltimagh team since 1914? Have we to wait till the boys come home'?[119] The legacy of the war would continue for some time. At the 1919 Annual Convention, a motion was put forward by the Dublin county committee that 'ex-soldiers be not admitted to membership of the GAA for a period of two years from the date of their discharge', and on the proviso that they were not in receipt of a pension from the army authorities.[120] Furthermore, at a meeting of the Wexford county committee in April 1920, 'a number of ex-soldiers wrote asking to join GAA clubs'. It was decided that if they had been GAA members prior to 1916 they could rejoin immediately, otherwise a moratorium of two years was put in place.[121]

GAA members' motivations for enlisting varied. These certainly included the cause of Ireland and Home Rule, religious freedom for Belgium, economic considerations, and simply the lure of excitement and curiosity. It is also likely that men were influenced by the actions of their comrades – in the GAA's case, their teammates.

However, from the limited sample of evidence available, it may be surmised that the monetary aspect was a considerable factor. Aside from farmers, who benefited from increased food prices during the war, many classes of society suffered, in particular labourers.[122] Prospects were so bleak in Derry, one newspaper wrote that 'enlistment or unemployment was the question a good many had to decide recently'.[123]

Indeed, among the cohort of men known to have enlisted, the socio-economic profile is strikingly similar. The aforementioned Martin Quigley, the Gaelic footballer player from Mayo who died in France in 1915, was in his mid-twenties, a general labourer and the son of a fisherman.[124] His family circumstances indicate that he may have felt economically compelled to support them by enlisting. Private Michael Cooper of Taghmon, County Wexford, was a keen Gaelic footballer.[125] A member of the Royal Irish Regiment, his medal card states that he arrived in France on 17 December 1915 and his death is recorded on 14 August 1917.[126] The census records of 1911 suggest that he was one of two sons living in a large household. Like his illiterate father, he was a labourer, and may have felt obliged to seek economic refuge for his family's sake.[127]

It appears that John Cunningham, who was awarded a Victoria Cross, worked as a railway porter. He was the son of a labourer and, according to the 1911 census, he was the eldest child living at home in the Thurles urban area of County Tipperary.[128] Doheny GAA Club's James Crowley, 'whose prowess as an accomplished exponent of Gaelic football playing has distinguished him on many a hard fought field from Jones's Road, Dublin to Skibbereen' was also a general labourer; he joined the Irish Guards.[129] Tyrone footballer Patrick Corey, of the Royal Inniskilling Fusiliers, was killed by shellfire at Bethine, France.[130] It appears that Corey, too, was a labourer and that he left his wife at home to fight at the front.[131] Like his father, John Fox too was a labourer, and according to a family member, financial considerations certainly played a part in his enlistment in addition to political motivations.[132]

It is clear that the First World War made an indelible mark on the Association. Fixtures were cancelled, players were lost, clubs were affected and officials clashed. Contrary to what some earlier histories of the Association suggest, the majority of GAA members during this time did not necessarily share the political views of Seán Etchingham, T. F. O'Sullivan and their like. The scale of enlistment of GAA members into the British Army highlights the importance of looking beyond traditional interpretations of the GAA's relationship with Irish nationalism. Some GAA members saw enlistment into the British Army as akin to treason, but countless others did not. The differences noted across clubs and counties reveal the Association's highly localised nature in terms of its cultural and political identities. For many, the GAA was a sporting organisation with a strong local ethos. It imbibed nationalist ideologies, encompassing the politics of John Redmond and Home Rule, along with the more radical nationalism of the period. This resulted in some members going to war, while others rejected the call. However, there were also those who were merely pragmatic. Going to war provided a livelihood, which took precedence over politics. This dichotomy between the political and the pragmatic, in its own peculiar way, may have ultimately allowed the GAA's hierarchy to distance itself from the politics of the Great War and remain focused on its *raison d'être* – the games.

CHAPTER 7

The GAA, Unionism and Partition, 1913–23

DÓNAL McANALLEN

Minutes of the adjourned 1920 Ulster Convention.

THE PROSPECT AND REALISATION of the partition of Ireland affected both the GAA and unionism in a profound manner. The sporting organisation saw the political division of the country as anathema to the national identity it championed, and resented the practical difficulties of having to deal with a new and heavily protected frontier in the course of its routine activities. Unionism metamorphosed from an embattled minority grouping around the island to an Ulster- and then six-counties-focused political philosophy and party in clear control of its own regional parliament. Consequently, at the end of this revolutionary decade, the GAA and unionism appeared, even more so than ever, to be polar opposites and guaranteed to remain so.

How and why relations between the GAA and unionists – as a people and a party[1] – became so strained in the period from 1913 to 1923 will comprise the essential thrust of this chapter. It will also aim to establish the extent to which their mutual hostility worsened from what it had previously been, and to what degree the developments of this decade determined their interaction in the longer term. Particular attention will be paid to Ulster, the heartland of unionist activity, with occasional reference to the more disparate unionist community in the other provinces.

• • •

Irish unionism and the GAA stood at variance with one another long before 1913. Their enmity was framed by their simultaneous emergence as dynamic forces in the mid-1880s, taking opposite sides on the all-defining Home Rule question. In truth, a trend of unionist detachment from hurling and kindred Irish sports was well in train for years before 1884. An eighteenth-century custom of ascendancy patronage for hurling in southern regions subsided after the 1798 Rebellion and the 1800 Act of Union, which tended to drive a social wedge between classes and reinforce religious divisions. Protestants played the northern variants of hurling, namely *camán* (or 'common(s)') and 'shinny', until the 1820s in many parts of Ulster – and indeed up to the 1870s, at least in the north-west – but disengaged gradually in tandem with post-1798 sectarian divisions, religious revivalism, greater enforcement of the 1695 Lord's Day Observance Act by the (Royal) Irish Constabulary, and a general disapproval of rough-and-tumble games as being indecorous and wasting time that could be spent on industry. Hence by the time of the Great

Famine (1845–9), voices of authority, conservative newspapers and even novelists were prone to depict hurling as Sabbath desecration or a cover for radical secret-society activities. Such images surely influenced the Trinity College men who reimagined and differentiated their sport as 'hurley' in the period between the 1860s and the 1870s.

For all that several northern Protestant natives were to the fore of Michael Cusack's mission to codify hurling and nurture the infant GAA, after his departure in 1886 such personnel were conspicuously absent, and the Association became more closely identified with nationalism. Cusack himself had set the tone by inviting Nationalist political luminaries Charles Stewart Parnell and Michael Davitt to serve as patrons of the GAA, alongside the fiercely patriotic Catholic Archbishop Thomas Croke. The fact that Cusack *et al.* categorised and organised it as a 'Gaelic' association – not merely 'Irish' or 'Celtic' – may have also imbued it with an implicitly racial creed that would discountenance those of Anglo-Irish and Ulster-Scotch ethnicities. Yet the greatest disincentives to unionist involvement in the GAA from 1887 were its reputation for Fenian infiltration and takeover, albeit somewhat exaggerated in police and media reports, as well as clerical sermons; the reintroduction in the early 1900s of the GAA's bans on members of the British Crown forces and on the playing of association football, rugby, cricket and hockey – four of the most popular games among young Protestant and unionist men; and the practical problem that the playing of almost all field sports on Sundays elicited vigorous conscientious objections from Protestant citizens.

If southern unionists were generally indifferent to the GAA, more explicit anti-GAA sentiment came to be expressed as Unionist politics became Ulster-ised from the early 1900s. Some of the new wave of northern Gaelic clubs encountered bands of sabbatarian vigilantes on their travels, and affrays ensued in the Lisburn, Banbridge, Cookstown and Markethill districts. Each of these incidents prompted parliamentary questions at Westminster, wherein Ulster Unionist Party MPs contested the rights of Gaelic teams to 'disturb' predominantly Protestant neighbourhoods on Sundays, as a riposte to Nationalist opposition to Orangemen parading the 'King's highway' through mainly Catholic areas. Such attitudes would resurface with the advent of the third Home Rule Bill in 1912. During a House of Commons debate on the recent sectarian riots and the mass expulsion of Catholic employees from the shipyards, James Craig, MP for East Down, directed his condemnation instead at a GAA provincial athletic event at Shaun's Park, Whiterock Road. The Sunday sports in 'the heart of Protestant Belfast' amounted to a 'provocative action', he alleged, which 'may go so far as to set alight a fire compared to which these riots and recent trouble are but a mere nothing'.[2] In August, a Gaelic sports meeting at Glenavy, County Antrim, sparked a protest by 200 sabbatarians 'against the invasion of the … district by Hibernians from Belfast', and some violent scenes ensued.[3] By contrast, the GAA's sporting affairs and accomplishments were not brought to the notice of Ulster Protestants. None of the three unionist daily newspapers in Belfast reported a word on Antrim's remarkable achievement of reaching two All-Ireland football finals in 1912.

While the 1695 Act was no longer enforced on sport in Ireland, and the Great Northern Railway's former veto on trains to Sunday games abated in the 1910s (but for an occasional wrangle about fees arising), unionists' objections and attendant legal barriers to Sunday play still obstructed the GAA in areas where suitable playing fields were scarce. Belfast Corporation's by-law against Sunday games rendered its allocation of a solitary Gaelic pitch at Falls Park unusable on the GAA's main day of play even in a Catholic-majority, built-up area. The Derry city fathers' regulations forbade Sunday games on the municipal-held Brandywell ground. So too did a clause relating to Clones Agricultural Society's showground, and the sabbatarians had 'a monopoly of the town parks' in Monaghan, to the ire of local GAA officials.[4] Protestant landowners who leased a field for Sunday games could be isolated from their peers; after one north-Monaghan Orangeman was reputedly penalised for doing so, local Gaelic teams organised matches to help to pay his legal costs.[5] Further south, in places like Cavan and Navan, friction endured between GAA boards and unionist-minded agricultural societies over the prices to lease their showgrounds for Sunday matches. Prohibitions on Sunday sport were not simply an Irish unionist issue; the strength of municipal sabbatarianism in Great Britain would hinder GAA units there for decades yet. At Westminster, however, the political classes made special allowance for Gaelic games in Ireland. During debate on the Week-day Rest Bill in May 1914, there was broad acceptance that admission fees should not be restricted for Sunday matches in Ireland as in Britain. Edward Goulding, an English Conservative MP, lauded the GAA's 'reasonable recreation and amusement for multitudes of people on a Sunday'; 'every one of us … are convinced that the Gaelic Athletic Association does great good in

Ireland'.[6] Statements from his party would soon become as sceptical as those of Ulster Unionists about the GAA.

The close association of the GAA with the Irish Volunteer movement in 1913–14 did much to confirm unionist preconceptions of the Association as a militant nationalist body. This was a very public partnership: thousands of GAA players enrolled; Gaelic officials, such as Ulster Council President Patrick Whelan, took prominent roles in the Volunteers; local battalions paraded at headline Gaelic games;[7] and rallies and drilling took place on GAA-leased grounds. A drill competition for sixteen Belfast companies of Volunteers as part of a sports day at Shaun's Park in July 1914 was described by *The Irish News*' Gaelic games columnist as 'a test of proficiency both for officers and men in … the elementary stages of the work before us'.[8] Once the Volunteers split in the autumn, some press organs speculated that GAA officials would side against the Redmondite majority and discourage members from enlisting to fight for the cause of 'small nations'. This was not a bizarre supposition, as the Association's rules had long debarred soldiers from membership. GAA officials steered clear of an overtly political stance at this time, however. At an Ulster Council meeting in late September, the acting chairman, P. L. McElgunn, denied the suggestion that they were 'anti-Party men' and opposing recruitment, stating simply that, 'Men of all ideas are in the GAA'.[9] It seems likely, then, that Ulster officials, more so than their southern counterparts, eschewed political standpoints so as to avoid antagonism from their many unionist neighbours.

While hundreds of GAA members around Ireland, including scores within Ulster, joined the Allied forces from the start of the First World War, unionists held to the view that the Association had set to work against the British war effort. After the withdrawal in April 1915 of a Laois motion to the GAA's Annual Convention to formally waive the ban on 'volunteering in the Army for the present European war',[10] Unionist politicians took aim at the Association. Sir Frederick Banbury, a Conservative MP for London, enquired what the War Office would do about the exclusion of British troops from GAA membership.[11] Few if any instances are known of this rule being enforced against recruits in the early years of the war. Radical figures were beginning to gain more influence in some urban clubs and county boards, but subversive activity in the Association remained quite small overall. The many policemen who observed GAA matches found little untoward, contemporary intelligence files indicate. Ulster Council officials decried the deployment of police reinforcements at an inter-county game at Clones in July 1915 as tending 'to cast suspicion on the Gaels of Ulster'.[12] The unionist view that the GAA sought to undermine the war effort continued to gain traction. The very fact that the Association carried on with its full programme of games, unlike the other sporting bodies that suspended competitions, provided sufficient ammunition for its critics. When parliament introduced the Entertainment Tax in early 1916 as a means to fund the Allied cause, Irish MPs secured exemption for bodies engaged in 'reviving national pastimes'. *The Times* of London remarked that '[t]here should only be one "national pastime" now, and if the Sinn Féiners want to have their hurling free of tax, they can go into the trenches and hurl – bombs.'[13]

In the wake of the 1916 Easter Rising, authority figures and leading Unionist politicians went further than ever before to identify the GAA as an inimical force on the home front. In parliament, Unionist leader Sir Edward Carson urged the Chancellor of the Exchequer, Reginald McKenna, to refuse tax exemption to the 'Gaelic Athletic League' [*sic*], as it was closed to the Crown forces but open to 'men who are in open rebellion against this country'. A day later, Sir John Lonsdale, MP for Mid-Armagh, added that it was 'largely supported by Sinn Féin, the notoriously disloyal section' and 'consistently hostile to recruiting'; it could not warrant tax exemption, he said, as nearly 100,000 people paid to watch a game in 1915.[14] (In fact, the biggest crowd was merely 27,000.) The mud seemed to stick, however. The Chancellor, having previously confirmed that 'bona-fide societies' who adhered to their 'avowed object' were exempt, declared in July that 'Gaelic League' [*sic*] games had 'no title to exemption'.[15] Pro-Union politicians' repeated use of misnomers tended almost to lump all cultural nationalist groups together in sedition. After the resigning Under-Secretary for Ireland, Sir Matthew Nathan, also pointed an accusing finger at the GAA for being 'anti-British' and political at a post-Rising inquiry at Westminster,[16] the Ulster secretary, Owen O'Duffy, echoed the Central Council's refutation of this 'falsehood'; 'I have been at hundreds of meetings ... and I never yet heard a word of politics'.[17]

The instinctive defence of the GAA as a deferential, law-abiding organisation was maintained by county officers. During the post-Rising period of martial law, police permits were required for events such as Gaelic games. In late May 1916, Monaghan applied for permits to set the ball rolling. Despite the sacrifice of principle, Ulster Council officials agreed that it was 'better to play under permit here to try to keep the game alive'.[18] The spectre of partition was already looming in some minds. Within days of the Lloyd George proposals for temporary partition gaining acceptance from the Ulster Unionists and the IPP in June, it was remarked in the Gaelic games column of *The Anglo-Celt*, in jest but quite revealingly, that Derry GAA officials were eager to bring off their tie with Cavan 'before they are "excluded" from the rest of Ireland'.[19] Banter about this border lit up the sidelines at Ulster championship matches that summer: when one Cavan supporter rejoiced aloud that 'Ireland' won a game, the retort came, 'Fermanagh is still in Ireland'.[20] The re-election in early 1917 of county officers from the nationalist establishment – from teachers to justices of the peace, with Catholic clerics as patrons – indicated that moderates remained in charge. From his Ulster GAA presidential platform, Patrick Whelan entreated the government to drop plans for compulsory tillage with national service, and instead to free Irish internees and send agricultural officials to consult with the GAA; working together, he projected, they could stave off famine, quell unrest and lay 'the foundations of a peace and prosperity guaranteed both to Ireland and England'.[21]

As months passed, and nationalist views hardened in tandem with the stiff statutory response to the Rising, GAA members adopted a more resolute position. Owen O'Duffy held a line of resistance against payment of the Entertainment Tax, claiming persecution and at the same time gloating at their success. Young adult members in particular were flaunting solidarity with the separatist movement. By early 1917, the emergence of new Gaelic clubs bearing the names of recent republican martyrs, fundraising matches for internees' dependants, political emblems at events, and the use of Gaelic games in places as cover for Volunteer military training[22] all emitted an increasingly strident outlook. The fact that a trickle of rank-and-file players, notably from several Belfast clubs, continued to join the British Army and die on the European battlefields counted for little to the GAA's critics.[23] Ulster Unionist politicians renewed and increased their accusations against the Association, no matter how exaggerated they might be. In May, South Tyrone MP William Coote asked the Chancellor of the Exchequer again to force the GAA to pay tax, and demanded a stop to the use of petrol by 'thousands of young men of military age who indulge in joy rides' to games every Sunday in Ulster; these games were 'largely organised for the purpose of spreading seditious teachings'. The

Chief Secretary for Ireland, Henry Duke, replied merely that no such complaints had reached the RIC.[24] One exception to the onslaught came in *Ireland's Saturday Night*, a sporting weekly from the unionist *Belfast Telegraph* stable, which introduced a Gaelic games column in about 1915 and highlighted stories of erstwhile GAA players in the trenches; from 1917 to 1920, this was the only regular source of news on Gaelic sports in Belfast, as the northern nationalist *The Irish News* took the peculiar decision to drop such coverage. The norm remained that the Belfast unionist dailies, including the evening *Telegraph*, were impregnable to GAA news.

Conversely, the leading organ of southern unionism, *The Irish Times*, expanded its coverage of Gaelic games over the course of the revolutionary decade. Although starting from quite a small base, the Dublin newspaper's willingness to reflect the rising popularity of these games – irrespective of their radical connotations – set it apart from the Belfast unionist dailies. Its attitude also appeared to demonstrate that unionist tolerance of Gaelic sports was greater in the south. It may be surmised, without empirical data on the subject, that even then southern Protestants were proportionately more likely than their northern brethren to play or support Gaelic games, and that those from small farms and Church of Ireland families tended to be more sympathetic than ascendancy figures or members of other Protestant denominations.

The hurling stick became re-politicised at this time by the Irish Volunteers, who found the *camán* ideal for drill; they could assemble under the guise of hurling and start to play when police came into view.[25] After a Volunteer struck and killed a policeman with a *camán* in 1917, the Dublin Castle authorities imposed a ban on marching with the stick in military formation. Like other official proscriptions at this time, however, this action if anything backfired and led to a greater profusion of *camáin* on the streets. Hurling clubs sprang up on virgin soil, such as pockets of County Cavan. Come election time in 1918, the hurling stick was infused with a new political symbolism. Volunteers armed with *camáin*, wearing uniform and parading in military formation marshalled Sinn Féin rallies and polling stations. Such actions at the South Armagh and East Tyrone by-elections in the early part of the year – Éamon de Valera was reportedly escorted by a 'Praetorian Guard of hurlers' in Dungannon[26] – appeared purposely intimidating to supporters of other parties. The influx of many of these men from the south[27] also tended to vindicate unionist preconceptions of hurlers as rebels 'invading' Ulster to spread sedition. Sinn Féin aficionados would justify brandishing them as self-defence from hostile Orange and Hibernian foes. This argument was less credible elsewhere. The areas of east Cavan where *camáin* were borne in parades coinciding with the June by-election (which led to numerous prosecutions for illegal assembly and drilling)[28] were overwhelmingly Catholic; and, ironically, John F. O'Hanlon, the IPP candidate who lost out, had a much stronger GAA track record (as a past county chairman) than his conqueror, Arthur Griffith. This iconic sporting symbol had, without the GAA's imprimatur, become ingrained in unionist minds and memories as a de facto republican emblem.

The more nonconformist the GAA grew, the more unionist wariness of it increased. In joining the chorus of nationalist bodies voicing resistance to conscription in April 1918, the Association adopted a more outspoken position. Unionist-controlled Armagh Urban District Council, whose city hall had hosted the recent Ulster GAA Convention, received complaints about lettings 'for Sinn Fein or disloyal meetings';[29] no more GAA functions followed. The authorities' proclamation of unpermitted public meetings and sports that summer apparently made it 'treasonable to play Gaelic games' – to quote Joseph Devlin, IPP MP for Belfast (Falls)[30] – but once the GAA pulled off its grand act of defiance on 'Gaelic Sunday' in August, Sinn Féin activists were encouraged to organise Gaelic football tournaments and sports days under GAA rules as a cover for their activities, so the dividing lines between the GAA and republicanism blurred further. The spate of Sinn Féin 'Gaelic sports events' from then on may have had the support of a rural majority in the southern provinces whose rapidly radicalised opinion would register at the general election in December, but around Ulster such occasions caused more divisions at local level. The Redmondite *Dundalk Democrat* decried the descent of Gaelic sports 'into the troubled sea of politics until they were simply recognised as so many Sinn Féin demonstrations'.[31] The appropriation of

Ticket for the Michael Barrett Sinn Féin Club athletic sports meeting, 1918.

the GAA's name and structures for political ends did not bypass northern unionist citizens either.

Notwithstanding these intra-nationalist tensions in its own ranks, the GAA was then engaged in an attempted *rapprochement* with its traditional rival athletic body, the unionist-inclined Irish Amateur Athletic Association (IAAA). Some northern unionist sportsmen took the view that the GAA was less radical overall in Ulster than in other provinces or at the level of the national hierarchy. After the increasingly emboldened Central Council took the radical decision in December 1918 to expel members who took the (newly introduced) Oath of Allegiance for civil servants, the Ulster president, Patrick Whelan, a justice of the peace, had to step down; and the prospect of many teachers and others being ejected caused much dissension among northern branches, with Cavan leading a minor revolt against it.[32] A wild rumour spread that the issue would force a split between Ulster and the rest of the GAA. Some northern-branch IAAA officials talked up this story as 'a good thing', and mooted a strategic alliance with any breakaway Ulster Gaelic body, as the Central Council had 'been captured by the Sinn Féiners'.[33] This distinction was misplaced. With the election of IRB Ulster centre Séamus Dobbyn as the new provincial GAA President, and Ulster Secretary Owen O'Duffy ascending the IRA ranks, the Ulster Council was effectively under revolutionary control from March 1919. O'Duffy's trenchant opposition to partition came into view at this point. He wrote to the press to criticise the recent 'Soccer propaganda' and 'bribes' of 'West Britishers' to convert Gaelic teams on the edges of the province; this, he alleged, was being rushed '[b]ecause the British Government is about to make the attempt to divide Ireland into two colonies', and the push for non-Irish games was aimed to 'make the world believe that the people of Ulster are different from the rest of Ireland'.

The GAA's entanglement with Sinn Féin continued apace, notably in areas of republican strength, as the War of Independence intensified and spread to Ulster in 1920. O'Duffy was arrested at an Ulster Council meeting in April. The provincial body became inactive and play ceased in several counties in the latter half of that year, as some players engaged in IRA activity, and travel to games and meetings became more hazardous for all GAA members amid military reprisals and unionist vigilantism. The danger of attack was greatest in Ulster. In north Armagh, a man returning from a sports day under GAA rules was killed by a sniper in August.[34] In unionist-majority towns, well-known GAA officials and nationalists were sharply exposed to loyalist wrath. After the IRA assassinated DI Oswald Swanzy of the RIC in August, hundreds of Lisburn Catholics' houses were burnt: first up, the family home of William Gilmore, the former Ulster GAA secretary (1909–11) and the lone Irish Volunteer in the town, who left for Dublin. On that evening, William Shaw, the town's only Sinn Féin councillor and ex-chairman of the Lisburn GAA club that had been forced to stop playing in 1904, was dragged outside and beaten by a mob.[35] In September, John McFadden, a brother of the acting Ulster GAA secretary, Patrick, was killed by a gang of RIC and Specials in another reprisal in Belfast; neither brother was a combatant.[36]

The response of Unionist MPs to Bloody Sunday, 21 November 1920, was to justify the actions of the Black and Tans and Auxiliaries in invading Croke Park and opening fire, causing fourteen deaths, and to endorse the view that Gaelic playing fields were legitimate targets for reprisals after IRA violence. Parliamentary debates about the events of that day focused at first on the IRA's assassination of fourteen British agents that morning. When Nationalist Joseph Devlin demanded answers about the Croke Park atrocity, he was opposed by a chorus of Unionist and English MPs, who jeered, 'Sit down'. He got involved in a brawl with Major John Molson, a Conservative Unionist MP, while other MPs chanted 'kill him'. The unionist *Belfast News Letter* endorsed the official explanation by the government that there was no reprisal and the crowd fired first.[37] These attitudes augured badly for the GAA in the new Unionist-dominated Northern Irish state.

In this state, created by the Government of Ireland Act in December 1920, the GAA would be isolated in an atmosphere of even more acute political prejudice. The six-county northern state was designed specifically in order to have a Protestant and unionist majority, who clung to the Union with Britain and rejected cultural connections with south of the border. The GAA in Ulster – staunchly nationalist, strongly Catholic in membership, a champion of the establishment of an all-Ireland Gaelic republic and at times apparently sympathetic to the use of physical force – seemed predestined to be an enemy of the northern state. The hostility between the two entities came quickly to the fore amid the enveloping turbulence.

FOLLOWING PAGES: Minutes for the adjourned 1920 Ulster Convention, at which Owen O'Duffy was arrested by 'military oppressors'.

Cardinal Ó Fiaich Library and Archive

The adjourned Convention of Ulster Prov. Council was held in Mr C' Oneill's Armagh on Sat 17th April. There were in attendance:-

Cavan.   B.C.Fay.
Fermanagh   Luke Clarke P.L. McIlgunn
Down.   Mr McKenney & Bennett.
Armagh   James Cooney.
Donegal   Joe Murray.
Antrim   P McFadden
Derry.   J McLaughlin & Campbell.
Tyrone.   Mr McIloogue.
     and Sec

On motion of Messrs McIlgunn & McLaughlin Mr B.C. Fay took the chair as Mr O Dobbyn had been taken by the enemy.

Minutes of previous meeting were read and adopted. The Sect. then reported the grant of £50 each from Munster & Leinster Councils to Ulster Cncl and also the offer of Cork Co. Bd of a further grant. Mr McFadden moved a vote of thanks to Munster & Leinster Councils for their generosity and this was supported by Messrs Murray & Clarke who also associated it to the energy of our Sect and included him in motion. Mr O Duffy replied on his own behalf and promised to convey thanks of Council to Munster & Leinster Boards.

The Sect then explained results of Annual Congress. Regarding College Competit he reported that while colleges were playing Gaelic It was next to impossible to get them to take part in Inter-College matches. After much discussion the Sect. was instructed to write Rev. P. O Daly. Mon. re College Council and to have a meeting called of same. The Sec. along with Mr Cooney + McFadden to attend same. County Sect. were also instructed to give all the help they could and even try to introduce college teams into Co. C'ships. Suggestions were also made to Council Delegates at College Cncl. Mtg. re St Michaels Enniskilln and the various Christian Bros. School.

The motion re Delegates at Prov. Councils was next dealt with and Sect. Explained that it was optional to adopt Ruling or not Mr McElgunn moved that Ulster Cncl in future be composed of 1 delegate from each County. He felt sure that in this way Council mtgs would be better attended and Mr McFadden seconded. and motion passed unanimously.

At this stage armed aliens surrounded the place of mtg and invaded the room. The Secty being taken away by the military oppressors. The Council deliberations were only suspended while members wished our Sect. God speed and good wishes for a safe return. For some time the meeting was carried on under the eyes of the oppressor as an armed guard was placed in the room. The Council decided regarding payment of delegates expenses that 3rd Class rail + hotel Expenses be paid from nearest Railway station.

On motion of Messrs McIlgunn + Cooney

The Unionist party's landslide victory – forty of the fifty-two seats – in the Northern Ireland general election of May 1921 effectively made for a one-party government; its parliament in Belfast opened weeks later. Nonetheless, the Unionist regime remained vigilant against ongoing IRA violence to the point of developing a siege mentality, and even a paranoia, about the official Protestant and British identity being undermined. The security forces, which were dominated in these early years by the undisciplined and explicitly Protestant B-Specials, kept the nationalist populace in check, and the continuing involvement of some prominent GAA members in the IRA provided justification for them to scrutinise and shadow the Association's activities. The heavy-handedness of the Specials towards GAA members was evident in a search of players and spectators at a game in Killowen, County Down, in January 1921;[38] and in April of the same year, when Specials shot dead brothers Daniel and Patrick Duffin, both members of O'Donovan Rossa GAA Club, at their home in Belfast. The former was also a member of the IRA; the latter was not. During another flurry of violence in the city in July, the RIC reported finding a rifle and 1,000 rounds of ammunition at St Gall's GAA Club hall, which the unionist press depicted as having been suddenly ravaged by fire. The club denied that any weapons had been found, and nationalists attributed the fire to arson in reprisal for an IRA ambush.[39]

While they tacitly accepted that the GAA was generally peaceful and law-abiding, the Unionist authorities could not but notice that the long-serving Ulster GAA secretary Owen O'Duffy was by mid-1921 the head man in the IRA in Ulster, as well as an elected TD. O'Duffy's platform statement in Armagh in September – that the IRA could 'use the lead' against loyalists who bore arms – resonated deeply among ordinary unionist citizens and doubtless tainted their view of any association with which he was involved.[40]

When the Ulster Council reconvened at last in October 1921, it had to contend with new and significant realities that had arisen during its fifteen-month hiatus – chiefly, partition and the creation of the Belfast government. The provincial council appeared to ignore these matters, as they are absent from its minutes of 1921–2; likewise with the Central Council. An unstated policy of non-recognition applied in respect of the border and the northern state. Some GAA members might have opted for more diplomatic terms than the Derry Gaelic games columnist 'Lámh Dearg', who called partition 'the greatest scheme of plunder ever conceived by our enemies', and derided the 'pigmy Parliament' in Belfast.[41] In any case, the term 'Northern Ireland' was to be avoided in meetings and documents. Ulster GAA members hoped for these arrangements to be short-lived, for they had a profound social impact on them: some lost their liberty, livelihoods or even their lives, and others felt forced to emigrate. The Boundary Commission offered a slim prospect of salvation, but officials like O'Duffy were plotting to wipe out the frontier through republican military activities.

The entangling of the GAA with the IRA campaign culminated in a major incident on 14 January 1922, which reinforced the most sceptical unionist views about the GAA. Ten members of the Monaghan Gaelic football team were arrested by B-Special constables at Dromore, County Tyrone, en route to the Ulster final in Derry. About half the team were in the IRA, including the Fifth Northern Division commandant, Dan Hogan,[42] and weapons were found in their cars. They claimed the right to carry the guns as members of the now de facto official army of the southern state, who required self-defence as they travelled through hostile Protestant areas. It seems, however, that they aimed to use the game as a cover for a reconnaissance mission in preparation for the jailbreak of three condemned prisoners in Derry Gaol.[43] O'Duffy, as Ulster GAA secretary and the IRA Chief of Staff, was ideally placed to coordinate events with his protégé, Hogan. A northern military court remanded the players in custody, without proof of their plans.[44] Their detention without charge triggered three weeks of tumult, starting with the IRA kidnap of forty-two border-region loyalists as hostages for the players, followed by the deaths of five B-Special constables and a Fermanagh IRA commandant and foot-baller (Matt Fitzpatrick) in a gun battle at Clones, and then a spate of thirty killings in Belfast.

This amounted to a nightmare start for the GAA within the new state. Unionist politicians seized the chance to portray the football game as a sham and the Association as an IRA front. In the northern parliament, Belfast MP Robert Lynn spoke of 'the so-called footballers … arrested … with arms and ammunition … and bombs and all the other paraphernalia generally associated with Gaelic football'.[45] At Westminster, Thomas Moles, a hardline Unionist MP, claimed the team had up to '20 bombs in their car, and a corresponding number of revolvers'. Politicians of other parties called for the footballers' release, however. Winston Churchill, Liberal MP and Secretary of State for the Colonies, read out a letter from

O'Duffy and asked why, if there were evidence of bombs being found, had the Belfast government taken 'the very lenient course of saying that they would not oppose bail' should the men request it.[46] The Lord Lieutenant duly advised that they be freed. James Craig, the Prime Minister in Belfast, initially vowed to resign if the royal prerogative were used over his head, but reluctantly he consented to their release in March.[47] Thus the first Northern Ireland government narrowly avoided being brought down by a GAA team. Unionist leaders would stay on red alert, however, to what they saw not as a sporting body but as a threat to security.

The passing of the sweeping Civil Authorities (Special Powers) Act in April 1922, as a means to stem the violence, spelt more bad news for the GAA. The Ministry of Home Affairs resisted the temptation, however, to include the GAA on its list of banned organisations issued in May. Remarkably, somehow there are no surviving Ministry files on the GAA as a security issue in its own right, whereas intelligence files concerning the Knights of St Columbanus and branches of Irish-language organisations are retained. The RUC said of an Irish-language body in Omagh in 1923 that it was non-political, but 'like the Gaelic League it may later develop on other lines. A very close watch … will be kept on it by the police.'[48] It can be surmised that a close watch was kept on the GAA for similar reasons. The police seemingly saw little difference between the GAA and the Gaelic League, and occasionally confused the two.[49]

Members of the Association, as community leaders, were persecuted, nevertheless. The Minister of Home Affairs, Richard Dawson Bates, used his special powers as repressive measures almost exclusively against the Catholic population to direct the internment without trial of over 900 nationalists, including numerous GAA members, between May 1922 and 1924. Many were detained on the prison ship *Argenta*. Just a small minority of them were active in the IRA, some of whom were GAA members too, such as Willie Byrne (Down), David Matthews and Hugh Corvin (Belfast). However, many GAA members of note who had no discernible IRA record were also interned.[50] Anyone deemed to act in a manner 'prejudicial to the preservation of the peace' could be detained, and this was interpreted to include influential promoters of Gaelic cultural activities, whose removal would further demoralise nationalism at local level. The internment of Dan Dempsey of Belfast, who was then on a committee to discuss the recruitment of Catholic policemen, typified the flimsy pretexts for some actions:

Has always kept the company of prominent Sinn Feiners. Is a prominent member of the Gaelic League and a great enthusiast of Gaelic Games. Has frequently expressed his views in favour of the Sinn Fein party and most likely is a member of the IRA but because of the position he occupies did not openly drill or march with them.[51]

The embellishment of evidence to justify internment became quite routine. John H. King, the Down board chairman, was a case in point. King was a solicitor and Sinn Féin supporter who had lobbied for the inclusion of south Down in the Irish Free State, but the RUC posited that he might have 'financed several Rebel schemes' and was 'chiefly dangerous from the point of view of an organiser and a man willing and able to finance any movement against the Northern Government'.[52] Under such logic, any GAA official or benefactor could be interned. J. J. McKenny, the Down secretary, and three well-known Fermanagh GAA officials suffered a similar fate.[53] Many GAA officials and other local nationalist leaders lay low or went 'on the run'. One of these, the recent Tyrone GAA board treasurer, Peter Tohall, was targeted for internment on the basis that he had been a Sinn Féin judge and had agreed to provide first aid to the IRA; then the police inflated his record, first to suggest that he supplied 'material for the manufacture of bombs', and then that he was 'an active IRA man'.[54]

The effect of such measures on the GAA was instant. From May 1922, organised games lapsed in south Armagh and south Down as teams feared to take to the field. In June, a referee urged the Newry and District League Committee to make no more fixtures 'until the times change … as we are surrounded by A, B and C Specials … Bessbrook did not turn up yesterday.'[55] For the rest of 1922 very few Gaelic games were played – GAA activities fell through in rural areas of the six counties, with Belfast and Derry City alone playing on. The advent of the Royal Ulster Constabulary (RUC) in June, to replace the RIC in the six counties, compounded the position. The Protestant-unionist domination of the RUC earned it a reputation of partisanship. The few GAA teams taking to the road now faced multiple stops on their way, such as the Derry football team that was detained overnight en route to Cavan for a game in August.[56]

Such perils, amid high sectarian tensions generally in the north-east and the disruption caused by the Civil War in the south for both the GAA at national level and some erstwhile Ulster members, ensured that the hibernation of the Association in several counties lasted for a couple of years or more. At no time was the GAA completely dormant throughout the six counties, but four counties had been inactive for a year or more by April 1923, when Ulster officials tabled a motion 'to direct the attention of Congress to the importance of keeping the GAA alive in the North-East counties'. Ulster secretary Patrick McFadden said 'the North was able to fight its own battles, but it should get the support of the 26 counties and did not.'[57] The Central Council soon rejected the more specific proposal to appoint a full-time (paid) special organiser for the six counties. There was already in these counties a sense of abandonment by the rest of Ireland in the sporting realm as in other matters – a theme that would recur for many years. Nevertheless, within a few months county board structures were back in operation everywhere but Derry. As a general northern revival got under way, the Association became more conscious of and forthright about its continued all-Ireland structure, in contrast to the introduction of partition in other spheres of life, not least in the division of Irish soccer into northern and southern associations in 1921.

On a practical level, however, GAA officials faced a series of difficult decisions regarding recognition of partition and the northern state. Without open debate, the long-standing ban on members of the Crown forces was retained but reinterpreted: members of the Garda Síochána and Irish army were admitted to the GAA, although technically they protected a British-imposed border and dominion status for the southern state, but RUC members and Specials were tacitly barred from the outset as front-line United Kingdom forces. The retention of this rule acted more as a token peaceful protest against the northern state than as an active weapon of exclusion. Once the National Athletic and Cycling Association of Ireland was formed at last as a united Irish athletic body in 1922, the GAA retreated from its initial insistence on a replica ban on Crown forces, and acceded to the new body admitting RUC athletes to compete alongside GAA members in track and field. Around 1922, the GAA hierarchy also covertly removed the ban on oath-swearing public servants,[58] after the Free State gained sovereignty. Despite the Oath of Allegiance no longer applying widely in the south, TDs still had to swear one before taking their seats, so the subtle deletion from the rulebook enabled eminent Cumann na nGaedheal figures to stay to the fore in the GAA without conflict. On the other hand, the Promissory Oaths Act (Northern Ireland), 1923, required all public servants, including schoolteachers, to swear allegiance.

Some northern nationalists initially refused to do so. The Central Council confirmed, after a query from Ulster, that 'the taking of the oath did not debar teachers from participating in GAA affairs'.[59]

As the security situation quietened down, the Northern government quickly came under pressure to stamp a strong Protestant ethos on the state. Northern sabbatarians pressed for legislation to restrict Sunday Gaelic games. While the Lord's Day Observance Act of 1695 remained in place – 'N.I. will never admit that a statute of William III is obsolete,' remarked one RUC inspector[60] – it had become obsolete in relation to sport. Minister Dawson Bates deflected early requests from backbench Unionist MPs to take action on this front: first, in October 1922, he declined to empower local councils to proscribe public amusements or games on Sundays in their areas;[61] then, in March 1923, he rejected the suggestion of Major David Shillington, Armagh MP, to use his special powers to stop a game near Lurgan on Easter Sunday. It was 'a very objectionable thing to have football matches played on Sunday,' Bates said, but '[t]he question is whether there will be a breach of the peace, and I am advised that there will not'.[62] He deferred to the judgement of RUC Inspector-General Charles Wickham that neither using the Lord's Day Observance Act nor new legislation would be advisable. Their caution surely owed much to the GAA's sheer manpower. If they recalled 'Gaelic Sunday' in 1918, when the GAA arranged nationwide matches in protest against the laws requiring permits to play, they realised that an outright ban on Gaelic games would be defied on a grand scale and backfire, so increasing the prospect of disorder, forcing more Protestant constables to work on Sundays and costing a great deal to police. Prosecution of players of Sunday games remained more commonplace in Great Britain. As long as Gaelic games avoided regular melees, they would be let play on. Yet no Unionist MP dissented from Bates' statement that they all objected to Sunday football, and a sizeable body of politicians and citizens viewed this matter as unfinished business.

On taxation matters, even more so, the Belfast government's early legislation worked to the disadvantage of the GAA. The Finance Act (Northern Ireland), 1922, removed the clause of the 1916 Finance Act that exempted bodies 'reviving national pastimes' from the Entertainment Tax. Belfast's Minister for Finance, Hugh Pollock, did not highlight the change, merely stating that the rewording would make 'the intention of the Act … more clear as far as Northern Ireland is concerned'.[63] The clause's deletion went unchallenged, as Nationalist MPs were boycotting the chamber, and escaped attention in the nationalist press. Only when customs officers came calling in autumn 1923 did the change dawn on northern GAA officials. The Ulster Council held that the Belfast parliament had acted *ultra vires*, as London retained ultimate authority over taxation, and instructed club and county officers to show the GAA rulebook to customs officers and cite the 1916 exemption.[64] The Tyrone county board also wrote to the British Prime Minister, Lloyd George, to make this case.[65] Brian Óg GAA Club of Cookstown suffered the first prosecution by Customs and Excise for evasion (in respect of four games) and was given a court fine, which the Ulster Council paid.[66]

Inasmuch as the Unionist government had a sports policy in its infant years, its main purpose was to present Northern Ireland as a hub of modern industry, a British tourist destination, and a place distinct from the rest of Ireland. Straight out of the blocks, the Motor Vehicle Races (Northern Ireland) Act 1922 facilitated road closures for rallies such as the Ulster Grand Prix. Though not yet actively discriminating against nationalist sports, the Belfast parliament gave them much shorter shrift than did Dáil Éireann. Whereas the Free State polity considered Gaelic games supporters when revising Sunday opening laws, the Intoxicating Liquor Act (Northern Ireland) 1923 closed all pubs on Sundays and removed the clause allowing bona fide travellers to get a drink. Private golf clubs (which had eminent Unionist members) could obtain licences to serve alcohol in their clubhouses on Sundays, but GAA clubs had no such premises. Restrictions on Sunday trading also prevented visiting parties from buying food on match days north of the border; even in nationalist-majority Newry, spectators would have to go hungry. In respect of customs, the Free State caused a bigger border bother in 1923. Those crossing into the twenty-six counties had to obtain customs passes. The lengthy form-filling and the fee payments affected the GAA possibly more than any other organisation. Ulster Council officials implored 'that no more prohibitive restrictions be placed on our own people in [the] Six County area'.[67]

On the whole, however, staging inter-county matches north of the border posed sundry practical disadvantages. Monaghan and Cavan venues continued to dominate the hosting of major Ulster championship ties, based on the belief that they would draw bigger crowds; only three of the provincial senior football finals in the period from 1921 to 1945 took place in the six-county state. The resultant gulf in infrastructure and wealth, probably combined with psychological factors, was replicated and accentuated on the field: Cavan and Monaghan exercised a complete hegemony of the football championship over that quarter-century, while Antrim, previously the most successful county in Ulster, drew blank.

Other public institutions in the six counties adhered to unionist and sabbatarian tenets that inconvenienced Gaelic sports teams. Due to an enduring Presbyterian ethos at Queen's University Belfast, a Gaelic football and hurling club formed by undergraduates in 1922 was denied recognition. The Students' Representative Council first considered preventing 'an unaffiliated Club from playing games on a Sunday, garbed in the Varsity colours', but then simply blocked its attempts to affiliate.[68] Without official status and funding, the club soon folded. Such obstacles began to disappear south of the border, where unionists who harboured doubts about the GAA had to come to terms with their minority position in the nationalist Irish Free State. Whereas a new hurling club at Trinity College Dublin was initially refused internal funding in early 1921, by the end of the next year the university came under pressure during a Dáil debate from Dan McCarthy TD, the GAA President, to cease its 'boycott' of Gaelic games or lose its statutory grant.[69] The Dublin University authorities approved a revived hurling club shortly afterwards, and Sir John Ross, recent Lord Chancellor of Ireland and 1870s Trinity hurley player, lent his blessing too. One student supporter, Brian Maginess of County Down, argued earnestly that hurling was 'purely' Irish and 'we must in our collegiate life become Irish or "go under"'; he would later become a Unionist MP and Stormont Minister for Home Affairs in the 1950s. Add in players such as Patrick O'Brien-Twohig (later CBE) and several future clerics – notably J. G. MacManaway, a future MP for Belfast – and one can see that the Trinity hurlers who lined out in 1923 were truly the first Protestant- or unionist-majority Gaelic sports team since the birth of the GAA. After the fanfare around the club's debut, it faded away.[70] Several contested aspects of the GAA's ethos, above all the retention of the ban on members playing rival or 'foreign' games, would act as barriers to the re-emergence of such men within the Association thereafter.

Local councils became the sites of the most obvious unionist discrimination against Gaelic games. Only the larger urban councils had the means to provide playing fields at this stage, but party politics and sectarianism took priority over the considerations of need and amenity. Partition heightened the significance of control of a local council and the divisiveness of apparently routine matters north of the border. Unionist councillors tended not to consider Gaelic games as worthy of allocation of playing facilities, viewing them not as sports but as nationalist political symbols, which should be suppressed as such.

Unionist-dominated Belfast Corporation, governing the most densely populated city, had the greatest duty of provision of sporting facilities. The dire need for Gaelic pitches in the city arose amid recent civil unrest: the Antrim GAA county board, in some disarray, could no longer afford the rent on its flagship ground, Shaun's Park, and due to a lull in games, the Falls Park Gaelic pitch was being used mostly for soccer. A Nationalist request to exempt Falls Park from the Sunday games by-law was dismissed by the corporation's Parks and Cemeteries Committee in 1920. When the board wrote seeking to retrieve the Falls Park Gaelic pitch in 1921, the same committee replied that no preference could be given to any association or individual for the use of pitches – despite having already laid out most of its football pitches with soccer dimensions and goalposts. The Gaelic pitch was restored, however, and the GAA board then pressed for a second pitch, as it catered for two distinct field sports. Over the next year the Parks Committee rebuffed this plea several times – on one occasion seeking formal legal advice as to whether hurling was legal under city by-laws – and later declared that Gaelic posts could be put up only with the consent of soccer clubs playing on the park.[71] A request to play schools' Gaelic games on Falls Park's former cricket ground was also rejected, lest it 'render the ground practically unplayable for cricket' in the future.[72]

Outside Belfast, the most notable public playing fields lay in the hands of the Derry city fathers, Derry Corporation (or 'Londonderry Corporation', to give them their official title). Under proportional representation, introduced in the 1920 local elections, Derry and several other local authorities in Ulster swung over to Nationalist control for the first time. The new regime opened up the municipal Brandywell ground for Sunday games. Up to 2,000 spectators attended the Derry Gaelic football final on a Sunday in 1921.[73] Gaelic games had never been played on a better maintained ground in the city. The venue was even appointed to host the Ulster football final in January 1922. Once the Belfast government abolished proportional representation for local elections, however, Derry Corporation and fourteen other councils, mostly west of the River Bann, were captured by Unionists in January 1923. This grand dispossession had a hugely depressive effect on nationalism, which rippled into cultural and sporting realms. The Derry City GAA board collapsed in the summer of 1923, just when the Association was regrouping elsewhere in Ulster. The corporation increased the fee for Sunday games at the Brandywell ground by 75 per cent, on the basis of covering extra caretakers' wages on Sundays, with just one Nationalist present to dissent.[74]

A mere eleven local authorities, mostly small in size, remained under Nationalist control. Even Nationalist-majority Omagh UDC appeared to reflect the Unionist resurgence when it decided to limit Sunday entertainments in its town hall, and to report youths to the police for kicking football near a fair green during Sunday church services.[75] Overall, it was clear that Gaelic games would remain politically divisive subjects for local councils, and public Gaelic pitches would be hard earned in the years ahead. By contrast, the opening of Breifne Park in Cavan town that July seemed to symbolise an extension of the handover of power south of the border from British to Irish rule. This was formerly Cavan Showgrounds, where Gaelic games on Sundays had previously been unwelcome. At the opening ceremony, Cavan county council chairman, Andy McEntee, rejoiced that the ground 'out of which in his younger days he had often been chased for kicking football was now their own property'.[76]

Speaking at the same event, Owen O'Duffy, now the Garda Commissioner in Dublin, predicted an equally bright future for the GAA north of the border. Alluding to the relative calm at the time, he quipped that 'the RUC have presented a set of medals to the Crossmaglen hurlers'.[77] Aside from the improbability of Crossmaglen ever having a hurling team, O'Duffy's statement misjudged the mood of the northern security forces. On that very same day in Crossmaglen, the presence of armed Specials in armoured Crossley tenders and Lancia 'cages' (vehicles) at the Armagh club football final intimidated and disgruntled supporters.[78] Regardless of the IRA's depletion, the Crown forces kept up constant surveillance and forcible handling of not just returning republican exiles and released internees, but nationalists in general. As well as being searched and cross-examined on the road, Tyrone supporters going to Clones in August also had rifles pointed at them;[79] and border crossings were dreaded ordeals for teams from the south. While some soccer fixtures were heavily policed too – and justifiably so against a backdrop of crowd incidents and arms offences at Irish League matches – constables appeared to expend more energy on GAA personnel and their warnings of possible trouble at games seemed confined to Gaelic sports.[80] A report by Ulster secretary Patrick McFadden in October 1923, that the GAA's northern revival was still 'hampered by many difficulties placed in the way … by administration of the Belfast government',[81] held far more weight than O'Duffy's view three months earlier. Getting on with the games quietly would be the priority for GAA players and organisers in the immediate time ahead.

• • •

Partition cemented the traditional position of the GAA as a steadfast or recalcitrant nationalist organisation. The northern province of the Association, formerly among the more moderate sections, had hardened in sentiment in response to the course of events over the revolutionary decade. The perpetuation of various contested rules and policies, the increased use of radical emblems and names, the presence of leading republican figures within its ranks, and the perceived disturbance of Sunday play were the GAA's hallmarks or guilty traits that reinforced the prejudices of unionist citizens by 1923. Southern unionists who still disliked the Association felt more inhibited to say so in their new climate, while a few who wished to assimilate at local level began to join in Gaelic games. North of the border, however, the Unionist government and unionist-minded authorities began to use their new or enhanced powers to obstruct nationalist bodies such as the GAA. Belfast rule became more adverse than Westminster rule for Gaelic sports.

The shadow of the revolution and partition would hang over relations between the GAA and unionism over the next century. The continued prominence of the ideology and symbolism of republican separatism and the litany of martyrs from these formative years within the discourse and iconography of the Association would become a constant point of contention for pro-Union citizens. Northern unionists, for their part, would be accused of engaging in or tolerating routine discrimination against the GAA and Gaelic sports simply because these did not conform to their desired image of a loyal Protestant and British six-county state distinct from southern Ireland. The residue of this mutual distrust lingers today and it is for this reason that unionists still form only a small minority within the GAA membership.

CHAPTER 8

The GAA, the 1916 Rising and its Aftermath to 1918

RICHARD McELLIGOTT

The Gaelic Athletic Association, Limited, shall be a st⌐
political and non-sectarian Association.   No politicak
of any kind shall be raised at any of its meetings and ⌐
Central Council, Provincial Councils, County Committees
shall take part as such in any political movement."

The Central Council, therefore, gives an unqualified de
ment of Matthew Nathan, that the Gaelic Athletic Associ
festo on the eve of the Prime Minister's visit to Dublir
    The Central Council goes further, and states, withou
ification or reservation whatsoever, that neither direc
the Gaelic Athletic Association any connection with suc
Prime Minister's visit, as was displayed.

Part of the statement issued by the GAA in May 1916, see pages 142–43.

B Y 1916, THE GAELIC ATHLETIC ASSOCIATION was one of the largest organisations in Ireland.[1] Politically, the vast majority of its members would have described themselves as constitutional nationalists who fully supported the cause for Irish Home Rule. In this, of course, the Association merely reflected the political opinions of greater Irish society. However, by 1916 the Association, at all levels, contained a growing number of influential and radical nationalists who were prepared to support an armed revolt against British rule. Though these individual members in no way represented the official position of the GAA, they did reflect the continuing emergence of militant cultural nationalism within Irish society in the two decades before 1916. Significant numbers of GAA members were actively involved in both the planning and execution of the Easter Rising. On account of this, the GAA and its members would find themselves increasingly targeted by the British government in the weeks and months after the insurrection. Therefore, like Irish society at large, the years between 1916 and 1919 would see the GAA's broad membership become increasingly politically radicalised. The impact of broader developments in Irish politics had, by 1919, turned the GAA into an active opponent of British rule in Ireland.

This chapter will investigate the role of members of the GAA in the execution of the 1916 Rising and the consequences of the British authorities' response to the uprising for the ordinary membership of the GAA. It will endeavour to show the processes that changed the GAA from a body that, in 1916, had members who happened to be politically active, to an organisation that, by 1919, was, of itself and in its actions and pronouncements, supportive of the nationalist separatist stance of those who wished to secure independence for an Irish Republic.

• • •

Perhaps it is not surprising that GAA members would be prominent in the Easter Rising, given the close involvement of so many GAA men with the Irish Volunteers. In November 1913, Eoin MacNeill had urged Irish nationalists to look to the example of the Ulster Volunteers and create a similar force to protect their right to Home Rule.[2] A week before, the *Dublin Leader* was already urging every GAA club to take the initiative in forming such a movement.[3] The RIC was worried about the potential for Irish nationalists arming, commenting that 'the Gaelic Athletic

Association could supply an abundance of first class recruits'.[4] Their fears proved justified. On 25 November 1913, a large public meeting was held in the Rotunda in Dublin at which the Irish Volunteers were formally established. The GAA's Secretary, Luke O'Toole, joined MacNeill on stage during the rally to address the 7,000-strong crowd.[5] Across Ireland, the Volunteers spread rapidly as nationalists, determined that Home Rule be realised, filled the ranks to protect its implementation from Unionist aggression. As the Volunteers became more widespread and started to recruit young and active men, it was inevitable that a large proportion of its force would be drawn from the GAA. The extent of this dual membership only increased as the Volunteers grew.[6] In areas like Kerry, the GAA played an instrumental role in the organisation and spread of the Volunteer movement.[7]

Yet the powerful unity of the Irish Volunteer movement was shattered by the outbreak of the First World War. John Redmond's open call for the Volunteers to enlist in the British war effort split the organisation in twain between Redmond's renamed National Volunteers and the Irish Volunteers faction under MacNeill's leadership.[8] By December, British intelligence estimated that out of a total force of 188,000 members, 174,500 had endorsed Redmond's position, but 13,500 had adhered to MacNeill.[9] While the vast majority of the GAA's membership within the Volunteers also stuck by Redmond, there is some evidence that the wider divide in the Volunteers permeated into individual clubs. Laune Rangers in Killorglin, County Kerry, almost fragmented because of a dispute among its members over the Volunteers split.[10] Despite the influence of the IRB within the GAA's leadership and their close connections with MacNeill's more radical splinter group, they had little influence over the loyalty of the Association's grass-roots membership. The GAA instead took the wise course of neutrality as far as the split was concerned. However, the editors of its official organ, *The Gaelic Athlete*, left few in doubt as to where their allegiance lay and decried Redmond's 'despicable imperialism' for causing the split.[11] Despite the Association's official stance of neutrality, by 1916 at least twelve individual county boards had clearly aligned themselves with MacNeill's Irish Volunteers.[12]

By now, the ruling Supreme Council of the IRB had already come to the decision to stage an armed insurrection against British rule before the end of the Great War. In May 1915, they set up a military coun-cil to plan such a revolt using the Irish Volunteers.[13] To aid the rebel-lion, a German arms shipment was arranged to land in Kerry in the days before its outbreak.[14] Aware of the potential of the GAA to aid its designs, the IRB had long sought to gain more influence in the Association. As Kerry was a lynchpin in the success of the venture, close links were established between the Rising's planners and local Volunteer leaders, many of whom were prominent local GAA officials. The IRB had remained a near-constant influence within the leadership of the Kerry GAA since the formation of its county board in 1888.[15] In this sense, the Kerry GAA contrasted with much of the rest of Ireland, where there were few overt links between the IRB and local GAA leadership. For example, by 1915 Austin Stack, the Kerry GAA chairman, had become the acknowledged head of both the IRB and the Irish Volunteers in the county.[16] As such, Kerry represented a county where the IRB could reasonably expect the cooperation of the local leadership of the GAA for its plans.

· · ·

In preparation for the Rising, Stack used the occasion of the All-Ireland final between Kerry and Wexford in November 1915 as a cover for an operation to smuggle a sizeable consignment of weapons from Dublin to Kerry, in order to adequately arm the local Volunteers. Tadhg Kennedy, a lieutenant in the force and a member of the Kerry county board, was put in charge of a group of Volunteers ostensibly travelling as supporters to the match. Once the weapons were secured, they were smuggled aboard the returning supporters' train to Tralee the following evening.[17] These weapons provided the bulk of the Kerry Volunteers' armament during Easter week 1916.[18] On a national level, a growing connection between the leadership of the GAA and the Irish Volunteers was apparent when, on the night of the same All-Ireland final, an informal conference between Volunteer leaders and the GAA's Central Council took place.[19] Police reports were in no doubt that the Irish Volunteers were increasingly supported by extremists within the GAA and that many of the Association's members were enlisting in the organisation.[20] Nonetheless, on a national level, it is difficult to say at this point how significant cross-membership between the GAA and the Volunteers was as an indication of the former's support for physical-force nationalism. It is as likely that many GAA members enrolled in the Volunteers simply to protect themselves from the growing prospect of British Army conscription, due to the losses being sustained in the war against Germany.[21]

Nevertheless, the leadership of the GAA in Kerry would play a significant role in the final plans for the rebellion. In February 1916 Stack was informed that the German arms consignment would be landed near Tralee by a ship, the *Aud*, which would arrive during the Easter weekend. Once the arms were ashore they were to be distributed among the Volunteers in Munster and used to prevent the movement of British reinforcements from the countryside into Dublin, where the main uprising would take place.[22] Stack effectively used local GAA connections to plan the landing. Patrick O'Shea, an All-Ireland winner with the Kerry team, was tasked with securing a trusted local harbour pilot to rendezvous and guide the German ship when it appeared off the Kerry coast.[23] In fact, so seemingly preoccupied had members of the county board become with Volunteer activity, the local press lamented that the GAA itself had become dormant in Kerry.[24] Despite the involvement of many within the Kerry GAA, it must be stressed that the vast majority of GAA members nationally and locally had little idea that an insurrection was being contemplated. Even in Kerry, those members who were part of the Volunteers' rank and file had little notion of what their leaders were undertaking.

The 1916 Rising would prove a costly failure in military terms and its repercussions would have serious consequences for the Association. The military council's plans for revolt began to fail almost as soon as they had been committed to action. For example, on Good Friday, two days before the rebellion was due to begin, the *Aud* was intercepted by the Royal Navy before it could land its weapons in Kerry.[25] Despite this setback, in Dublin it was decided to press ahead with the insurrection.

It is clear the Association as a body was no active participant in the rebellion nor had its national leadership possessed any inside knowledge of its secret planning, although the contrary has often been forcefully argued by historians of the GAA in the decades following Irish independence.[26] Like the greater Irish public, the overwhelming membership of the GAA was caught off-guard by the Rising. Nothing better illustrates this than the fact that less than twenty-four hours before the rebellion broke out, the GAA held its Annual Convention as usual in Dublin's City Hall. However, among those in attendance was Harry Boland, the President of the Dublin GAA and a leading member of the city's IRB and Volunteers, who would take an active part in the uprising.[27] The following morning, as he prepared to join the main rebel garrison in the GPO, J. J. Walsh, chairman of the Cork GAA, recounted that he met the GAA President,

The annual Convention of the Gaelic Athletic Association Ld. was held at the Council Chamber City Hall Dublin on Easter Sunday 23rd April 1916. Ald Nowlan Presiding The following member of the Central Council Athletic Council & Various Prov Councils as well as delegate from each County were in attendance

63

LATE MR. F. B. DINNEEN

At the opening of the proceedings the Chairman referred sympathetically to the death of Mr. F. B. Dinneen, and said that the Association had sustained a great loss by his unexpected demise. He proposed: "That we, the members of the Gaelic Athletic Association in convention assembled, desire to place on record an expression of our profound regret at the sad demise of our old colleague, F. B. Dinneen, and we desire to tender to his relatives our sincerest sympathy in their sad bereavement; and that copies of this motion be sent to his relatives and the Press."

Mr. Patrick M'Grath, Tipperary, Secretary Munster Council, who seconded the motion, said that he had the pleasure of Mr. Dinneen's uninterrupted friendship for at least thirty-five years. He knew the great interest Mr. Dinneen had taken in the Association, to which his death was a great loss.

Mr. Jas. Harrington, Cork; Mr. John Kelly, Chairman Limerick County Board; Mr. J. J. Hogan, President of the Leinster Council; Mr. Thos. Kenny, President of the Connaught Council; Mr. P. Whelan, J.P., President Ulster Council; Mr. M. Brennan, Chairman Roscommon County Board; Mr. J. O'Brien, President of the Munster Council and Mr. H. Boland, Chairman County Dublin Committee, also associated themselves with the motion and paid a warm tribute to Mr. Dinneen's great work for the Association.

The motion was unanimously adopted.

The minutes of last annual Convention having been taken as read, the report and balance-sheet of the Central Council for the past year were considered. The accounts showed that the gross receipts for the year ending February 29, 1916, were £1,937 18s 7d, and the total disbursements £2,132 9s 5d, being an excess of £194 10s 10d of disbursements over receipts.

The Croke Park accounts were given separately, and showed that the total receipts for the year ending February 29th were £524 18s 1d, and the expenditure £317 18s 1d, leaving a credit balance of £207.

The Secretary's report dealt with the progress of the Association during the year.

On the motion of the Chairman, seconded by Mr. M. F. Crowe, trustee, the report and statement of accounts were unanimously adopted.

Election of Officers.

The election of officers was next proceeded with. The Secretary announced that there was only one nomination for the Presidency, viz., Alderman Nowlan (outgoing), and he had great pleasure in declaring Ald. Nowlan re-elected (applause). The Secretary also announced that there were only two nominations for the two trusteeships, viz., Messrs. D. Fraher (Waterford), and M. F. Crowe (Kerry), the outgoing officers, and he had great pleasure in declaring these two gentlemen re-elected (applause).

The Athletic Council report and balance sheet was next considered. The accounts showed that the gross receipts for the year ending February 29th were £332 10s 5d, and the expenditure £366 2s 7d, leaving a balance in hands of £14 4s 6d. The balance in hands at the commencement of the season was £47 16s 8d. The report of the Athletic Council Secretary referred to the great progress made in the Athletic Department during the year, and stated that two world's records were made by John O'Grady (Co. Limerick), viz., the 28lbs and the 56lbs. The report stated that 41 meetings were held in Leinster, 24 in Munster, 19 in Connacht, and eight in Ulster, showing a slight decrease in Leinster, Munster, and Ulster, and an increase in Connacht. It also stated that 16 All-Ireland Athletic and seven cycling championships were held during the season, and also that a number of provincial cycling and athletic competitions were held in the various provinces under the auspices of Sports Committees. The National Cross-country championships, held at Larkfield on March 28th, were also referred to. The number of athletes registered for the season was given as 375, as against 609 for the preceding season.

On the motion of Mr J. J. Keane the report and accounts of the Athletic Council were unanimously adopted.

Provincial Council Accounts.

On the motion of Mr J. J. Hogan, the report and statement of accounts of the Leinster Council were adopted. The total receipts for the year were shown as £1,514 3s 3d, and the expenditure £1,447 5s, showing a credit balance of £66 18s 3d.

Mr. James Miller seconded the adoption of the accounts, which were passed without discussion.

On the motion of Mr. P. Whelan, J.P., seconded by Mr. Dempsey, the accounts of the Ulster Council were passed. The receipts were shown as £327 18s 3d, and the expenditure £305 2s 8d, leaving a balance to credit of £22 15s 7d.

The Munster Council accounts were next proposed. The receipts showed that the total cash received for the year was £1,443 1s 10d, and the expenditure £1,254 10s 10d, showing a credit balance of £26 7s 3d.

The receipts of the Wolfe Tone Memorial Tournament, held by the Munster Council,

[handwritten margin note:] the motion of Harrington to Nolan

The UCD team that won the Sigerson Cup in 1915. Éamon Bulfin, the man who raised the tricolour over the GPO on Easter Monday 1916, is fourth from left in the back row wearing what appears to be a goalkeeper's jersey.
UCD SPORTS CENTRE

Alderman Jim Nowlan, and several other GAA officials as they were heading home from the Annual Convention.[28] On returning to his home town of Kilkenny that evening, Nowlan was arrested for his membership of the Sinn Féin movement, which the authorities now believed was rebelling against them.[29]

Hundreds of politically active GAA members within the Irish Volunteers took part in the Rising. William Nolan has identified 302 players from 52 separate Dublin GAA clubs who were numbered among the rebels' combined force of around 1,300 men and women. There is evidence of a large degree of participation by individual Dublin GAA clubs, with sixty-nine members of the St Laurence O'Toole club alone taking part in the fighting.[30] By Tuesday, GAA men were stationed in all major rebel outposts in the city. In the GPO, Walsh was joined by the likes of Domhnall Ó Buachalla, the then captain of the Kildare footballers and leader of the Maynooth Volunteers, who would go on to become the Governor General of the Irish Free State.[31] Another occupant of the GPO was Éamon Bulfin, captain of UCD's 1915 hurling team (which won the Fitzgibbon Cup) and commander of the university's Volunteer company. Bulfin was the rebel given the privilege of hoisting the Republican tricolour over the roof of the GPO, once the position had been taken.[32]

In the south-east of the city, the Dublin Volunteers' Third Battalion, under the command of Captain Éamon de Valera, took up positions centred on Boland's Mills. Among the garrison were several players of the Fontenoy, Sandymount and St Andrews GAA clubs.[33] Ironically, in what would be one of the first actions of the Rising, some of these men would soon attack a unit of the Irish Association of Volunteer Training Corps, recruited from members of the IRFU. This force consisted of part-time military reservists, many of whom were professionals deemed too old to enlist for active service.[34] They had been on a field exercise in Wicklow when they heard of the rebellion and were cautiously making their way back to their depot in Beggars Bush barracks. A detachment under the command of the IRFU's President, Francis Browning, was ambushed by the Volunteers on Haddington Road. Browning and four other IRFU members were cut down.[35]

Outside of the city itself, GAA men were also active in the other rebel actions that took place during Easter week. For example, the commander of the Dublin Volunteers' Fifth Battalion, stationed in north county Dublin, was Thomas Ashe, a former captain of the Lispole GAA club in Kerry and founder of the Lusk GAA club.[36] With a force of sixty men, Ashe commanded one of the most successful actions of Easter week. On Friday 28 April, he attacked a large RIC force of fifty men in Ashbourne, County Meath, killing ten officers, wounding a further eighteen and capturing the rest, with the loss of only two Volunteers.[37] In Galway, 500

Volunteers assembled on Easter Monday and carried out some limited attacks on local police barracks. The majority of these men were hurlers and members of local GAA clubs.[38] Meanwhile, in Wexford, Volunteers led by prominent local GAA men Seán Etchingham and Seamus Doyle used the pretext of an Easter Sunday GAA match in Wexford Park to cover their turnout for the Rising.[39] They managed to advance upon and hold Enniscorthy for several days before surrendering.[40] In all, five of the fifteen men executed for their part in the Rising had GAA connections.[41] Other prominent rebels captured, such as Stack, Boland, Walsh, Ashe and Michael Collins, had been local and national administrators within the organisation.

• • •

The members of the Association who were active in the rebellion were radical nationalists, in the main IRB men, long committed to the overthrow of British rule in Ireland. They neither represented nor reflected the political views of the national membership of the GAA in 1916. However, this overlap between radical nationalists and GAA members is perhaps easy to explain. Because of their political outlook, men like Boland, Walsh or Stack would naturally have joined any movement with nationalist credentials, either to cement their own identity or to use as cover for recruitment into the IRB.[42] Thus, in addition to attaining office in the GAA, such men were just as likely to be fervent supporters of bodies like the Gaelic League.[43] Historically, many prominent officials within the Association had been given to delivering pronouncements that seemed to support a brand of physical-force nationalism, and the impression given (and often intended) was that the speaker's views were also those of the GAA.[44] The tenor of such declarations could only serve to attract men of the physical-force persuasion into the Association, and those advocates often became proportionately more prominent in the affairs of the GAA than, for example, the moderate constitutional nationalist supporters of the Irish Parliamentary Party (IPP).[45]

In the immediate aftermath of the Rising, public opinion across Ireland decried the rebels. Likewise, the vast majority within the rank-and-file membership of the GAA censured their actions.[46] Nevertheless, the months after the rebellion witnessed the GAA and its members becoming increasingly politically radicalised. This radicalisation was in part due to the response of the British authorities to the Association in the weeks and months after the revolt. In their attempts to discover the cause for the rebellion, the British government quickly turned their attention to the GAA. It is easy to understand why they would have targeted the Association as an active participant in the rebellion. Many of its leading figures were men of extreme nationalist views and had been arrested and sentenced for their role in the Rising. In addition, the GAA, since its inception in November 1884, had been actively identified as a semi-seditious body by the British authorities. An IRB element had always been apparent within its national leadership and periodically, as in 1887, had attempted to take full control of the GAA's ruling Central Council. This move led to the Association's near destruction as politically moderate members became alienated from its ranks, while the Catholic Church began to actively denounce it.[47] When the GAA experienced a period of revival and renewed growth in the early twentieth century, the IRB began again to secure key positions within it. However, learning from the mistakes of the past, they adopted a more subtle strategy, forgoing any open recruitment of GAA members, and preferring to use their influence to get members elected onto the Central Council and county boards. Given this continued IRB element within the GAA's higher echelons, it was only natural that the British authorities would target the Association in connection with the Rising.

On 25 April 1916, martial law was proclaimed across the country, and the holding of matches or sporting tournaments was strictly prohibited. As a result Gaelic games were suspended.[48] About 3,400 men and women across Ireland were arrested and deported in the days following the Rising for their supposed involvement with the rebellion.[49] Due to the close connection between some leading members of the GAA and the Irish Volunteers, those targeted for arrest included hundreds of ordinary members of the GAA.[50] Many found themselves deported to special internment camps such as Frongoch in north Wales. The detention of so many young men, several with little previous involvement in organisations like the IRB or the Irish Volunteers, brought them into contact with the emerging revolutionary political doctrine.[51] Due to their shared incarceration, many GAA members also became politically radicalised. Internment proved an excellent training camp for the Volunteers. It allowed officers to subject their men to proper military drill. The realities of incarceration also turned them into a mentally tougher force.[52] William Mullins, an internee and footballer with the Tralee Mitchels GAA Club, stated: 'I am fully convinced that Frongoch made our whole organisation into what it eventually reached. The comradeship that developed and the knowledge … [of] the military aspect of things was a binding force for the future. John Bull made an awful blunder when he put us all together there.'[53]

Owing to the numbers of Gaelic players interned in the camp, Gaelic football contests were arranged to keep up discipline, fitness and morale among prisoners.[54] Indeed, the boredom of prison life and lack of other distractions ensured that even former sceptics took up Gaelic games. Dick Fitzgerald, the former All-Ireland winning Kerry captain and Michael Collins, a previous member of the London GAA who had fought in the GPO, organised a series of GAA tournaments.[55] Two matches were played daily and a league competition was also organised among four teams, with each competing in six games. The teams were called after the leaders of the Rising. The fourth team, nicknamed 'The Leprechauns' due to the small stature of the players, was coached by Dick Fitzgerald and actually won the competition.[56] Inter-county contests were also arranged, and the main pitch in Frongoch was renamed Croke Park. The final of one tournament pitted the Kerry and Louth internees against one another, with Kerry winning by a point.[57] If Frongoch became a school of revolution, it is significant that Gaelic games were predominant. The concentration on Gaelic games could be seen as a deliberate statement symbolising the prisoners' commitment to the struggle for Irish independence and a rejection of British rule.[58]

A Royal Commission on the rebellion in Ireland, set up to investigate the Rising, concluded that the whole affair was perpetrated by the Irish Volunteers and asserted that its entire leadership consisted of separatists drawn mainly from four anti-British bodies, of which the GAA was one.[59] The Irish Volunteers were said to have practically full control over the Association.[60] Yet, as a consequence of the government's internment of the more extreme nationalists within the Association, it was the moderates within the Central Council who were left to deal with the charges levelled by the Royal Commission.[61] In response, they issued a press statement vehemently denying the accusations.[62] In the political climate of the time, it was obvious that the GAA wished to disassociate itself as much as possible from the Rising to avoid any further government crackdown on it or its members. The statement was thus devoid of any sympathy for the rebels or their deaths. The GAA, like every other major nationalist body in Ireland, showed no immediate empathy with those who took part in the rebellion, or their cause.[63] The IPP did not consider the GAA itself as having played any role in the rebellion. Indeed, the Irish MP and long-standing GAA member Thomas Lundon called on the Prime Minister to let GAA games resume in those parts of the country unaffected by the Rising in Dublin.[64] Yet some within the GAA were proud that the Association had been implicated, an act which seemed to reaffirm its nationalist credentials. The former GAA Secretary, Maurice Moynihan, noted that any national organisation worthy of its name had been drawn into the inquiry and it would 'be most uncomplimentary to the Association if it were omitted'.[65]

Between July and August 1916 the majority of the internees were released. By now Irish public opinion had begun to turn against the British establishment. This public reaction was influenced by the harsh execution of the rebel leaders, the mass arrests and internments without trial, as well as the continued imposition of martial law and the undiminished fear that Irishmen would soon be forced into conscription for the British Army.[66] As early as June 1916, the authorities had been reporting a shift in nationalist opinion in Ireland towards empathy with the rebels.[67] Once restrictions on sports events were lifted, GAA matches provided some of the earliest opportunities for displays of this growing surge of empathy.[68] In July, the Tipperary hurlers played a match wearing rosettes symbolising their sympathy for the executed leaders of the Rising, an action greeted with wild cheers by the crowd.[69] Soon the authorities were noting that '[a] discontented and rebellious spirit is widespread [which] frequently comes to the surface at Gaelic Athletic Association tournaments'.[70] Following the rebellion, British authorities conducted a campaign of harassment against the GAA on both local and national levels. In some areas, the police continued to obstruct GAA activity months after the ending of the Rising. By September 1916, it was still reported in Kerry that local police were forcing entry into GAA events.[71] The arrest and detention of many within the Association also hardened members' views of the British government. The rise of the Sinn Féin party between 1917 and 1918 would provide the catalyst for the political radicalisation of Irish society and with it the GAA.

• • •

At a special meeting of Central Council held at Croke Park on Sunday, 28th May 1916, Mr. J.J. Hogan presiding in the absence of Ald. Nowlan, arising out of the press reports before the Rebellion Commission by those giving evidence endeavouring to connect the G.A.A. with the Irish Volunteers and Citizen Army, the following report was drawn up to be handed the Press, copies to be also sent to the Chairman, Rebellion Commission:

<u>Lord Hardinge's Commission</u>
<u>Special Meeting of Central Council</u>

At a special meeting of the Governing Body Central Council of the Gaelic Athletic Association, held on Sunday, May 28th, at headquarters, Croke Park, Dublin, the Secretary, amongst other matters, drew attention to a series of allegations vide Press reports, made before the Rebellion Commission now sitting.

After some consideration and discussion it was decided to issue the following statement:

The position of the Gaelic Athletic Association in relation to politics is clearly defined in the following rule, which, as far as the Governing Body knows, has been stringently acted on:

"The Gaelic Athletic Association, Limited, shall be a strictly non-political and non-sectarian Association. No political questions of any kind shall be raised at any of its meetings and neither Central Council, Provincial Councils, County Committees nor clubs shall take part as such in any political movement."

The Central Council, therefore, gives an unqualified denial to the statement of Matthew Nathan, that the Gaelic Athletic Association signed a manifesto on the eve of the Prime Minister's visit to Dublin in September 1914. The Central Council goes further, and states, without any qualification or reservation whatsoever, that neither directly nor indirectly had the Gaelic Athletic Association any connection with such opposition to the Prime Minister's visit, as was displayed.

Since the Gaelic Athletic Association is non-political it follows that the members thereof are at perfect liberty to join any political organisation they may choose to be identified with. And hence the Central Council finds that many members of the Association are attached to the United Irish League, All-for-Ireland League, Irish Volunteers, National Volunteers, and various other national associations. The statements, therefore, that the Gaelic the Gaelic Athletic Association. They have always been admitted to all such gatherings provided they were prepared to pay the fee charged the general public.

The Central Council strongly protests against the misrepresentations of the aims and objects of the Gaelic Athletic Association as tendered to the Commission by Sir Matthew Nathan and other witnesses, and thinks that all such allegations should, at least, be accompanied by definite proofs.

The statement issued by the GAA in May 1916 in response to accusations by the Royal Commission on the Rebellion in Ireland that the GAA participated in the planning of the 1916 Rising.

The Rising had been greeted with disbelief and anger by the Irish people. The membership of the Association had overwhelmingly shared these sentiments. But the draconian reaction of the authorities swiftly changed public perception and generated a renewed hatred of British rule in Ireland. With popular opinion moving against the IPP and its links with the British government, Sinn Féin was in a unique position to capitalise on the new national mood.[72] Though Arthur Griffith's organisation had no involvement with the Rising, the British authorities succeeded in vesting his Sinn Féin party with a role of authority in Irish nationalism it had never achieved by itself, simply by branding all rebels 'Sinn Féiners'.[73] Moderates like Griffith thus had an opportunity to exploit this new-found, if misplaced, fame for the small organisation.[74] As early as the autumn of 1916, the authorities were identifying a widespread public belief that political freedom from Britain could be achieved more quickly by adopting the Sinn Féin policy of defiance rather than by the old IPP policy of cooperation.[75] By 1917, it was apparent that the transforming political landscape was also impacting on the membership of the GAA. In fact, GAA events frequently showed some of the earliest examples of this changing political mood. In Kerry in January 1917, a Lispole supporter coming from a match in Dingle was arrested and sentenced to six weeks' hard labour for shouting 'Up the Sinn Féiners, [they] are winning and they'll win.'[76] Meanwhile, in Ulster, several GAA clubs were rechristened in deference to the martyrs of 1916, including clubs named for Pearse and O'Rahilly in Tyrone.[77]

In June 1917, the British government commuted the sentences of all those still arrested and held after the Rising. GAA men like Austin Stack and Thomas Ashe were given a hero's welcome on their return home.[78] In the weeks that followed, Stack and Ashe toured Ireland, promulgating the Sinn Féin message and imploring young men to reform the Volunteers and make it a powerful force again.[79] Such appeals were the beginning of an attempt within Irish nationalism to unite the Irish Volunteers under the Sinn Féin banner. This process was cemented in October 1917 when Éamon de Valera, the new President of the Irish Volunteers, replaced Arthur Griffith as President of Sinn Féin.[80] In August, both Stack and Ashe were arrested for making seditious speeches in public.[81] In protest, they began a hunger strike that resulted in Ashe's death due to injuries sustained while being force-fed by prison officers.[82] Nationalist public opinion in Ireland was outraged.[83] Those within the GAA were similarly appalled by the death of their former member. The Dublin county board issued a damning statement 'deploring the killing' and resolving to have representatives of every GAA club in the city at the funeral.[84] His public funeral in Dublin was the largest ever seen in the city.[85] Ashe's death was a major catalyst for a huge expansion of the Sinn Féin movement. By December, police reported that nationally the party had over 1,000 clubs and 66,000 members.[86]

It is clear the death of Ashe had just as profound an effect on the membership of the GAA as it had on broader Irish nationalism. Increasingly resentful of the British authorities' attempts to curb the popularity of Sinn Féin, many of its adherents within the Association used their influence at both national and local level to indoctrinate members into the new political grouping, and throughout 1917 there was a significant correlation between local GAA and Sinn Féin membership.[87] By May, Sinn Féin's popularity was said to be so great that it 'virtually dominated' the GAA.[88] In Clare, the county board began the process that saw de Valera nominated to contest the by-election for Sinn Féin in July 1917.[89] In the same year, the Clare footballers entered their matches under a banner proclaiming 'Up de Valera'.[90] Meanwhile, prominent GAA officials such as Stack and Boland were appointed to Sinn Féin's ruling executive.[91] The Association also hoped to capitalise on the new patriotic spirit that was enflaming Irish public opinion. Its Central Council issued letters to county boards to re-form clubs no longer in existence 'and take advantage of the present feeling throughout the county by establishing such clubs with the object of wiping out soccer and other foreign games'.[92]

However, the rising tide of Sinn Féin nationalism did not lift all GAA boats. In Kerry, there is evidence of some resentment towards the status Sinn Féin had achieved by undermining and destroying the popular support of the IPP. For example, 1917 marked the reappearance of widespread agrarian disturbances in rural Ireland, as thousands of farm labourers and holders of uneconomic land became both progressively politicised by the Sinn Féin movement and increasingly envious of the wartime profits that many farmers were accumulating.[93] Within the Keel GAA club, differences arose between the younger farm labourers who fully supported Sinn Féin and the older members, mostly local farmers, who had greatly profited from the prosperity the war had brought them and were happy with the political status quo. Such men retained a strong allegiance to IPP MPs. The dispute resulted in the club splitting in 1917.

The Sinn Féin supporters renamed their team the Keel Sinn Féiners, in reference to their political allegiance.[94] Likewise in Louth, the *Dundalk Democrat* bemoaned the fact that local GAA matches were now seemingly nothing more than Sinn Féin demonstrations.[95]

While a strong GAA was not necessarily a prerequisite for an area developing into a centre of revolutionary activity,[96] one cannot deny the

The 1917 Clare football team, which entered matches marching under an 'Up de Valera' banner.

involvement of hundreds of GAA members in the reorganisation of the Irish Volunteers that occurred during 1917. It was probably inevitable that many of the local leaders would be young men of some social stature. These 'natural leaders' were in many cases the captains of the local GAA team.[97]

• • •

In April 1918, a massive German offensive on the Western Front forced the British government into an attempt to extend conscription to Ireland. Naturally, once news of their intentions broke, it caused outright revolt among representatives of all shades of Irish nationalist opinion.[98] A Special Meeting of the Central Council unanimously declared: 'That we pledge ourselves to resist by any and every means in our power the attempted conscription of Irish manhood and we call on all members of the GAA to give effect to the terms of [this] … resolution'.[99]

Huge public demonstrations were held across Ireland to resist conscription, and on 23 April a general strike effectively brought the country to a halt.[100] In the face of such mass public resistance, the British government was forced to postpone the implementation of conscription indefinitely.[101] The attempt to enforce conscription led to an enormous uptake in enlistment in the Irish Volunteers in order to resist the measure, by force if necessary. This had the natural effect of feeding large numbers of GAA members into the Volunteers. In north Kerry, it was reported that hurling matches were being used to mask the convening and drilling of several local Volunteer contingents.[102]

Faced with growing political unrest, Emergency Rule was introduced to Ireland, and all public gatherings and political rallies were banned. In addition, the Sinn Féin party was proscribed, along with the Irish Volunteers and the Gaelic League.[103] The absence of the GAA from the list of proscribed organisations is evidence that, although the Association's membership undoubtedly overlapped with Sinn Féin, up until this point the GAA was able to officially maintain a discernible distance between itself and the party.[104] Yet, the English *Daily Chronicle* argued that the authorities had made a grave error in not proclaiming the GAA 'an eager and lively organisation of revolutionary propagandists'.[105] Though the GAA was not suppressed, the rules banning public gatherings were framed to include GAA matches.[106] Within a week, games run under its auspices were being broken up by the police.[107]

Until this point, it seemed clear that despite the changing political stance of many within the Association, at an official level, the GAA had remained cautious of committing itself too strongly to the political opinions of the majority of Irish nationalists, for fear of alienating its own more moderate members. Perhaps this can be best seen in the GAA's decision in November 1916 to actively support and run tournaments in aid of the Irish National Aid and Volunteer Dependants Fund.[108] The fund was initially set up by Kathleen Clarke, the widow of the executed rebel Thomas Clarke, to provide monies to support the families of those killed or imprisoned after the Rising. In 1917, Michael Collins took over as secretary and the fund was increasingly used to support all political prisoners jailed on account of their Sinn Féin or Volunteer activities.[109] Very quickly, the GAA became the principal source of finance for the National Aid initiative. In February, a special GAA subcommittee chaired by Boland was set up to plan a national tournament of inter-county contests for the National Aid fun. Eleven counties pledged to compete in the tournament, which went ahead between 11 and 18 March.[110] As William Murphy has noted, espousing the cause of nationalist political prisoners throughout 1917 was a way for the GAA to allow its membership to demonstrate a degree of sympathy for political radicals without the Association itself becoming identified with their aims.[111]

By the summer of 1918, matters had altered significantly. The aftermath of the conscription crisis highlighted the extent to which a broad swathe of Irish society had become fundamentally opposed to the continuation of British rule. The protests and strikes that were held that April had shown the way forward for those within the Association who hoped to utilise it to discredit the British administration in Ireland. Emboldened by this example, the GAA followed the same template and began to organise its own mass, peaceful protest. In response to its games being banned, the GAA ordered all of its clubs and county boards to organise an extensive programme of Gaelic matches, to be held across every county on Sunday, 4 August.[112] This mass protest of games, dubbed 'Gaelic Sunday', initiated a trial of strength between the government and the GAA.[113] At 3 p.m., between 1,500 and 1,800 matches took place, in almost every county in Ireland. The newspaper *Sport* reported that as many as 4,000 teams and anywhere between 45,000 and 100,000 players participated in the matches; practically every affiliated hurling and football club in the country was involved.[114] Faced with such mass disobedience, the authorities were powerless.[115] The success of the event put an end to the British government's interference with the running of the GAA, and the following week Gaelic matches resumed as usual. It has been stated that Gaelic Sunday represented the largest, most widespread and successful act of public defiance against British rule in Ireland in the period between 1916 and 1922.[116] While this can certainly be argued, it is noteworthy that the occasion on which the Association acted with the greatest vigour

Michael Collins (right) talking to members of the Kilkenny hurling team before the 1921 Leinster hurling final, Croke Park, 11 September 1921.

to oppose the British state only occurred when the state threatened the GAA's livelihood by targeting its games.[117]

Ireland's political landscape underwent a significant upheaval in late 1918. In unison with greater Irish nationalist opinion, the broad membership of the GAA fully supported this power shift. The attempted introduction of conscription by the British government cemented Sinn Féin's place at the head of popular nationalist political opinion. In that December's general election, the party won 65 per cent of the vote outside Ulster.[118] Following on from their electoral promise, the Sinn Féin representatives assembled in Dublin and established a new legislative assembly, Dáil Éireann, dedicating themselves to working towards establishing a free Irish Republic.

With the broad base of Irish nationalism now fully in support of Sinn Féin, the GAA began to firmly align itself with the movement. During the same week that de Valera took his place at the head of Ireland's new legislative assembly, the Association held the final of its tournament in aid of the Volunteer Dependants Fund at Croke Park. De Valera attended and received a rapturous reception from the crowd of 25,000 present.[119] Further evidence of the GAA's Sinn Féin leanings, especially among its leadership, was provided by the 1919 Annual Convention ban on civil servants who had been required to take the Oath of Allegiance to the King.[120] This ban was an instance of the GAA being used directly as a weapon against the British state in Ireland.[121] The episode clearly shows how those in control of the Association had further endorsed the policy of 'social ostracisation' now advocated by Sinn Féin. They used it against sections of their own membership who they saw, by their employment, as contributing to the British administration in Ireland. In view of such policies, there can be little doubt that by 1919 the GAA had taken an increasingly radical position, and had in effect become an ideological opponent of British rule in Ireland.

In the three years after Easter 1916, much of the GAA's membership had gone through a process of political radicalisation. Within the Association, widespread support for the IPP had been destroyed, and in its place was an overwhelming support for republican aspirations for an independent Ireland. By 1919, the GAA, as an organisation, had become firmly committed to Sinn Féin's objective of establishing an Irish republic. During the subsequent Anglo-Irish War, hundreds of the Association's members would be active in the fight for Irish independence.

CHAPTER 9

The GAA in a Time of Guerrilla War and Civil Strife, 1918–23

MIKE CRONIN

Match ticket for the 21 November 1920 challenge football game between Dublin and Tipperary.

WRITING IN HIS MEMOIR, *Over the Bar,* Breandán Ó hEithir recalled that, as a young boy, 'I associated the GAA almost completely with history. This was because my father had been in Croke Park on Bloody Sunday … [he described] the panic when the shooting started, the stampede that flattened a galvanised fence, leaving him with a scar on his kneecap.'[1] The young Ó hEithir was, in many respects, correct. The GAA, while successfully overseeing its vibrant and popular games, is about history. Such histories are multiple and richly layered. They cover memories of games and sporting endeavours; the lives of emigrant Gaels playing in far-flung corners of the world; the broad social, economic and political context of the Association; and, most importantly in the context of this book, they have given the GAA a central role in the years of the Irish revolution.

The story of the GAA and the revolutionary period is most evident, and daily rehearsed, at Croke Park, the scene of Bloody Sunday, where those killed are memorialised and the event is highlighted in the museum and the associated stadium tours.[2] The events of 21 November 1920 transformed Croke Park, as it 'was now more than merely a playing field: it was martyred ground'.[3] As horrific as Bloody Sunday was, it served to elevate the place of the GAA within the national psyche and, if anything, led to a later overstating of the role of the Association in the revolutionary period. As William Murphy noted, 'the role of the Gaelic Athletic Association during the Irish revolution has received more, if fragmented, attention than most aspects of the association's history'.[4] The years of war and civil strife from 1918 to 1923 undoubtedly had an impact on the ways in which the GAA could function. In this, the GAA was not alone, as many aspects of Irish life during the period – whether travel, day-to-day business or social life – were affected by disruptions caused by fighting and political upheaval.

And yet it has to be remembered that the Irish period of war and revolution was highly localised, and its effects, in comparison with the various ethnic and nation-building struggles happening elsewhere in Europe at the time, were limited. Irish life was both dislocated and transformed during the period from 1918 to 1923, but, in comparison with events in Russia, Turkey, Armenia, Mexico and other countries, a semblance of, and, for the most part, commitment to a democratic civil society was evident on all sides. So, while the events of these years had a dramatic effect on the life of the GAA, it has to be remembered that it still exists as a continuous and active organisation, and is never in danger of disappearing from the national consciousness.[5]

During the First World War, some 200,000 Irish-born men were in the armed services, and of these approximately 30,000 were killed.[6] These men were drawn from all counties of the island, with the result that the Great War and its years of mass mobilisation had a powerful impact on families, villages and towns across the country. For the GAA, the First World War had its most direct impact in terms of young men of sport-playing age being the very ones who went to war. The period from 1914 to 1918, then, was one of absence, during which many young men were away fighting, and clubs often struggled to put teams on the pitch. The absences and the deaths of the First World War were traumatic for those families and communities that were affected, but the actual fighting (until Easter week 1916) was elsewhere, beyond the shores of Ireland. So, while the First World War impacted greatly on Ireland and on organisations such as the GAA, it was different from the experience of the period from 1918 to 1923. Comparatively, the Irish loss of life during this latter period was far smaller: the War of Independence (1919–21) was responsible for approximately 1,400 deaths; sectarian violence in the North between 1920 and 1922 accounted for 557 deaths; and the Civil War (1922–3) took some 1,300 lives.[7] The killing was highly localised, with half of the total deaths occurring in the cities of Dublin, Belfast and Cork. A quarter of all deaths took place in Limerick, Kerry, Tipperary and Clare.

It is in these figures, and their geographical concentration, that the Irish experience of these years can best be understood.[8] The Irish wars were primarily focused on the three major urban centres on the island, and in Munster. While Ireland spent much of the period under restrictive military laws that affected everyone, for some parts of the country the war had little impact in terms of military activity and fighting. In areas where the fighting was regular, the life of the GAA was clearly affected. In Tipperary, for example, the Mid-Tipperary board was unable to meet for seven months, and when they did convene in December 1922, only seven clubs were represented. As the board secretary noted, 'owing to the disturbed times, the trenching and blocking of roads, and the much too frequent use of the revolver ... fixtures fell through, leaving the sport on the wane in the county'.[9] That said, the continuance of the games, even in such trying circumstances, was a key aim of the GAA. When military restrictions caused the cancellation of all GAA fixtures across Tipperary in August 1919, the South Riding county board, in a creative use of the county boundary, decided to play all of its scheduled fixtures at Darinlaun 'on the County Waterford side of the river'.[10]

A major switch during the revolutionary period was in the style of the warfare, and the overriding sense of terror that accompanied much military activity. As David Fitzpatrick noted:

> the code of honour and fair play observed by the rebels of 1916 ... rapidly disintegrated as the 'War of Independence' degenerated into a morass of ambushes and assassinations in the years preceding the Truce ... the Civil War caused further mutations, as anti-Treaty 'Irregulars' attempted to maintain guerrilla resistance in the absence of widespread popular support, while the new government applied state terror through systematic executions on a scale never attempted by the old regime.[11]

The wars in Ireland had a direct impact on Irish society that the First World War did not, in that they affected day-to-day life in areas where the conflicts took place, and had a direct psychological impact on those that they touched. During the years between 1918 and 1923, the GAA, a sporting organisation with strong nationalist ties, had to try to organise its games and maintain its stated apolitical stance in the face of war, terror and the control of daily life by a raft of emergency legislation. During this period, the membership of the GAA comprised a majority of non-combatants who were nonetheless affected by the conflict and a minority who were involved in IRA activity (the number of GAA members active in the IRA has been estimated at 0.006 per cent of the IRA's total active membership; and it has been suggested that 'there is little evidence to suggest a strong link between the two'[12]). In essence, the GAA during this time, as an organisation, can be seen as a cultural supporter of the move towards national liberation, but one whose membership was largely not militarily engaged. However, with the signing and ratification of the Treaty by January 1922, those fighters who were members of the GAA subdivided into those supporting the new state and those opposing it.

During the revolutionary period's fighting, dislocation, apparent national victory, and then divisive fall into Civil War, the GAA managed to keep the organisation going and keep its games alive. A key element in the success of the GAA in terms of its internal cohesion and ability to organise games was its clearly stated apolitical stance. While individual members of the GAA took part in the fighting, the Association itself tried to remain free of politics. For example, while the secretary of the Cork county board, Patrick O'Keeffe, was charged in 1920 with possession of a live Mills bomb during the War of Independence,[13] he subsequently went out of his way to make clear his apolitical line when arrested in 1923 during the Civil War. He informed the *Irish Examiner*, 'I have not even personally interfered in politics, and all times have kept the name of the GAA immune from such.'[14] The actions of O'Keeffe are in many ways a microcosm of GAA attitudes during the period. The struggle against the British from 1919 to 1921 was one the GAA, while officially neutral, did in fact support. Gaelic Sunday in 1918, when Gaelic matches were held across the country in defiance of the laws requiring permits to play them, stands as evidence of the GAA's opposition to British rule. The Association's sympathies are also made clear by its decisions, whether nationally or at county level, to commemorate Irishmen killed in the conflict – such as the decision to postpone all games after the death on hunger strike of Terence MacSwiney.[15] In the Civil War period, however, the GAA refrained from all such actions; strict neutrality, at the national level at least, was the key aim. In a fight between Irishmen, the GAA could not take sides for fear of endangering the future cohesion of the organisation.

For the GAA, then, disruption undoubtedly occurred during this period, but its games were still played and every national championship in football and hurling was completed, albeit belatedly. Alongside the organisation of its games, the period of war and civil strife led the GAA to moments of political action (for example, Gaelic Sunday), thrust some of its members into the political and military limelight, and brought the war directly into its own home (notably on Bloody Sunday, 1920). In all this, however, it has to be remembered that the GAA was but one social and cultural organisation around which the winds of war and revolutionary politics swirled. Similar histories could be written about the Catholic Church or the Gaelic League in the revolutionary period, and the role that their members played in creating an independent Ireland. The GAA is an important organisation in the history of the revolution, but it is not unique. As William Murphy concluded, 'the GAA appears to have been a playground of the revolution more often than it was a player in the revolution.'[16]

So what exactly did happen to the GAA during the period from 1918 to 1923, and how, despite the turmoil of these years, was the Association, as Diarmaid Ferriter suggests, 'able to recover relatively quickly'?[17] The first thing to note is that during this period many features of GAA life continued as normal, apparently undisturbed by the fighting and associated upheaval. For example, in February 1923, a W. Ryan wrote to the *Irish Independent* to complain about high admission charges for entry into GAA matches. He wrote, 'I believe that the principal cause of small crowds at the various matches is the high charge for admission to the arena … for Sunday's hurling contest the enormous fee of 5/- is asked for admission to the stands. This is really exorbitant.'[18]

As well as ticket prices, the constant concern about foreign games was also a regular gripe during the period. In March 1921, at the GAA convention in Dublin, Mr McGovern from Cavan proposed a motion that 'Central Council be instructed to take steps to have our national games given at least as much prominence in the Irish daily press as is given at all times to foreign games'.[19] At the organisational level, issues around timings and the weather were to the fore. At the Meath GAA Annual Convention in May 1919 there was a debate over the start times for matches, and whether referees should enforce the stated throw-in time. The chairman of the county board argued that referees should only allow matches to start fifteen minutes late in the case of a delayed or incomplete team being in place. After that, the team that failed to take the pitch should be disqualified. He was challenged by Mr Eggleston, who asked, 'and if it is raining?' The decision was taken that if games were indeed delayed by bad weather, and that was reflected in the referee's report, then the county board could consider the matter and choose either to allow the result to stand or order a rematch.[20]

And if it was not timings and weather that caused consternation to the GAA faithful, it was the perennial issue of venues and railway excursions. In July 1923, the Munster Council decided that the provincial hurling final between Limerick and Tipperary, set for 12 August, would be held in Limerick. The letters pages of the press quickly filled with arguments against a final being held in Limerick, arguing that either Cork or Thurles were easier to access. A Galway Gael wrote to the papers asking whether 'we shall have the chance of witnessing such a great contest' and asking that the councils of the GAA do something to ensure that train excursions would be put in place for travelling fans.[21] What was apparent, from the other staple of GAA business, the balance sheet, was that crowds, while lower than before, were still turning up to Croke Park. The attendance at the 1915 All-Ireland football final had been 27,000, whereas the delayed 1918 final (played in February 1919) attracted a reduced gate of 12,000 and the delayed 1921 final (played in June 1923) attracted 11,700. Despite this reduction, Croke Park generated £4,786 in gate receipts in 1922 from the seven matches it hosted. Overall, the GAA had £3,942 on account at the end of the financial year, despite what the *Irish Independent* referred to as 'the unsettled conditions prevailing'.[22]

So, despite the undoubted and very real problems that the GAA faced, it is clear from the national and provincial newspapers of the period that in many respects the Association went about its business as normal. Issues that had always caused consternation and debate in clubs, county boards, the newspapers and at Annual Conventions did not disappear because of the conflict, but rather continued along as normal. It is also important, by way of context, to note that the GAA was not a fully formed and uniformly organised body during this period. At the start of the First World War, the GAA had been in existence for three decades; the organisation had journeyed through the years of the Parnell split and its devastating aftermath, and by the early years of the twentieth century had slowly begun its recovery. While the First World War, followed by the political conflict on the island, had a debilitating effect on some aspects of the GAA's development, there were areas of the country – particularly in Ulster – where the Association was already, without the onset of conflict, struggling to get off the ground and lay down deep roots. The county boards for Antrim, Tyrone and Donegal had only been formed in 1900, 1904 and 1905, respectively, and it is clear that the number of affiliated clubs, and matches played, in the first decade of these boards' existence was low.[23] Throughout this period, the Annual Convention discussed the weakness of the GAA in these areas and what steps might be taken to remedy the situation.[24] To assess and understand the life of the GAA from 1918 to 1923 is also to acknowledge that this was, in certain parts of the island, a weak and disjointed organisation that was far from flourishing. While the upheaval undoubtedly hampered attempts to develop the games and structures of the GAA in those slowly developing counties, its impact was therefore less marked in those places than in other parts of the country where the Association was strong and the conflict concentrated.

One of the most significant steps publicly taken by the GAA during this period was its organisation of Gaelic Sunday in 1918. During the summer of 1918, there were increasing reports of police interference with GAA matches, and a number of incidents where events had become violent. The GAA was informed by Dublin Castle that none of its games could be staged unless a permit was obtained. The GAA conceived the Castle decision as a direct attack that was informed more by prejudice against the Association, as it was part of the broad nationalist front, than by any serious concerns about crowds gathering to watch sporting contests. The GAA chose not to comply with the order, and informed all provincial councils and county boards that they were not to apply for permits. To underpin the seriousness of the situation, the Central Council also ruled that anyone who did apply for a permit would be automatically suspended from the Association. In July, the stand of the GAA in not applying for permits was made clear when *The Irish Times* reported that,

> although the GAA has not been proclaimed and although GAA matches – football and hurling and camog for ladies – did not come under General Shaw's order inasmuch as all the important games were not to be played in 'public places' practically all fixtures have been proclaimed in the absence of permits from the police, which had not been applied for.[25]

In order to actively oppose the Castle ruling, the GAA decided to organise Gaelic Sunday for 4 August 1918, when matches would be held across the country. All matches would take place in full public view, and no official permission would be sought from the authorities. In the lead-up to Gaelic Sunday, it was made known by Dublin Castle that Gaelic matches were no longer part of the restrictions on public gatherings.

Despite this, the GAA decided to go ahead with its planned matches and the day 'was to be used as a show of cultural nationalism so that the authorities might know not only the seriousness with which the GAA viewed the ban on Gaelic games, but also realise the sheer numbers of people and the clout which it had at its disposal'.[26] In the event, some 1,500 football, hurling and camogie games were played, involving 45,000 athletes.[27] The police, apart from two RIC men who paid into a game in Athlone as spectators, stayed away from these Gaelic gatherings, and the day passed off peacefully. Andrew McGuire and David Hassan have argued that Gaelic Sunday was unusual in the revolutionary period, as it was an event that the GAA controlled. They state that the events of 1916 and Bloody

GAELIC ATHLETIC ASSOCIATION.

Croke Park,
D u b l i n.
22nd July, 1918.

Dear Sir,

At a Meeting of Central Council held on Saturday last
the existing situation regarding the playing of the Matches
was considered, and the following decisions arrived at:-

I.   That under no circumstances must a permit be
      applied for either by Provincial Councils, Co. Committees,
      Leagues, Tournament Committees, Clubs, or by a third
      party such as Secretaries of Grounds, etc.

II.   Any individual or Club infringing the foregoing order
      becomes automatically and indefinitely suspended.

III. Orders 1 and II apply also to sports promoting
      bodies and registered Athletes and Cyclists.

IV.   You are directed to summon within the next 10 days
      a Meeting consisting of one Delegate from each Club:
      (a) to inform them of these orders and for transmission
      of same to their respective Clubs; (b) to arrange for
      Sunday, August 4th, at 3 p.m. (old time) a series of
      Matches throughout your County, which are to be local-
      ised as much as possible.

V.   Having regard to the abnormal circumstances, and to
      the fact that I have received applications from Soccer
      and Rugby Players, the Council decided with a view to
      propagandist work to grant an amnesty to all such
      persons, but they must apply to your Committee for
      reinstatement on or before September 1st., and I shall
      be glad if you will give this matter all the prominence
      possible.

      I may add that the advertising of these Matches is in
the discretion of your Committee, who will of course be guided
by local circumstances, but should you be disposed to publicly
advertise, you must not do so before the Thursday or Friday
preceding the match.

Yours truly,

L. J. O'TOOLE.

Statement issued by the GAA organising 'Gaelic Sunday', 4 August 1918.

Sunday were products of the time, and that the GAA 'took no direct role in either happening'. Rather than trying to shoehorn the GAA into the pantheon of Irish revolutionary bodies and individuals, McGuire and Hassan contend that 'merely having revolutionaries in its ranks does not a revolutionary organisation make'. Instead of dealing with the links, if they exist at all, between the GAA and the wars of 1919 to 1923, they argue that tangible events such as Gaelic Sunday, which the GAA directly organised and controlled, should be assessed, as they reveal the 'GAA directly engaging with the British authorities and asserting itself in the political landscape'.[28]

It is clear that Gaelic Sunday was an impressive show of strength by the GAA and, in terms of getting bodies out onto the playing fields of Ireland, was highly successful. Given that the British had cancelled the ban on GAA activity prior to Gaelic Sunday, the show of strength was not strictly required. However, the Association took the day to have been a victory over the British authorities. As GAA Secretary Luke O'Toole told the Annual Convention in 1919:

> the ban on public gatherings was aimed at the Association in particular. It was a challenge to the independence of the Association, and it was promptly accepted ... the spirit [of Gaelic Sunday] was taken up whole-heartedly by every county, the value of whose assistance in forcing the withdrawal of the order was recognised by their Association.[29]

While an exercise, perhaps, in counterfactual history, O'Toole's desire to see Gaelic Sunday not simply as a show of strength, but as a victory over the forces of British law and order, was important in announcing clearly – if any such announcement was necessary – where the sympathies of the GAA would lie in the coming conflict.

In 1919, the GAA Central Council took the decision to ban any civil servants from membership of the Association if they had taken an obligatory Oath of Allegiance to the Crown. The Central Council decision was ratified at the GAA Annual Convention in Dublin in April 1919. This decision was highly contentious. While it made sense from a GAA point of view – how could the Association object to British rule in Ireland if it contained in its ranks thousands of men who had sworn allegiance to the Crown? – the decision forced ordinary working men to choose between their sporting allegiance and their livelihood. At the Annual

Convention that ratified the ban, James Nowlan introduced the motion in straightforward terms: 'no matter what a man did for the Association the moment he took the oath of allegiance he ceased or should cease to be a member.' The Annual Convention was largely supportive of the motion, but was challenged by Mr Henesey of Dublin, who was also chairman of the Civil Servants' Association. He pointed out the inconsistency of the GAA's stance, arguing that the issue of civil servants taking an Oath of Allegiance was no different from the Association paying income tax to the British state. He also stated that while 'soldiers discharged got absolution from the GAA the civil servants seemed to be nobody's child'.[30]

Despite the passage of the motion and confirmation that civil servants taking the oath would be banned from membership, the rule was difficult to implement, and seen by many as a harsh response to a situation in which civil servants actually had little choice. Before the close of the 1919 Annual Convention, amendments were offered to try to ease the way for civil servants. In the end it was 'decided that the decision of the Council on the question of civil servants and the oath of allegiance, be the law of the Association in the future; [with] an amendment which sought to provide that those who had taken the oath under duress up to November last be retained in membership, those taking it in the future to be debarred from membership'.[31] At a stroke, the GAA solved a problem of its own making. While the ban on civil servants who had taken the oath was driven by an ideal of national purity, it was unworkable and punitive. In accepting the amendment and positioning civil servants as unwilling actors in the oath process, the GAA avoided punishing its membership for something that was effectively beyond their control. The amendment debate had made clear distinctions between the police and members of the judiciary, who had taken the oath voluntarily, and civil servants, who, it was argued, had taken it under duress. The issue dropped from the headlines after the amendment, but the whole issue had been one where the GAA had attempted to take a position against those 'men who clung to their soft jobs and deserted their country by swearing allegiance to a foreign king'.[32] In attempting to make a political statement against the Oath of Allegiance and the reach of the British state, the GAA had run the risk of alienating part of its membership. The whole saga reinforced the need for the GAA to tread very carefully when its actions potentially created division in its own ranks.

The most notorious event during the revolutionary period was undoubtedly Bloody Sunday, 21 November 1920. The day had begun with

A special Meeting of Central Council
was held at 68 upper O'Connell St. on
7th December 1918 Ald Nowlan Presiding
the following members of the Council
were in attendance. Messrs M. F. Crowe
M. Collins P. D Breen & J. O'Toole Sec
The Minutes of the previous meeting were
read & Signed.

The first business occupying the
attention of the meeting was the Consideration
of the position of the Civil Servants having
taken the oath of allegiance, the question
was discussed for a considerable at some
length, the meeting were unanimous
that the Council should take action in a
matter. The President Suggested that the
enforcement of the Suspension be left in
the hands of the Various Co Committees
Mr Collins & Mr P Breen maintained that
the Council should give a lead in the
matter, and not leave the onus on
Co Committees. The following motion
was eventually drafted

That is was incompatible with the principles of the association for any member to take the oath of allegiance, and any member having done so, is hereby relieved of membership pending next all Ireland Convention.

The motion having been read over by the Secy the chairman inquired of all the members present were unanimous in favour of the motion. and all having approved of the same, the ~~motion was declared carried~~ on the motion of Mr Croke seconded by Mr Collins, the motion was passed unanimously

The all Ireland football Semi final Mayo & Tipperary was fixed for Croke Park on Jany 12th Mr K. Collins referee
The all Ireland hurling Final was fixed for Jany 26th with Mr Walsh as referee
The football final was fixed for Feby 16th
The Council also fixed the Leinster football final for Jany 9th so as to permit the final being played on

the killing of fourteen suspected British spies, and culminated with an attack on Croke Park during a Dublin versus Tipperary challenge match, which led to the deaths of thirteen spectators and one player, Michael Hogan.[33] The day was one of the bloodiest in the War of Independence, and the GAA was unwittingly at the heart of it. One of the spies, John Joseph Fitzgerald, who was killed that morning at 28 Earlsfort Terrace, was, 'like Michael Hogan, from a well-known Tipperary GAA family'.[34] In the afternoon – despite rumours and later justifications that Croke Park was targeted due to the presence of IRA gunmen in the crowd – those who died were ordinary Dubliners attending a football match. The GAA was undoubtedly a victim of the war on Bloody Sunday. There was no link between the killings in the morning and those who attended the game in the afternoon.

What is significant about Bloody Sunday is that it allowed the GAA to act as a martyr, an organisation that had been singled out by the British for bloody reprisal. It was selected not for anything it had done that day, but rather because a large gathering of Gaels, who the authorities identified with the broad nationalist front, made an easy target. Bloody Sunday would raise the GAA in the national struggle to the position of victim at the heart of the narrative, along with all those who had paid the ultimate price for national freedom. The games of the GAA, which had always been imbued with nationalism, were elevated by the events of November 1920 so that the Association became the ultimate symbol of sport in the national service, and Croke Park became a shrine to those who had been killed there. Never again could the GAA be simply a sporting body.[35]

Months after the events of Bloody Sunday, after a further upsurge in violence, the War of Independence ended in a truce in July 1921. In practical terms this meant that those GAA men who were in prison for IRA activity, where they had often played their games, returned home, and the fundraising that the Association had done on behalf of those affected by the conflict drew to a close.[36] The Truce was followed by 'an astonishingly rapid return to normal life by the community generally, a process from which the GAA at once benefitted'.[37] While the games of the GAA sprang back into life and as near a full fixture list as possible, except in Munster, the issue of the Anglo-Irish Treaty and the divisive Dáil debates of December 1921 and January 1922 created a political headache for the GAA. While GAA men prominent in politics took different sides on the issue of the Treaty and the ensuing Civil War, the GAA seemingly did nothing. The Annual Convention of 1922 had empowered the Central

Council to call a Special Convention later that year if circumstances warranted such, but this never happened. Effectively, those running the GAA threw their weight behind the administration of the newly created Irish Free State and never allowed open debate on the issue of where the Association stood on the Treaty issue. Both Marcus de Búrca and W. F. Mandle argued that, while the Central Council did include anti-Treatyites (such as Frank McGrath, Stephen Jordan and Dan O'Rourke), their voices were not prominent and in effect the more powerful voices (such as Dan McCarthy, Eoin O'Duffy and J. J. Walsh), who were allied with the pro-Treaty side, won out.[38] The GAA, then, embraced the new state and rapidly became part of the establishment. Those who opposed the Treaty viewed the GAA stance with suspicion, but equally they largely returned to the sporting fold after the end of hostilities in 1923.

During the Civil War, the day-to-day operations of the GAA were negatively affected, as they had been during the years of fighting against the British. In Leinster and Munster there were few fixtures played between June and October 1922. While games in Leinster began again in mid-October 1922, the situation in those counties of the south-west controlled by anti-Treaty forces meant that there was little sporting action in Munster. In the midst of the fighting, in December 1922, the Cork county board asked the Central Council to convene a Special Convention to see if the GAA could assist in bringing the Civil War to an end. In the event, a special subcommittee was formed that would take the views of both sides in the fighting and ascertain if there was any common ground that might lead to a cessation of hostilities. On 23 January 1923 the subcommittee reported to the Central Council that its mission had failed, and that there was no benefit in holding a Special Convention. While the GAA had attempted to find a solution to the conflict, it was simply not influential enough to bring the two sides together. If, then, the Association found that it could not act as peace broker, its most important aim for the duration of the conflict was to ensure that the bitterness of national division did not infect the GAA, and that it held its own community together around its games as best it could.

The ending of the Civil War in May 1923 allowed the GAA to begin anew, despite the large number of men held in prison. The fixtures in Munster began again in earnest, and by the end of 1923 the various championship schedules there had been played out and were up to date. The GAA had survived the conflict intact, and continued to stress its apolitical nature throughout 1923. The Central Council banned the sale of political literature at Croke Park, embargoed the employment of bands that had not been approved and prohibited the collection of funds for political campaigns at its grounds.

In post-Civil War Ireland, the GAA had to regroup, re-energise its games and organisation, and hope that the bitterness of the split did not fester in its clubs and committees across the island. Where the GAA had been shaky in the years prior to the revolution, it continued to struggle. The GAA's organisation in Ulster remained weak well into the 1920s, and counties such as Kildare and Fermanagh were slow to regroup. In Kerry, where feelings ran high about those ex-combatants held in internment camps, teams refused to play until political prisoners were freed. That said, once regrouped, Kerry proved all-powerful and won the 1924 All-Ireland in football.[39] The only split that took place within the GAA in the wake of the Civil War was in Clare. The split was over the issue of the executions by the state of Clare footballers and anti-Treatyites Con McMahon and Patrick Hennessy, and led to the emergence, in 1924, of rival county boards. On one side was a pro-Treaty group led by Father Michael Hamilton; the other 'board' contained the anti-Treatyites. For a year the two groups ran rival competitions, but eventually the split was healed in the summer of 1925. Despite these local issues, and rumblings from various parts of the country about what stance the GAA should take on the continued detention of republican prisoners, the GAA emerged from the Civil War intact, and was able to heal any lingering wounds quickly.

The most significant symbol of the GAA's emergence from the years of conflict was the hosting of *Aonach Tailteann* (or the Tailteann Games), the Irish Olympics, at Croke Park in 1924 (and again in 1928 and 1932). For the event, the state gifted the GAA £10,000 for the refurbishment and enlargement of Croke Park. While Sinn Féin boycotted the event, the opening ceremony was held in front a large crowd of spectators and athletes from across the Irish diaspora. It was widely covered in the international press as symbolic of Ireland's emergence from years of war and as a public announcement of independent nationhood. The image of the GAA leadership seated on the reviewing stand at the opening ceremony, alongside the Catholic hierarchy and various government ministers, illustrated that the Association had survived the war years as a united organisation and had taken its place at the heart of the new state.[40]

CHAPTER 10

The GAA and Irish Political Prisoners, 1916–23

MARK REYNOLDS

A Gaelic football game in progress in Stafford Jail, *c.* 1916.

I N THE FORMATIVE YEARS OF THE GAA, there was a tenuous connection between the Association and Irish political prisoners: two of the original patrons, Charles Stewart Parnell and Michael Davitt, had previously been imprisoned for political activities;[1] the issue played a role during the 1887–8 split and reconstruction;[2] and, in the context of the 'Ranch War',[3] Rule 8 (exclusion of the British military) was amended in 1909 to exclude jail warders from membership of the GAA.[4] Following the 1916 Rising, the relationship between the GAA and political prisoners evolved, and the Association became actively involved with prisoners and in prisoner welfare issues. This relationship manifested itself in three different ways between 1916 and 1923: first, Gaelic games were played in the various internment camps and prisons; second, the Association publicly supported the plight of the internees and prisoners; and, third, the Association contributed to the various prison welfare funds.

. . .

The internment and imprisonment of republicans was a constant feature of the period from 1916 to 1923. In the aftermath of the 1916 Rising, approximately 1,800 Irishmen were interned in Frongoch (North Wales), while during the War of Independence (1919–21), the main internment centre was the Ballykinlar camp (County Down), which housed 2,000 men, with the Rath camp in the Curragh (County Kildare) also holding internees. During the Civil War (1922–3), internment was introduced to the North of Ireland in May 1922, with the Provisional government also introducing internment to the Irish Free State in September 1922 and using the Curragh camp in Kildare as the main holding centre. Gaelic games were played in the three major internment camps (Frongoch, Ballykinlar and the Curragh) that operated between 1916 and 1923. In the aftermath of the 1916 Rising, and throughout the War of Independence internees exclusively played Gaelic games, whereas during the Civil War, Gaelic games were played alongside other codes, including soccer and rugby, by the Curragh internees. (When internment was introduced to the North of Ireland in 1922, the vast majority of the internees were held aboard the prison ship *Argenta*, where the cramped conditions did not allow for the playing of sport.) This section will look at the playing of Gaelic games in the various internment camps and, to a lesser extent, the prisons, to highlight the role and importance of Gaelic games to the internees and prisoners.

Gaelic football competitions were organised and played by the intern-ees in all three of the major internment camps. Among those interned in Frongoch were the inter-county footballers Dick Fitzgerald (Kerry), Frank Burke (Dublin), Frank Shouldice (Dublin), Paddy Cahill (Kerry), Brian Joyce (Dublin) and Seamus Dobbyn (Antrim). While there were some complaints about the unsuitability of the hilly camp for football matches, the internees quickly adapted to the landscape and established a dedicated football pitch, albeit one that sloped towards one set of goals, called Croke Park, where they enthusiastically held a large number of Gaelic football matches on a daily basis.[5] A Gaelic football competition was organised among four Frongoch teams, with each team playing six matches: teams from the South Camp wore a blue stripe while teams from the North Camp wore red stripes. Three of the teams were named after the executed leaders of the 1916 Rising, but it was Dick Fitzgerald's team, called 'The Leprechauns' due to the small stature of some its players, that won the competition.[6] Football competitions were also organised along inter-county lines – in early July 1916, a 'Gaelic football and athletic carnival' was held in the camp, with Kerry's one-point victory over Louth being the 'principal feature' of the carnival, while later in the month, on 16 July 1916, representatives of Dublin beat Wexford by 1–08 to 2–03 in the 'Frongoch (Leinster) Championship'.[7]

In Ballykinlar, despite the fact that there was no designated recreation space for the first few months, an inter-hut Gaelic football competition was quickly established. The various huts formed Gaelic football teams and played matches with footballs bought with money raised through a five-shillings-per-hut levy. In the beginning, due to a lack of space, huts were only allowed to field ten men each, with matches played at twenty minutes per half, and three games played per day. In the aftermath of the fatal shooting on 17 January 1921 of two prisoners, James Tormey and James Sloan, for standing too close to the Ballykinlar perimeter wire,[8] the Ballykinlar prisoners named their club the Tormey-Sloan GAA Hurling and Football Club. Frank Carney, honorary secretary of the Ballykinlar camp, wrote to the Dublin county board in October 1921 forwarding the affiliation fees for the Tormey-Sloan GAA Hurling and Football Club, registering the club colours as 'plain black' and stating that 'the membership at present was about 100, and they intended running an intermediate and junior football team and a junior hurling team on release'.[9]

An inter-county Gaelic football competition was also played in the Curragh camp during the Civil War. In October 1922, in front of a 'full gathering on the sidelines', the Kildare internees beat the Dublin internees, by 3–06 to 1–05, in the final of the 'series of inter-county football matches amongst the prisoners at Droichead Nua (Newbridge) Internment camp'.[10] One of the players on the Kildare team of internees, Bill Gannon, had only months previously, in February 1922, played with Kildare in Croke Park as they won a football tournament in aid of the republican prisoners. Gannon subsequently became the first man to lift the Sam Maguire Cup when Kildare won the All-Ireland football title in 1928. While hurling was not permitted in Frongoch, Ballykinlar or the Rath camp, as the authorities feared the hurls could be used as weapons against the prison guards, the sport was played in the Curragh camp during the Civil War.[11] Gaelic games during this period were, however, played alongside soccer and rugby. When Todd Andrews, a member of the Dublin IRA, was interned in the Rath camp during the War of Independence, his dislike of Gaelic games, the only games tolerated by the mainly rural internees, stymied his relations with his comrades. When Andrews was again interned in the Curragh camp during the Civil War, Dublin men this time constituted a majority in the camp, and soccer and rugby flourished, with Gaelic football ranked only third in terms of popularity.[12]

Athletic competitions were also popular among the internees, particularly in the Frongoch and Ballykinlar camps. In August 1916, an 'eventful' afternoon of sports 'under GAA laws' was held in Frongoch that 'excited great interest and gave an opportunity to many athletes to display their prowess in a goodly number of contests from the favourite 100 Yards Dash to the 16lbs "push"'.[13] When accusations were later made in the House of Commons about the substandard quality of food within Frongoch, Major Newman was able to point out that the internees were so well nourished that they regularly engaged in athletics and sports events. In May 1921, the Ballykinlar No. 2 Compound sports committee challenged the No. 1 Compound to a sports tournament, a challenge that was duly accepted. Several athletic competitions were scheduled and the compounds began holding trials to pick the best men to represent them. Leo Henderson wrote from Ballykinlar to the Central Council of the GAA that there were '15 events coupled with a tug-of-war competition' planned for the 'Ballykinlar Athletic Competition' and he requested that the GAA provide medals for these events. The Central Council agreed to provide

'15 gold medals for the various athletic events and silver medals with gold centres for the tug-of-war competition', and directed Luke O'Toole, Secretary of the GAA, to write to Henderson and explain 'the conditions under which the medals were being presented, namely to the winners of the inter-camp competition'.[14] When the British commandant refused to allow the inter-compound competition to take place, Henderson informed the GAA Central Council of its cancellation, but the GAA refused to accede to his suggestion of supplying the promised medals to the No. 1 Compound.[15] At the same meeting, the GAA also refused, albeit with much regret, a request from 'Mr E. Smyth, Ballykinlar Camp' to furnish the camp with gymnasium equipment as 'the present financial position prevented [the GAA] from complying with the request'.[16] Later in the year, however, in October 1921, the Leinster Council agreed to cover the cost of prizes, not to exceed £10, for a boxing tournament held in Compound No. 2.[17]

Throughout the period between 1916 and 1923, Gaelic games were also played by those in prison, as distinct from those in internment camps, but, for practical reasons, the games did not flourish as they did in the camps. As with the internment camps, hurling was not allowed, and while football was popular among the prisoners, handball and rounders flourished. The two sports, which were more suited to the confined exercise yards of conventional prisons, were played in Reading, Lincoln and Birmingham prisons.[18] In conventional prisons, perhaps more so than in internment camps, the prison authorities encouraged the playing of Gaelic games, as the playing of sport expended energy and aggression that might otherwise have been directed at the guards themselves.

The playing of Gaelic games in internment camps and prisons served a number of important functions. The purpose of the internment camps was one of containment rather than punishment or rehabilitation, with the internees granted de facto prisoner-of-war status. The prisoners' leaders in the camps established a routine of military discipline among the internees – programmes, including Gaelic games, were initiated to stimulate the men physically, mentally, politically and culturally. For many internees, Gaelic games provided much-needed relief and staved off the boredom

FOLLOWING PAGES: Minutes of the Central Council meetings, 13 May and 3 July 1921, at which the GAA agreed to provide medals for the Ballykinlar Athletic Competition.

A special Meeting Central Coun
was held at Croke Park on Sunda
13th May 1921 Mr James Nowlan
Presiding the following member
of the Council were in attendance
(Messrs P McDonnell (Treasurer) P D Bre
J J Keane & L J O Toole Secy.

The meeting was called to decide
what action should be taken in
reference to Hospital Sunday. aft
the question had been carefully consider
It was decided that owing to prevailing
Conditions existing no inter County
Matches be arranged but the
Various Leagues in Dublin together
with the Co Committee be requested
to arrange a series of matches
the proceeds to be retained for
the Hospital Sunday fund.
An application was received from
Mr Henderson Ballykinlar Camp
explaining that in No 1 their Camp

Athletic Competitions were being
held and also inviting the Council
to present medals to 15 events Coupled
with a tug of war competition. The
Council unanimously decided to
provide 15 gold medals for the various
Athletic events & Silver medals with
gold centres for the tug of war Competition
the Secy was directed to write to
Henderson explaining the Conditions
under which the medals were being
presented namely, to the winners
of the inter Camp competitions at
Special meeting of the Standing
Committee

C. MacCarthy
11th Sept 31

A Special Meeting of the Ground &
Standing Committee present Breen McDonnell Keane Nowlan
at Croke Park on 3rd July 1931.
a further letter was received from
Mr Henderson stating the inter Camp

Competition would not likely be
held and suggesting that the
promised medals be given to
No 1 Camp. the total meeting
unanimously decided to adhere
to their previous order that the
medals be presented only for the
inter Camp Competition
A letter was also received from
Mr Smyth Bally Keilar Camp
making application for the supply
of an Gymnasium out fit &
Equipment the Seay was directed
to inform Mr Smyth that the Councel
much regretted their present finacial
position prevented them from
Complying with the request.
The Seay explained to the meeting
the possibility of Mr Farquaherson
House & yard being offered for sale, after fully
considering the matter It was decided
to approch the deal with the view of purchasing
or If Mr Keane would Consider let

over the property in trust for the Gaa
the matter was left in the hands of the
Chairman & Secy to make the necessary
arrangements.

D. Mac Carthaig
11th Sept 1921.

Teams posing for a photograph in Stafford Jail, *c.* 1916.

that normally accompanies an unspecified period of detention. When several Kerry internees were released from Frongoch in July 1916, they reported that 'taking everything into consideration … they had a fairly good time. Concerts, football matches, and other amusements broke the monotony of their deportation.'[19] Gaelic games were also used as a cultural weapon by those interned by the British. Against the backdrop of British captivity, Gaelic games were played as a means of reaffirming an Irish identity. *The Kerryman* reported that 'the intense Gaelicism of the Irish prisoners of war at Frongoch Internment Camp is clearly demonstrated in their eager attendance at Irish language classes … and their zest in pursuing the Gaelic games arranged by well-known G.A.A. men in their midst.'[20] The need for this cultural reaffirmation was not as urgent, or needed at all, when the situation changed to Irishmen being interned in

Ireland by the Irish government. It is likely that this was one of the reasons that games other than Gaelic games were played enthusiastically by the Civil War Curragh camp internees.

Gaelic football teams formed in the internment camps were also used for commemorative purposes following the conclusion of the Civil War. An 'Internees Inter-Camp' football competition was played in St James' Park in Dublin on 28 June 1924,[21] with Gormanston (3-03) beating Tintown (2-03) in the final of the tournament.[22] In Westmeath, a June 1924 commemoration of 'the men who died in the service of the Republic since 1916' featured an exhibition football game between the Westmeath football team and a team of ex-internees, won by Westmeath on a score of 1-04 to 0-04,[23] while in August 1924 a football match was played in Wexford Park between teams representing Dublin and Wexford ex-internees.[24] Following their release, a group of Kerry internees challenged the Kerry football team to a match; when the challenge was accepted, the match was fixed for Tralee, on 10 February 1924, with the Kerry county board using the match as a trial to pick the county team to face Cavan in the upcoming (delayed) 1923 All-Ireland semi-final. When the former internees were beaten, on the score of 0-05 to 1-00,[25] they requested a replay which they subsequently won 4-04 to 0-04.[26] Due to this, many former republican internees lined out on the Kerry team that included Con Brosnan, a captain in the Free State Army, for the 1923 All-Ireland football semi-final, played in Croke Park on 27 April 1924, and for the subsequent 1923 All-Ireland final.[27] It was members of this Kerry team who took part in a football match between a team of former Curragh internees and a team consisting of internees from other internment camps and Kerry footballers, to celebrate the arrival of Austin Stack in Tralee on 27 July 1924. The Curragh internees won the game 0-04 to 0-02.[28]

· · ·

When the GAA agreed, in November 1916, to send representatives to a proposed Dublin Corporation Convention for the formation of a Political Prisoners Amnesty Association, they did so only after the GAA President, Alderman Nowlan, ruled that such involvement 'could not be considered as relating to politics'.[29] In 1916, the rulebook of the GAA stipulated that the Association was a 'strictly non-political and non-sectarian Association' with 'political questions of any kind' not allowed at any GAA meetings,

HOME FROM FRONGOCH.

WHAT LIFE IN A WELSH DETENTION CAMP IS LIKE.

SATURDAY.

The following Kerry prisoners who were arrested by the military in May, and who were subsequently deported, were released from Frongoch Detention Camp on Thursday:

TRALEE—Messrs. P. J. Cahill, P. J. Hogan, T. J. McCarthy, E. Barry, W. Farmer, W. Mullins, M Doyle, J. Wall, T. Slattery.

DINGLE—Messrs. M. J. Moriarty, T. Moriarty.

GORTATLEA—Mr. Henry Spring.

BALLYMACELLIGOTT—Messrs. John Byrne, T. McEllistrum.

CORDAL—Mr. T. T. O'Connor.

The Tralee and Dingle men arrived here yesterday by the mid-day train from Dublin and were welcomed by an immense crowd of friends, the fair sex predominating. The others came out at intermediate stations. The released men are in the best of health and spirits and are none the worse for their varied experiences of Irish and English detention prisons.

There was a large force of police, under D.I. Britten, stationed at the different entrances to the Tralee station, but everthing passed off quietly. A member of the Urban Council who was not permitted to leave the station premises at the same time as others had a few interchanges with the Head Constable.

The released men were first imprisoned in Tralee gaol, then removed to Richmond Barracks and subsequently to Wakefield military prison. After some weeks in the latter place, they were transferred to Frongoch Detention Camp where they had a good deal of liberty and had nothing to complain of as regards the food. There were about 2,000 Irishmen interned at Frongoch and taking everything into consideration the released men say they had a fairly good time. Concerts, football matches, and other amusements broke the monotony of their deportation. On one or two occasions they were permitted to have a route march through the districts in the neighbourhood of the camp, which is picturesquely situated, being partly surrounded by mountains about the height of Cahirconree. To the west they could see the peak of Snowden, which is the highest mountain in England or Wales. Their detention barrack was an old distillery, along which ran the river Bala. One of them said their camp reminded him of the Sportsfield at Killarney, the Bala being something like the Flesk, the grounds surrounded by trees and the mountains close at hand. They got on remarkably well with their military guards who gave them a good deal of latitude. But romantic scenery and friendly guards did not make them perfectly happy. The desire to be back once more amongst their relatives and friends—the call of the Motherland—was always with them.

The following are still at Frongoch:—

TRALEE—Messrs. Dan Healy, Jack O'Reilly, S. H. Ruttle, J. Mehnn, M. J. O'Connor, A. Cotton, J Horan.

O'DORNEY—Mr. Mortimer O'Connor.

CASTLEISLAND—Mr. D. O'Mahony.

CAHERCIVEEN—Messrs. Denis Daly, J. O'Donoghue, M. O'Connell, J. Clifford.

KILLARNEY—Messrs. Dick Fitzgerald, Spillane. Horgan, Sullivan and Shea.

The most of those are expected to be released shortly.

All sorts of occupations are represented at Frongoch—Engineers. University men, Doctors, Civil Servants, a Clerk of the Union, School Teachers, business men of all descriptions and newspapermen galore.

A first-hand account of life in the Frongoch camp, *The Kerryman*, 29 July 1916.

and all GAA units banned from participating 'in any political movement.' Throughout the period from 1916 to 1923, the GAA had to differentiate between political matters (which debarred GAA involvement) and national issues (which allowed GAA involvement). The GAA viewed the treatment and welfare of Irish political prisoners as a non-political national issue and, until the Civil War, the Association was comfortable issuing statements in support of the prisoners.

During the period from 1916 to 1921, several GAA units publicly professed their support for political prisoners. The North Tipperary board, at their February 1920 meeting, appointed a committee to collect funds for a suitable presentation for their imprisoned secretary, Widger Meagher, who 'was in jail undergoing a sentence of six months for a breach of the D.O.R.A.'[30] Frank McGrath, the Munster delegate to the Central Council, was included on this presentation committee, despite the fact that he had been 'recently deported to Wormwood Scrubs'. When McGrath was released from Wormwood Scrubs to see his ill father, on 17 March 1920, he was re-elected as the Munster delegate to the Central Council[31] and ultimately nominated as the GAA President at the 1920 Annual Convention, with his address appearing on the ballot as 'Wormwood Scrubs Prison'.[32] During the 1920 Mountjoy hunger strike, the Dublin county board postponed their 14 April 1920 meeting 'as a protest against the treatment of the Irishmen in Mountjoy Gaol',[33] an act that was very much in keeping with the one-day trade union-led general strike observed throughout Dublin the previous day. There was also a degree of symbolic reaction on the part of the GAA to the various high-profile deaths that took place within the prisons between 1916 and 1921. When Thomas Ashe died on hunger strike on 25 September 1917, the Dublin county board strongly condemned his death, postponed all scheduled games and arranged for all Dublin football clubs to be represented at his funeral, with members encouraged to carry hurls. Similarly, Alderman Nowlan, J. J. Keane and O. C. Harty represented the GAA at the 31 October 1920 funeral of Terence MacSwiney, who died as a result of force-feeding while on hunger strike in Brixton Prison on 20 October 1920.

Throughout the Civil War, the GAA attempted to portray itself as a neutral organisation and did not issue any major statements in support of the republicans interned and imprisoned by the Provisional government. In the aftermath of the Civil War, however, the issue of prisoners had serious consequences for the GAA. Rather than GAA units freely demonstrating

The weekly meeting of the Co. Dublin Committee was held on Tuesday night, at 65 Parnell street, Mr. A. C. Harty, V.P., presiding. Also present—Messrs. Thomas C. Murphy, Jos. Delaney, Jos. M'Mahon, P. Doyle, John M'Grath, M. P. Keogh, Jas. M'Evoy, Thos. Hayes, Thos. Smyth, Thos. Stanley, H. O'Neill, M. Phelan, P. Kenefick, R. Mockler, T. J. Lonergan, N. Caffrey, J. Kirwan (Hon. Registrar), L. J. O'Toole (Sec. Central Council), and Alderman D. O'Toole (Hon. Sec. and Treasurer).

New Clubs.

The following new clubs affiliated—M'Bride F.C. and Crumlin Independent F.C. (Minor). The Hon. Sec. stated that several other clubs were in process of organising, and would probably be affiliated at next meeting.

Next Sunday's Fixtures.

The Hon. Sec. stated that the re-play of the All-Ireland Junior Football Final had been indefinitely postponed, and the following programme was confirmed for Sunday next, 30th inst.:—

At Croke Park:

Intermediate Football Semi-Final—St. Sylvesters (Malahide) v. McCrackens (Ballsbridge), 12.30. Mr. T. J. Lonergan.

Junior Football (Final A Div.)—St. Marys (Saggart) v. Round Towers (Clondalkin), 1.30. Mr. N. Caffrey.

TRANSFERS.

The following transfers were sanctioned—Thos. Cassidy, Glasthule Mitchels, to St. Benedicts (Dalkey), and Patrick Doherty, Patrick Hurley, John Maxwell, Patrick May, Thos. Mockler, Rd. Buggy, and Jas. Doyle from O'Rahilly H.C. to Con Colbert H.C.

GENERAL.

Erin's Isle F.C. were granted permission to play a friendly with St. L. O'Tooles F.C. at an Aeridheacht at Finglas Bridge on Sunday next. Con Colbert H.C. were granted permission to play Hearts of Steel H.C. in the Park, and James Stephens were granted permission to play Erin's Hope at St. Patrick's College ground.

The objection by Croke F.C. to Donore F.C. arising out of their Minor Football Championship tie was postponed until next meeting, when it will be finally dealt with.

The deputation appointed to wait on the different colleges and schools in the city and county made a report of their visit to the various institutions which was considered satisfactory. A full resumé of the interviews will be published later.

A grant of £2 was made to a player of the Limerick team injured in match on September 9th.

The Leinster Council notified that the Leinster Football Final, Dublin v. Wexford, had been fixed for Croke Park on Sunday, October 14th, at 12.15, and in response to a request the committee decided to render all possible assistance to the Council on the date of the final.

The Committee had under consideration arrangements for the proposed tournament at Croke Park on Sunday, October 21st, for the benefit of a well-known Dublin Gael. Mr. J. J. Hogan (Chairman Leinster Council) attended in connection with the matter, and the following programme was arranged for October 21st:—

At Croke Park:

Football—North Co. Selected v. South Co. Selected.

Inter-County Football—Dublin (Geraldine Selection) v. Louth.

The team to represent the North Co. will be selected by St. Sylvesters, and Stars of Erin will select the team for South Co.

The question of making further fixtures for the tournament was postponed until next meeting, when definite arrangements regarding the fixtures for October 21st will be made, and the Committee appeal to the Gaels of Dublin for their assistance in making the tournament a success.

On the motion of Mr Lonergan a sum of £3 was voted to Mr Jno W Donovan as expenses for remaining in Dublin for the Leinster Football Final.

A sum of 10/- was voted to Mr P McDonnell (O'Tooles) for special expenses from Carlow to Dublin for his Match; and £1.10 to Thos Daly as expenses for the Dublin v Kilkenny Match.

Messrs Kirwin, Keogh & Hanlee were appointed as a Deputation to wait on Donnybrook C Y M S on Friday 28th Sept

A C Harty
2/10/17

Special Meeting 28 Sept 1917

A special meeting of the above was held at 65 Parnell street last night to make arrangements to have all hurling and football clubs in Dublin represented at the funeral of the late Mr. Thos. Ashe. Mr. Eamon Hynes presided over a large attendance of delegates, practically all clubs in the city and county being represented.

Mr. A. C. Harty, V.C., proposed:—"That we, the representatives of the Gaels of Dublin, deeply deplore the tragic death of Mr. Thomas Ashe, a member of our Association, and a brilliant and gifted young Irishman, and that we tender to his relatives and friends our expression of sincere regret. We strongly condemn the inhuman practice which resulted in his death, which we consider a disgrace to civilisation."

Mr. E. Hynes (Hon. Chairman, S.H. and F. League) seconded the resolution, which was passed in silence.

It was decided that all clubs should meet at Croke Park on Sunday morning at 11 o'clock to be marshalled there, and proceed to the place allotted to them at the City Hall. Mr. H. Boland, Hon. Chairman, was appointed Chief Marshal of the G.A.A. section, with Messrs. A. C. Harty, V.C., and E. Hynes assistant Marshals. It was agreed that all clubs that could do so should carry camans, and it was arranged to place a wreath on the grave from the Gaels of Dublin. The Chairman, in bringing the meeting to a close, appealed to all members of the G.A.A. to turn out in full force at Croke Park on Sunday morning.

It was unanimously decided to cancel the Championship Fixtures arranged for Croke Park on Sunday Sept 30th on account of the Funeral

A C Harty
2/10/17

their support for the prisoners, GAA club, county and provincial teams came under strenuous pressure from republicans to cancel Gaelic games as a means of protesting against the continued detention of republicans. Between 14 October and 23 November 1923, a series of related hunger strikes were initiated by the republican prisoners in Mountjoy, Cork, Kilkenny and Dundalk prisons and the internees in the Curragh camp, in an effort to secure their unconditional release. Throughout this two-month period, republicans actively attempted to influence, and sometimes force, the GAA to support the prisoners publicly by cancelling scheduled games. In October 1923, the Ballywilliam Sinn Féin Club publicly called 'on the Co Boards of North and South Tipperary to further suspend all fixtures of the G.A.A. pending the release of the prisoners and also that all other public amusements cease'.[34] In Waterford, four 'prominent local republicans' entered the Waterford Sports Field and appealed to the Gaelic football and hurling players not to play their scheduled matches while the hunger strike was in progress. After a 'heated parley ... during which heated interchanges took place between Republicans and [GAA] officials' the matches were postponed.[35] In November 1923, several GAA grounds in Cork were vandalised, with stands and dressing rooms burnt and goalposts cut down by men with the 'evident intention of preventing Gaelic games from being played while the prisoners are on hunger strike'.[36] There was, however, some support from within the GAA for the cancellation of fixtures in support of the prisoners. When the pro-Treaty Kilkenny chairman, Thomas Walshe, refused a November 1923 appeal from Kilkenny Sinn Féin to postpone all fixtures until the prisoners were released, on the grounds that the appeal was 'not only political, but it is a shade worse – it is party political', two Kilkenny clubs, Clomanto and Callan, both intimated that they would not take part in the county championships until the prisoners were released.[37]

This republican pressure on the GAA intensified the following year and almost caused the collapse of three delayed 1923 All-Ireland championships. In June 1924, the Kerry football team came under public pressure from republicans not to compete in the 1923 All-Ireland senior football final, scheduled for 13 June 1924, until all political prisoners, including the Kerry GAA chairman, Austin Stack, were released

FACING PAGE: Minutes of the Dublin county board meeting, 28 September 1917, at which the board made preparations to be fully represented at the funeral of hunger striker Thomas Ashe.

from prison. The Kerry county board and the Kerry footballers held a 'prolonged conference' on 10 and 11 June 1924, with the decision taken to 'postpone the match … so as to prevent a split amongst the team, and save the G.A.A. in Kerry from a general split.'[38] The Central Council met on 14 June 1924 to discuss the matter and, in the absence of the Kerry representative, Dick Fitzgerald, who was delayed and joined the meeting after the decision had been taken, ruled that Dublin be awarded a walkover in the final. This was despite an appeal from the Kerry secretary, Din Joe Bailey, who wrote that Kerry's decision not to partake in the final was the 'lesser evil' of the two options, with the alternative being 'playing with a depleted team with no chance of victory, and smashing the unity of the GAA in Kerry'.[39] Encouraged by this success, Moss Twomey, IRA Chief of Staff, sent orders to all IRA volunteers across the country to approach GAA county teams and county boards, and request that they withdraw from their respective competitions; ultimately the IRA was hoping to use the GAA to embarrass the Irish Free State by organising a mass boycott of the 1924 Tailteann Games.[40] Within a fortnight, the Central Council effectively had to write off the 1923 All-Ireland senior hurling final between Limerick and Galway, scheduled for 29 June 1924, when Limerick refused to play as their players had been 'influenced and warned not to travel'[41] and Galway would not accept a walkover from the governing body.[42] The Cork county board decided, on 2 July 1924, that the Cork team would not contest the All-Ireland junior hurling final until the prisoners, including their chairman, Seán McCarthy, were released,[43] which resulted in the Central Council awarding the final to Offaly, who had informed the council that they were willing to compete.[44]

In addition to the All-Ireland finals, the cause of political prisoners was also affecting club, inter-county and inter-provincial competitions throughout June and July 1924. Two Kilkenny clubs, Callan and Glenmore, refused to play in the south Kilkenny hurling championship,[45] while the Nil Desperandum and UCC clubs were both unwilling to take part in the Cork senior football final.[46] The Louth county board, at the behest of Sinn Féin, withdrew from their scheduled Leinster senior football semi-final fixture against Dublin,[47] while the Munster Council, unhappy with the treatment meted out to Cork, Limerick and Kerry, refused to select hurling and football teams to represent the province in the inter-provincial trial matches for the 1924 Tailteann Games. Having suspended the Cork county board and threatening to impose financial penalties on the Limerick and Kerry county boards, the GAA held a Special Convention on 10 August 1924 at which it was agreed to withdraw the (threatened) financial penalties on the Kerry and Limerick teams and to remove the suspension on the Cork county board. A resolution was also passed directing the Central Council to proceed with the 1923 finals,[48] with the Central Council fixing the hurling final for 14 September 1924 and the football final for 28 September 1924.[49] By the time these 1923 finals were played, the vast majority of the Irish prisoners had been released and the furore over their continued detention had dissipated.

• • •

In the immediate aftermath of the imprisonment and internment of those suspected of being involved in the 1916 Rising, several fundraising organisations were established, with the Irish Volunteer Dependants Fund (IVDF)[50] and the Irish National Aid Association (INAA)[51] being the two most prominent. While the GAA, at national level, became officially involved in fundraising for prisoners in November 1916, Gaelic games were used to raise funds for political prisoners at a local level even before the Rising – a Gaelic games tournament was held in Athenry in June 1915 for the benefit of Seán McDermott, who had been imprisoned under the Defence of the Realm Act.[52] In the aftermath of 1916 Rising, two challenge football games, between Lees and Macroom and between Clondrohid and Cill na Martra (Kilnamartyra), were played in Cork in July 1916 to raise funds for the 'maintenance of the dependants of the O'Connor brothers, New Street, who were arrested in connection with rebellion affair and interned'. *The Southern Star* called the brothers 'prominent supporters of the Gaelic movement in all its phases' and reported that the 'attendance of the public was a solid recognition of the worthiness of the object, and the tournament was financially a marked success'.[53]

The Central Council of the GAA, in November 1916, agreed to stage an All-Ireland competition in aid of the 'Irish National Aid and Volunteer Dependants Fund' (popularly known as 'National Aid')[54] and established a subcommittee to 'act in conjunction with the National Aid Committee for the carrying out of the tournament'.[55] National Aid also established their own GAA subcommittee that circularised all GAA county boards requesting that they organise local tournaments as a prelude to an inter-county tournament, with 'a set of gold medals suitably inscribed' offered to the winners. When the Dublin county board received this circular from National Aid, the board fixed the first round fixtures for 4 March 1917, cancelled all other fixtures in Dublin that day and appealed 'to all supporters of the G.A.A. in the county to give the tournament their support'.[56] Despite this appeal, match reports from the time indicate little interest in the National Aid hurling and football competitions – the Dublin hurling and football finals, won by Collegians and Lawrence O'Tooles respectively, were played in Croke Park on 29 April 1917 in front of 1,000 spectators.[57] The first round of the Leinster inter-county football championship, between Dublin and Louth, was held in Dundalk on 27 January 1918 and although the press called the match 'exciting', it was reported that 'little interest was taken locally in the fixture, and the attendance was very small'.[58] The Leinster football final of the competition, between Dublin and Wexford, was played in Croke Park on 31 March 1918 in front of 'only 1,000 spectators, who braved an incessant downpour'.[59] The hurling competition fared somewhat better – 4,000 attended the Leinster hurling final, which was played in Croke Park 'in ideal weather'.[60]

Financially, the National Aid tournament cannot be deemed to have been a success. In November 1917, National Aid's GAA subcommittee reported that they had received £434 3s. 11d. from the GAA,[61] which, presumably, consisted of funds raised through local tournaments, including those held in Louth[62] and Dublin,[63] and outright subscriptions.[64] However, by March 1918, National Aid felt compelled to write to the GAA to ascertain the exact position of the fund.[65] In January 1919, National Aid again wrote to the GAA asking 'for at least a refund of the £100 advanced in connection with the tournament'.[66] The Central Council, at their 25 January 1919 meeting, seemed to consider the 'original fund now closed' and, noting that it had contributed 'over £700' to the fund, decided to send a deputation to 'wait upon the National Aid committee with the view of having whatever funds accrue from the remaining ties of the tournament devoted to those civil servants (male and female) whom [sic] refused to take the oath of allegiance.'[67] This GAA deputation offered National Aid £150 (that included the £100 advanced by National Aid) of the £700 collected.[68] National Aid, 'having regard to the delay which has already taken place, and to the fact that the accounts of this Association will soon have to be closed, and further that losses may be incurred by offering the consideration of this matter any longer', reluctantly accepted the offer but stipulated that 'the name of the National Aid Association be in no further way identified with any tournament matches held … under the G.A.A.', following the National Aid All-Ireland hurling final, scheduled for 9 February 1919.[69] This hurling final, held in Croke Park, attracted a crowd of between 7,000 and 8,000, who saw Dublin defeat Limerick, 5-02 to 2-01.[70]

Within one week of closing the National Aid fund, the GAA agreed to support the Irish Republican Prisoners' Dependants Fund (IRPDF), an organisation founded in September 1917 and consisting predominantly of Sinn Féin personnel.[71] This 'switch' from National Aid to the IRPDF was indicative of the changing outlook of the GAA; at the 1918 Annual Convention, a motion led by Harry Boland was passed censuring the Central Council for negotiating with the British Military and the IPP on the respective matters of transport and the Entertainment Tax.[72] This represented a shift in GAA support from constitutional nationalism towards the more militant position of Sinn Féin. (Interestingly, it was the Dublin county board, with Harry Boland as chairman, who, in April 1916, originally suggested canvassing support from the IPP in their opposition to the Entertainment Tax.[73]) Instead of an All-Ireland competition, county committees were requested to 'run friendly matches or local tournaments on the same lines as National Aid' but with all contributions registered through the Central Council.[74] On 6 April 1919, an estimated 20,000 to 25,000 people attended a football match in Croke Park between Wexford and Tipperary in aid of the IRPDF: many republican dignitaries attended this match, including Éamon de Valera (who threw in the ball to start the game), the Lord Mayor of Dublin and 'a good sprinkling of military officers and men, including many representatives of the overseas forces'.[75] The ill-fated Dublin versus Tipperary football game of 21 November 1920 (Bloody Sunday) was also, according to the Leinster Council secretary John Shouldice, 'organised by the Volunteers Dependants Fund Committee' for the benefit of the relatives of imprisoned or dead republicans.[76]

Between the July 1921 Truce and the outbreak of the Civil War in June 1922, the IRPDF continued to use Gaelic games to raise funds for its cause, with the GAA raising £543 9s. 6d. for the fund in 1921.[77] In February 1922, the IRPDF staged a charity football game in Croke Park between Tipperary and Kildare, and advertised this game in the newspapers under the somewhat inappropriate headline 'Desperate Shooting at Croke Park

(L–r): Michael Collins, Commandant Seán MacEoin and Harry Boland at Croke Park for the 25 September 1921 hurling match between Laois and Dublin, in aid of the Irish Republican Prisoners' Dependants Fund.

(For Goals and Points) on Sunday Next'. In a sign of the emerging political divisions and tensions, the IRPDF invited 'Republicans, Free Staters and Separatists (Sinn Feiners All!!)' to 'Adjourn to the Old Venue for a Few Hours Relaxation.'[78] The game itself, won by Kildare, was attended by between 10,000 and 12,000 spectators, including many wounded IRA men, despite the 'wet and uninviting' weather. Kathleen Clarke, TD, presented the Irish Republican Prisoners' Dependants Fund Cup[79] to the Kildare captain, George Higgins, after the match.[80]

The IRPDF was associated with the anti-Treaty republican side following the outbreak of the Civil War. Speaking in January 1924, after the conclusion of the Civil War, President Cosgrave claimed that the IRPDF 'was seized on behalf of the irregulars on the outbreak of civil strife and … used as a cloak for furthering the activities and propaganda of the Irregulars throughout the entire campaign of destruction',[81] a claim denied by the IRPDF secretary, Kathleen Barry.[82] While the GAA, at national level, never overtly claimed its support for the Treaty, throughout the Civil War

Alderman Kathleen Clarke, widow of executed 1916 leader Thomas Clarke, presenting the Irish Republican Prisoners' Dependants Fund Cup to the Kildare captain, George Higgins, on 28 February 1922.

period, the GAA was an enthusiastic partner of the Irish Free State in the planning of the 1924 Tailteann Games, with Croke Park as the epicentre of the games. Furthermore, in May 1922 the GAA decided that county boards could, if they so chose, accept affiliations from National Army teams for inclusion in county championships,[83] while in June 1922 the Association agreed to provide two cups to the National Army for its hurling and football competitions.[84] As the Civil War came to an end, the GAA banned 'any collections or sales of literature of any political or other nature' in Croke Park, in response to the many complaints it received from patrons of the stadium.[85] While the minutes of the Central Council meetings do not record any requests from the IRPDF for help in their Civil War fundraising activities, one can say with certainty that had any request from the IRPDF been received, it would have been rejected as the GAA sought to develop its relationship with the Irish government and the National Army, while at the same time proclaiming its neutral non-political position.

GAA fundraising recommenced following the conclusion of the Civil War, albeit at a much more local level. In August 1923, the Louth county board, in response to a request from the Drogheda Prisoners' Dependants Fund, agreed to run a countywide club tournament in aid of the fund,[86] and in October 1923 the county board agreed to allow a football match take place as part of a bazaar the fund had planned for November.[87] This fundraising continued as the prisoners began to be released – the Dublin county board held a football match between 'city born' (chosen by Lawrence O'Tooles club) and 'country born' (chosen by Kickhams club) footballers in Croke Park on 3 February 1924 in aid of the Released Prisoners Fund.[88] This match, won by the 'country born' footballers on a score of 4-06 to 2-03, was well attended and raised a 'substantial' amount 'in aid of the Dublin area prisoners'.[89]

Fundraising for Irish internees and political prisoners was the form of support most amenable to the GAA, with the Association a most enthusiastic fundraiser in the pre-Civil War period. Fundraising was also the most public form of support undertaken by the GAA: pre-match advertisements regularly appeared in the newspapers for GAA fundraising games and tournaments. The crowds at these games, although modest at first, grew and attracted republican dignitaries, which in turn led to increased publicity, including, on at least one occasion, a British Pathé camera crew. The Civil War, however, changed the dynamics of fundraising and, as discussed, the enthusiasm with which the Association had raised funds for political prisoners came to an almost complete halt.

· · ·

While the role and importance of the GAA in the Irish independence struggle from 1913 to 1923 has been the subject of some debate and much revisionism, it can be argued that the relationship between the GAA and political prisoners represents one of the only direct and tangible links between the GAA and the nationalist movement. The GAA, as an organisation, never endorsed the Volunteer movement; it did not take part in the planning or undertaking of the Rising (and actually sought to disassociate itself from the Rising in the immediate aftermath); and, while the organisation was affected by the War of Independence and Civil War, it never became a direct participant in either of the conflicts. (While de Búrca maintains that Bloody Sunday firmly linked the GAA to the 'underground nation', it must be remembered that apart from being a victim, the GAA played no other role in the day's proceedings.) It was GAA support for political prisoners, its fundraising ventures in particular, that firmly and publicly linked the GAA to the nationalist struggle, maybe even more so than the Association's continued ban on the British military and the short-lived (and somewhat unpopular) ban on Irish civil servants who took the Oath of Allegiance. Throughout the entire revolutionary period, the GAA's main concern, despite the political turmoil, was the promotion and administration of Gaelic games and ensuring that the Association survived. Supporting political prisoners in nineteenth- and twentieth-century Ireland, as William Murphy has noted, was an 'activity which allowed mainstream nationalists indicate a certain degree of sympathy for radicals without becoming entirely identified with their aims'.[90] This template of support worked for the GAA, so much so that it was redeployed during future bouts of internment and imprisonment introduced during the Second World War, the Border Campaign and the 'Troubles'.

CHAPTER 11

Camogie and Revolutionary Ireland, 1913–23

EOGHAN CORRY

A 1924 Ladies Hurling Match at Nenagh, as published by the
Cork Weekly Examiner.

Томбгаск in north Wexford is one of those places for which the descriptor 'hamlet' or 'village' is a considerable overstatement. It is a crossroads, little more, with one of those character-laden rural pubs we often take for granted, Pat Coleman's Rebel Arms, peeking across the Slaney floodplain to an All-Ireland championship medal-winning view of magnificent Mount Leinster. This is as suitable a place as any to start the search for an explanation of how camogie reinvented itself in the 1910s. Tombrack sent its team, captained by Anty O'Neill (the first generation of a great Wexford GAA family that provided two Leinster Council secretaries and the referee of the 1947 Polo Grounds football final in New York), to play a team from Glasnevin in August 1913, in the earliest stages of the revival of the Camogie Association.[1]

On the face of it, the first three decades of camogie history were not particularly successful. It was the 1930s before the game emerged to establish itself as a resourceful second-tier sport in the Irish sporting landscape. But it is its presence in isolated hamlets like Tombrack that gives us a clue as to the largely undocumented revolution that enhanced the lives of Irishwomen during the decade of revolution. Camogie had a relatively high profile in the national and provincial press at the time, but the scattered and inconsistent coverage may not reveal the scale of the activity. Overworked sports journalists went for the lowest-hanging *fraochán* – matches between urban clubs in Jones' Road, The Thatch, Drumcondra, Phoenix Park, Richmond Hill, the Mardyke and the O'Neill Crowley Ground at Victoria Cross.

Beyond this documented reportage, camogie had a secret history, preserved in fading photographs and the fireside memories of the countrywomen who sustained the camogie revival – one of the several concurrent revolutions in Irish sporting, political and popular culture that marked the revolutionary decade.

The word 'camogie' created great resonance during this period. Decades later, Samuel Beckett famously purloined it for one of his wordplays.[2] A British Army communiqué characterised a riot in Cork in June 1917 as being instigated by 'the camogie contingent'. The participants were, according to the military, returning from a camogie match between Plunketts and Clan Emer at the O'Neill Crowley Ground on Western Road accompanied by the Pipers' Band 'when they launched an attack on the county jail, stones being thrown and some windows broken. Cheers were raised for the prisoners still there and these were answered from within the prison walls.'[3] One can imagine the disdain this phrase conveyed: the presence of women in a protest zone was a combination of the things that the regime hated most. Currents that could be retrospectively described today as supporting democracy, suffragism, nationalism, trade unionism and linguistic revivalism were all, to one extent or other, mixed up together in that group of women.

One is struck by the spirit of these camogie pioneers, in an age when history, physiology, psychology and economics collided. They seemed to be fighting on all fronts at once. A surprising number of them were involved in the political struggle; many were suffragettes and many were involved in the trade union struggle. But even if we confine ourselves to looking at their role in shaking up the sporting culture that prevailed at the time, their achievements were considerable.[4]

At this time, and in so many of the succeeding decades, sports culture was arranged to reflect an unrelenting male dominance. The concerns of the new camogie players about their image, what clothing should be worn on the field, whether they should publicise their activities and whether to allow competition, so evident from contemporary newspaper coverage, were shared by pioneer ladies' hockey players in England.[5]

Although the slogan 'mainstream is male stream' was first coined by sports sociologists decades after the Camogie Association was ash-clattered into existence, in accounts of the infant sport you can detect the camogie players' faltering steps into a culture where sport, assumed to reflect masculinity, was organised in patriarchal institutions and founded on a mythology of female frailty.[6]

A Game of Our Own (Dublin, 2011) is the title of the official history of the sport compiled by Mary Moran, a past President of the Camogie Association (and, equally importantly, a woman who restored Cork camogie's position at the top table of the sport in the 1970s). It expressed the separatist goal of the early pioneers. They did not seek any status within the GAA; they set out to build their own structures unrelated to anything that was happening in male sports. Hence, camogie does not fit as easily as it might first appear into the debates and controversies of women's sports history. Nevertheless, there is no shortage of expression of camogie's unequal struggle against male-dominated cultural, media, political and clerical opposition, and, even within the Gaelic family, no scarcity of sporting obstacles.

Mary Moran's list of some of those obstacles will be familiar to anyone who has attempted to organise sport for females:

> A lack of players with leisure time to play; a dearth of funds; difficulties in obtaining use of playing pitches; absence of public support; problems with transport and communication; no previous experience of organisation; girls moving away on marriage; child bearing and rearing; burden of work in rural areas, and public opinion against women's participation in sport hindered development. [7]

Allen Guttman provides a useful international context:

> Women have never been totally excluded from sport, but they have – until quite recently – seldom been granted the same opportunities as men. Opportunity came only after a prolonged struggle on the part of female athletes and their male supporters (who were seldom as numerous as the women's male opponents). [8]

Camogie personnel of later eras may have focused a lot on these obstacles and not on the sport's achievements, which were considerable. They achieved participation and attendance levels that were above the European norm for other female sports. They managed to secure press (and later broadcast) coverage at a high, if inconsistent, level. The external obstacles the organisation faced were augmented by a lack of continuity among officials at local level, and by clashes between the strong personalities among the few long-term officials who did serve the game. Camogie did not prosper in the 1910s and 1920s. What was achieved in the decade of upheaval was survival.

The interpretation of the first bank of camogie historians, Mary Moran and Pádraig Puirséil, was that camogie was founded in two waves, one led by the Keating Branch of the Gaelic League between 1904 and 1906, and the other by Crokes GAA Club in Dublin between 1910 and 1912. We can safely assume that Pádraig Puirséil's interpretation was shared or inspired by his wife Úna Bean Uí Phuirséil (formerly Agnes Hourigan), lifelong champion of camogie as distinguished player, commentator, administrator and, from 1976 to 1979, President of the Association. Mary Moran's comment is that:

what Keatings did in the earlier years, Crokes did in 1910 and afterwards. It is probably true to say that were it not for the intervention of Crokes Gaelic Club, the game would not have survived. [9]

Both were important wellsprings, and understanding them is key to understanding the earliest phase of camogie history.

Keatings was not just any branch of the Gaelic League – it was one of the most active, founded by revivalist writers Tadhg Ó Donnchadha ('Torna'), Seán Ua Ceallaigh ('Sceilg'), Risteard Ó Foghlú and Shán Ó Cuiv. Máire Ní Chinnéide, a draper's daughter from South Great George's Street and a past pupil of Muckross who is best remembered nowadays as the collector and editor of the memoir of Peig Sayers, was prominent among the women who first began to play hurling in Drumcondra in 1903. She was the first student to win an Irish scholarship at the Royal University (later to become UCD), graduating in 1901. Her colleagues in Drumcondra were also graduates of the Royal University, which had become the second university to allow women to graduate:

> Máire Ní Chinnéide was a classmate of brilliant women under-graduates like the late Agnes O'Farrelly, the late Mrs Hannah Sheehy Skeffington, her sister Mrs Kettle, and Senator Mrs Helena Concannon. In those days, the Royal University was merely an examining body. Lectures were given in several colleges like Eccles Street and Loreto College for the girls, and, for the boys in the Jesuit College, now Newman House, on St. Stephen's Green. Rallying place of the university students was the Sheehy's Sunday evening 'at home.' It was there she thinks that the announcement was made that the shy and retiring young student, James Joyce, had received a cheque for £15 for an article in an English magazine. There was general jubilation. [10]

Ó Donnchadha supplied the name for the new game played by these women: *camógaíocht. Camóg* would later be equated to a younger or smaller hurling stick. Ó Donnchadha was a scholar of old Irish, in which the word *camac* was an alternative name for *camán*. It was also common in Welsh as a description of a stick-and-ball game. [11]

The rules, too, appear to have been drawn up by men. Stopping the

The 1904 Cuchullains Camogie team. The dress and the shape of the *camán*, as seen here, were standard for camogie players at the time and for the foreseeable future.

ball with the skirt was deemed to be a foul. Séamus Ó Braonáin modified the rules of hurling to make the pitches and goals smaller. His overly narrow 10-foot-wide goal was widened to 15 feet within seven years in 1911 (field hockey and shinty goals are 12 feet wide; hurling goals are 21 feet wide), but many other aspects of his slimmed-down model endured. The modified field and goal sizes, along with the elliptic team formations (of 1-2-3-3-3-2-1), survived until 1999. Both meant that camogie necessitated modifying GAA fields for its matches. This created difficulties on the occasions when camogie fixtures were staged alongside high-profile GAA events, such as when the All-Ireland final replay was staged as a curtain-raiser to the Oireachtas hurling final at Croke Park in 1967, or when the 1958 All-Ireland final was played some time after the All-Ireland senior hurling semi-final between Tipperary and Kilkenny – and after most of the attendance had departed – to allow the appropriate posts to be constructed. The most contentious feature, particularly for women in traditional hurling counties such as Cork, Kilkenny and Tipperary, the bar at the top of the point posts, was not introduced until 1929 and survived until 1979.

The spherical team plan reflected the phalanx tactics of the early football and hurling that Ó Braonáin played; as Jimmy Brennan, he won four All-Ireland senior football medals with Dublin. It was outmoded in both sports by the 1920s, and indeed camogie was evolving to use the open spaces that Ó Braonáin's team formation had inadvertently created, especially as played by Antrim in the 1940s and 1950s, and by Nell McCarthy's Dublin teams. Ó Braonáin was to enter into another stage of camogie history when he intervened to have commentary of the All-Ireland camogie final broadcast on Radio Éireann from 1940, after he became the national broadcaster's third Director of Broadcasting.

The moderated rules raise some fascinating questions in themselves. Were these inhibitions imposed on the women members by men? They were a product of the culture from which camogie emerged, but tennis and hockey did not moderate their rules for ladies, although golf's separated tees are of the same vintage and have survived. We can see evidence of the role of men as administrators of the women's game, and the tensions this created, in later decades. The issue of men putting shackles on female sport was a feature of the decade. Sporting culture internationally held it as axiomatic that women would not be up to the task of full-scale athletic participation. It was 1928 before the Olympic movement allowed any women's athletics at all, and 1984 before they allowed women's races over 1,500 metres. One final point from the Keatings era: some retrospective attention may be focused on the fact that the Sinn Féin GAA club, which affiliated in 1906, largely concerned itself with camogie. The personnel indicate no connection with the emerging political party, but the emergence of the nomenclature of the political movement is apparent.[12]

As with the Keatings, Crokes was not just any GAA club. It was one of the most active, and famously the most insurrectionary in 1916: thirty-two of the forty male members of the club participated in the Rising. The February 1911 quarterly report devotes considerable time to off-field activities such as Pádraig Ó Ceallacháin's language classes, the *aeridheacht* (open-air entertainment) in Richmond Hill and their plans for a journal.[13] Crokes founded a camogie branch at the end of 1910, and finding they had not enough opposition, set about rectifying the situation.[14] They knew from the experience of Keatings that they needed to broaden the base of the game. Club members Seán O'Duffy and Cáit O'Donoghue utilised their access to gatekeepers of the contemporary media – especially John Wyse Power, editor of the *Evening Herald*, and the sports pages of *The Freeman's Journal* organised by P. P. Sutton – to generate some pre-publicity. The notice in *The Freeman's Journal* – with its assumption of the indispensability of male direction – suggests that the target audience was urban:

> This healthy game, which suggests a blend of hurling and hockey, was introduced a few years ago in Dublin, and it provoked some most interesting contests between local clubs. Only a little organisation should be needed by men to preserve it as a means of recreation for many hundreds of indoor workers in Dublin.[15]

Crokes also secured wide reportage of the revival meeting at the Gaelic League Hall, 25 Rutland Square, on 21 April 1911 – a date that sits proudly as the birthdate on the Association's Facebook page and leads to interesting purchase suggestions in the targeted advertisements for the page's administrators.

One is struck by how similar these newspaper reports of the second attempt to found the Camogie Association are to those of the foundation of the GAA on 1 November 1884: a series of letters of support from influential figures in social and academic circles, with little emphasis on

Action shots from a 1924 Ladies Hurling Match at Nenagh, as published by the *Cork Weekly Examiner*.

the forms and structures of the new body. The ten clubs that attended the inaugural meeting of *An Cumann Camóguidheachta* included a cross section of the 'Irish-Ireland' cultural vortex in the city: Ard Chraobh, Drumcondra Keatings, and Kevin's Gaelic League branches; Colmcille's, Fianna, St Margaret's and Crokes GAA clubs; the Emmett choir; and Inghinidhe na hÉireann. Often depicted as an amateur theatrical group, Inghinidhe na hÉireann was founded by Maud Gonne in 1900, and became a branch of Cumann na mBan when it was unveiled as an auxiliary to the Irish Volunteers in April 1914.

The tone of the proceedings was an epistolary series of endorsements. Anita Lett of Davidstown, County Wexford, commented:

> If only girls could be induced to play more games we would not see so many, as we do now, unable to work, run, or even walk with ease or grace. Besides this, I feel their health would be vastly improved with healthy outdoor exercise. I hope, however, that should games amongst girls be developed to any great extent, that they will not fall into the error which has become the curse of football among men – that is, that while 15 play, 15,000 look on.[16]

The key to extending the narrow camogie base of 1904–6 was the appointment of a unionist president; in truth, more a patron than a president. Elizabeth Burke-Plunkett was a Galway woman, a daughter of George Edmond Burke of Danesfield in Moycullen. She was the wife of Arthur Plunkett, the state steward to the colonial administration in Dublin Castle and one of the few remaining Catholic peers in 1911.

She appears to have been seen as a compromise figure in 1910s Ireland: a little too close to Dublin Castle for Maud Gonne and her circle, but influential among a middle-ground constituency torn between the obsession with class and status of the colonists and the egalitarianism and dissenting spirit of the reformists. Her circle of friends included, on the one hand, Field Marshal Douglas Haig, Horace Plunkett and Chief Secretary George Wyndham, and, on the other side of the Home Rule question, figures such as Charles Stewart Parnell, Michael Collins and Éamon de Valera. She was something of a touchstone for cultural and social groups, using her status as Countess of Fingall to promote Irish industrial, charitable and cultural groups. She became the first President of the Irish Countrywomen's Association. Her patronage of camogie

Gaelic League Hall

25 Rutland Square

21st April 1911.

In response to a circular issued by the Croke Club, and the further co-operation of Miss Cáit ní Donncaḋa, a large number of delegates from camoguidheaċt the clubs and Gaelic League branches, as well as members of the outside public, attended this evening at above addr to consider the best means of fostering and popularising camoguidheacht. Among those present were: Mrs Hamilt Foxrock, Mrs O'Nolan (Máire de Buitléir), Cáit ní Donncaḋa Mr S. Sloan, Tomás Mac Oirreaċtaiẓ, Seán O'h. Uicuile, and representatives from the Ard-Ċraoḃ, Keatings, Kevin Colmcille, St Margaret's, Inġinıṡe na h-Ġreann, Drumcond Emmet Choir and Fianna

On the motion of Cáit ní Donncaḋa, seconded by Mr S. Sloan, Mrs Hamilton was moved to the chair.

After having thanked the meeting in a few brief sentences for the honour thus conferred, Mrs Hamilton proceeded to read several letters cordially approving the formation of an association that would have for its primary object the promotion of a pleasant pastime for Irish girls. The first letter submitted was from

ABOVE AND FOLLOWING PAGES: Minutes of the 21 April 1911 meeting at which *An Cumann Camoguidheachta* was formally established. THE CAMOGIE ASSOCIATION/ AN CUMANN CAMÓGAÍOCHTA the Countess of Fingall, and read:

"I will be delighted to do anything I can to help what I consider a splendid work, for I believe if we could make the boys and girls lives in Ireland more happy and cheerful we would keep many more of them at home. I will gladly be President of the Association and do all that I can to further the objects for which it is being founded. I regret it will be impossible for me to attend to-night's meeting."

Maire de Buitleir wrote to say that "it was with great pleasure and interest she had heard that some patriotic women and girls were taking steps to organize open-air games and other recreations for themselves and their fellow-countrywomen. The old classic ideal of a healthy mind in a healthy should be aimed at in modern Ireland, as it had been aimed at and achieved by our ancestors." She hoped that as a result of the Conference a widespread movement would be created to popularize out-of-door national games.

Mrs Lett, of Wexford wrote stating she was very glad to hear the subject of games for girls was being taken up. She thought if girls could only be induced to play more games they would become ever so much more strong and healthy, and acquire, what very few now possessed, considerable grace and ease of carriage. Anything she could do to make the pastime popular she would willingly do. She deeply regretted her inability to attend.

At this juncture a telegram arrived from the Emerald Camog Club, Dundalk, which read "Wish your meeting every success. Kindly send us particulars. Can we do anything to help? For our own part we will do all we can here to forward the game".

The reading was greeted with applause.

Mrs Hamilton then in a few neatly-expressed sentences, congratulated the meeting in having for its first President the Countess of Fingall. She believed that under her presidency the proposed Association would have a very brilliant and successful future, and since camo-guidheacht was such a pleasant, health-giving pastime she had little doubt that within a few years it would be practised widely throughout the whole country. She welcomed with her whole heart, the idea of an Association and bespoke for it immediate and lasting success.

Her remarks were seconded by Tomás Mac Aosa, who acted as Sec. to the meeting, and he was followed by Mrs O'Nolan, Cait ní Dhonnchadha, Tomás Mac Oireactaig, and Mrs Sloan, all of whom strongly supported the founding of an Association. The proposition that An Cumann

Camoguidheachta be and is hereby established was then put to the meeting and carried unanimously

Mrs Hamilton formally proposed and Cáit Ní Donncá seconded, Lady Fingall as President. The motion was carried with enthusiasm. Tomás Mac Aosa proposed and Mrs O'Nolan seconded, that Mrs Hamilton be a Vice-President, and Cáit Ní Donncása proposed and Mr S Sloan seconded that Mrs O'Nolan be also a Vice-President. Both motions were carried unanimously. The positions of Hon Sec. and Hon. Treas. were allotted to Tomás Mac Aosa and Mr Geo Hughes respectively.

It was resolved that the Executive Committee for the time being consist of the above officers and one represent-ative from each affiliated club, the affiliation fee for each club to be 5/- yearly.

It was decided after a brief discussion to leave over to the new committee the revision of the old rules governing camogudheacht, and a similar decision was arrived at regarding the framing of laws to govern the Association

The feasibility of a competitive league was considered, but in view of the paucity of existing clubs and of the immaturity and inexperience of An Cumann Camógui deacta, it was deemed adivsable to postpone the instituting of such a league for at least some while, and to devo instead all attention to the growth, development and popularization of the game itself. Toward the attainment of this end. an admirable suggestion from Seán Ó h-Uptuyle that an Organizer be appointed by the Association to wait on Gaelic League Branches and kindred bodies to request that they (assist An Cumann Camóguíṡeacta by) forming camóguíṡté clubs within their respective societies, was readily approved and adopted by the meeting.

With regard to committee meetings, which it was suggested be held fortnightly, the Hon Sec. was instructed to write to the Committee of the Ard-Craobh, Connpas na Gaeilge, to request their permission for the holding of such meetings in the Library attached to the Branch.

Votes of thanks were passed to the Coisde of the Ard-Craoi for its great courtesy in placing the Hall at the disposal of the meeting, and to Mrs Hamilton for her kindness in presiding.

The meeting then dissolved.

Cataoppleac

17ᵃᵈ Aibreán 1912.

E. C. Hamilton

17.4.'12

was the result of a friendship with Máire Ní Chinnéide that had been forged through theatrical circles. She was accorded the presidency of the Camogie Association, but never attended a single meeting, sending an annual apology to the Annual Congress. In her absence, Vice-President Éibhlín Nic Aitéinn (Elizabeth Hamilton) chaired the meetings. Máire de Buitléir also held a vice-presidency, and Tomás Mac Aodha of Crokes became Secretary of the Association.

Support was also sought by the Association from Agnes O'Farrelly, She was of a more familiar gene pool – a close friend of Roger Casement, she was later to preside over the foundation meeting of Cumann na mBan. A Cavan woman, her legacy to camogie included the foundation of the UCD camogie club and persuading William Gibson, 2nd Baron Ashbourne and President of the Gaelic League, to donate a cup for the inter-varsity competition. She later became the third President of the Camogie Association.

The organisers of that first meeting of the Camogie Association cited contemporary ideas, not just about exercise, in their bid to extend the game as far as possible beyond the Gaelic League and the GAA. Newly elected Vice-President Elizabeth Hamilton from Foxrock thought it

> an admirable idea that ladies should have some form of recreation of their own that would, while giving healthy enjoyment, counter-act the evil effects of town life, and make them physically and otherwise better and nobler women. She believed it was a great pleasure and boon to be able now and again to cast aside the cares and worries of everyday life and throw oneself wholeheartedly into some entertaining and delightful pastime.

The revival was successful beyond the ambitions of the founders, on the evidence of the following year's convention in the Oak Room of the Mansion House. The Dublin League, which Crokes had hoped to establish, was up and running, while details were heard of activity in Laois, Wexford, Louth, Meath, Dublin, Wicklow, Westmeath, Kilkenny, Cork, Limerick, Tipperary, Clare, Kerry, Waterford, Roscommon, Galway, Monaghan, Antrim, Down and Cavan. Clubs, together with representatives from Cork, Louth, Wexford, Kerry, Roscommon and London, joined the cluster of nine local Dublin clubs.[17]

A letter from Douglas Hyde read to the meeting declared:

Such a game, besides being so good in itself, is of more value to Irish girls than any foreign game can be because it appeals to what is instinctive and hereditary in Irish blood. I read a most remarkable article a couple of years ago upon the improvement in physique and, indeed, all round of the Swedish girls since they took up skating as a national pastime. I hope you can effect something of the same good by popularising camóguidheacht.[18]

The Association's growth spurt was largely devoid of structure. Wexford and Cork established county boards, with Cork's chaired by Mary MacSwiney, sister of Terence MacSwiney (Republican Mayor of Cork in 1920 who would die on hunger strike in Brixton Prison later that year). It was Cork's county board that was to host the most explicit link between the game and the women's suffrage movement, a lecture by P. S. Ó hÉigeartaigh in April 1914, in which he told the camogie board that

The modern movement for the suffrage and its allied movements are merely symptoms of woman's awakening to full consideration, and claiming a soul of her own. In a just civilisation there should be no differentiation on a sex basis, legally, economically or politically, we could not get the best out of a nation while its women, the mothers and educators of the children, were shut out from free citizenship.[19]

Dublin, the other city where the game was played most conspicuously, had no county board. The loss of access to Richmond Hill in the spring of 1913 was a big blow to both Crokes GAA and the Dublin Camogie League – a blow from which camogie did not recover until they got a field in Phoenix Park in 1924. As a result, Dublin's league of 1913 was not completed, and the game retreated to the series of challenge and exhibition matches that had sustained it before the revival of Crokes. It was 1915 when Dublin formed a county board, so that a deputation could march at the funeral of O'Donovan Rossa.[20]

The activity of the Association elsewhere was sporadic and inconsistent. Mary Moran wryly comments, 'the level of activity varied from getting a team together to compete in an Aeridheacht to a number of clubs participating in regular competition.' In most places, camogie was a carnival event, accorded the status of the annual tug-of-war matches or horseshoe-throwing contests between burly agricultural labourers: a once-a-year activity conjured up for the new village fetes of rural Ireland, the increasingly prolific *aeridheachtaí* of the Gaelic League, which were becoming a phenomenon of the age in their own right.

Camogie's impact on these events can sometimes be understated. The more practised Cork and Dublin city clubs travelled to participate in these affairs and often to play local teams. At the *aeridheachtaí* in Kinsale and Dunmanway, the camogie match was regarded as the highlight of the programme. 'Come and see the cailíní hurling', exhorted the newspaper advertisement for the great camogie match to help liquidate the debt of the village hall in Coachford. Even in regular competitions in the city, camogie was an attraction in its own right. A camogie match was on the undercard for two hurling matches at Cork Athletic Grounds that started long after the advertised hour, 'which prevented the camogie match, the chief attraction, being up to time'.[21]

Was the camogie movement of the Crokes era proactive or reactive? It would be hard to imagine the newly (comparatively) empowered, confident young university graduates of the post-Parnellite generation not being influenced by the developments in female sport elsewhere.

Irishwomen were among the first to embrace the sports movements that had found their way onto the island from three main sources of inspiration: England, the US and mainland Europe. Ahead of women in other cultures, Irishwomen had been participating for half a century by the time rules were formulated for camogie. Women played croquet at a high level from the 1840s. In 1854, they achieved a near dominant position in the ancient but newly organised sport of archery. Women riders participated in the hunter shows from the 1860s on. Irishwomen were pioneers of ladies' golf; the Irish Ladies' Golf Union was the first in the world when it was founded in 1893, with its members May Hezlet, Rhona Adair and Clara Mulligan quickly gaining international prominence. Ireland won the first ladies' home international in 1907. Irishwomen were also pioneers of women's tennis, staging the first women's championship at Fitzwilliam Lawn Tennis Club on 5 June 1879 (May Langrishe from Celbridge, the youngest competitor at fifteen years of age, was the first national female tennis champion in the sport's history). Lena Rice, from County Tipperary, won the Wimbledon singles title in 1890, and Mabel Cahill, from County Kilkenny, won two successive singles titles at the

US National Championships in the 1890s. The first national women's body in hockey, the Irish Ladies' Hockey Union, was founded in 1894. Ireland participated in the first ladies' hockey internationals. The first two matches were between what was effectively an Alexandra College team, calling itself Ireland, and a Newnham and Girton College team, calling itself England, at the Alexandra College ground on 10 January 1895 and in Brighton on 10 April 1895. This would be followed by the first official hockey international in 1896.[22]

The Freeman's Journal of 3 March 1896 remarked:

Time, which proves everything, has revealed the existence of a thirst for strong exercise in women that is not to be assuaged by golf. Of course the delightful winter pastime of Hockey has found its way into both sexes. Four years ago the game, confined to men, was represented by less than half a dozen clubs; at the present moment there are between twenty and thirty men's clubs, some three or four for membership of which ladies are also eligible, and a fair number of exclusively ladies clubs. There are some who, remembering the comparative neglect that has overtaken the once popular Hurley in Dublin, have their misgivings as to the fixity of tenure more sanguine admirers prophesy for the newcomer; but the boasted superior science of the modern game and its special adaptability... should tell for a long life to the less exacting and kindred pastime.[23]

Pitch and goal sizes were not modified from the men's game for ladies' hockey, as they were for camogie, but the goal width for both genders was only 2 feet wider than the original camogie goal and the pitch length was 50 yards, compared with 60 to 100 yards for early camogie.

We get a delicious sense of the excitement generated by the *aeridheachtaí* from newspaper accounts, like this one from Dunmanway in June 1914, which prompt recognition that the camogie revival had a wider social relevance than simply a sports-specific movement:

The majority of the spectators having never seen a match between the members of the gentler sex were enthusiastic over the display and as each player with her caman swiped at the ball there were numerous shouts of encouragement from the side-line. While the match was in progress many and varied were the expressions of opinion along the line. Here was the interested follower of his club shouting to the player to mind her place; here was the delighted old Doheny footballer enjoying the rare sport to him of seeing girl knock girl or crack her with the caman on the shin in real earnest; here also was the old grandmother with her grandchildren expressing her indignation at the conduct of the hussies.[24]

When the Cork camogie authorities decided to move matches from Sundays in August 1913, a letter writer complained:

> How can the Camogie Association expect to make the games popular if they intend to abandon matches on Sunday – the very day when our working people are free to witness them?[25]

There came an astonishing reply:

> As an ex-member of a prominent city camogie team I can authoritatively say that this decision has been arrived at because of the 'rough working class crowd' which patronises these matches when certain teams are playing. These teams are mainly composed of girls who work for their living, but because they work and are held in the esteem of the working class, this aristocratic Association, in order to prevent these teams from playing on Sunday, abandons the Sunday matches and thereby debars the rough working class crowd from following them.
>
> Surely, this action of the Camogie Association is what I consider unpatriotic, and is one which calls for condemnation from any Irishman. This Association was founded for the purpose of fostering our Gaelic games, but instead of giving every class an opportunity of witnessing them they intend to make them a society affair for the benefit of our city half-holidayers.[26]

Anonymous letters to the paper were the internet forums of the time and cannot be regarded as authoritative, but debate and controversy of this kind certainly gave more publicity to the new game.

Another hint of the class politics of camogie can be gleaned from the second controversy of that summer, the 1913 Cork camogie final between Clan Emer and Redmonds. The original match was scheduled for a Wednesday night, and a large crowd gathered for a match that fell through. It was contended that Miss Lombardi, the captain of the Redmonds team, sailed for America and that a good many of the players proceeded to Queenstown to give her a send-off, and as a result were in no condition to play the match. Miss Cassilly of Redmonds subsequently protested that Redmonds were five players short on the occasion, as all their members 'were not shop girls who could get off and she did not think her club should be asked to play with five substitutes'. Another big crowd saw Redmonds win the replay.[27] 'Large crowds' were reported at several of the matches. Receipts were £60 for a Cork versus Kilkenny inter-county match (admission 6d., enclosure 1s.), suggesting 2,400 attended.[28]

The inter-county matches that were organised during the decade of upheaval – Dublin against Louth, Lancashire against Wexford, Cork against Kilkenny, Kilkenny against Waterford, and Louth against Monaghan – were make-believe. All counties except Cork and Dublin were represented by one-club teams such as Dundalk Emer's and Kilkenny Deirdre's (for the latter of which Annie Gargan – sister of Matt Gargan, winner of five All-Ireland hurling medals – played).[29]

We do not have to look far to see how often camogie clubs extended their remit beyond the provision of sports facilities. As politics became more charged, Carrigdubh and Fáinne an Lae played a match to help finance the Defence of Ireland Fund in September 1914. In 1918, Toomevarra Cumann na mBan also organised a camogie tournament as a fundraiser, and Nenagh Cumann na mBan started a camogie club. In Meath, a robust lady with strong republican connections refused to accept the command of the local Cumann na mBan, but instead volunteered to play in goal for its camogie team.[30]

It was fifteen more years before plausible inter-county matches and a viable county board structure emerged. The provincial structure had been the foundation stone on which the GAA revival of 1900 to 1903 was constructed. But, while it suited Gaelic football, it did not suit camogie at all (or even hurling, leading to the aberration of Galway reaching the All-Ireland final in 1928, 1955 and 1958 without playing a match). For a later generation of camogie commentators, Úna Uí Phuirséil (Agnes Hourigan-Purcell) and Mary Moran among them, it was a source of disappointment that All-Ireland camogie championships arrived so late – twenty years after the foundation of the Association, as opposed to three years in the case of the GAA and nine years in the case of ladies' hockey.

(Ladies' hockey had been given a fillip by the introduction of inter-provincials in 1899, but found it difficult to sustain them in the 1900s).

An All-Ireland championship with county teams would have been as much of an aberration in 1910s camogie as it would be in ladies' hockey today. The game was effectively played in two cities and in a scattering of isolated parishes throughout the country – attempting to survive on rulebooks from Dublin and whatever matches they could arrange – such as Tombrack, Kilpatrick (which inaugurated a club) and Shanballymore, where a camogie match was also staged in 1914.[31]

Camogie was seen as an alternative home-grown sport for women, with all the predictable political connotations. The *Cork Examiner* of 21 July 1913 explicitly claimed that 'the game of camogie was organised so that the lady members of the Gaelic Association could have an Irish game to play instead of English hockey'.[32] As such, it was more vulnerable than the GAA or the Gaelic League to the disruption caused by social and political events, which brought it to a halt in growth areas like Belfast, and slowed it elsewhere, when the *aeridheachtaí* that had served to sustain it were disrupted. Where it did survive, it was because of vocational teams, rather than Gaelic League or GAA-based clubs. Camogie served as something of a museum piece in subsequent decades – a reminder of structures that had featured in the infant GAA, but that had been lost over time.

Hurling had been energised and influenced by the Gaelic League movement in the 1900s. Counties like Derry had no recent hurling presence before the Gaelic League revival. Gaelic League branches no longer fielded clubs by the end of the 1910s. Camogie retained the professional, vocational aspect of early GAA clubs, when teams like Young Irelands (playing out of Guinness' Brewery), Commercials (based in Limerick drapery houses) and Kickhams (with a membership from the Dublin drapery trade) had won championships or played in All-Ireland finals.

While the GAA clubs of the 1920s settled on the current structure based around communities and parishes, camogie retained the vocational element, with teams based in factories and looser work alliances or employers, until the 1960s when camogie too made its transition to a parish-based structure. Three of the greatest players in the game – Kathleen Mills, Kathleen Cody and Sophie Brack – owed their prominence to playing for the CIÉ club where their fathers worked. There are signs that the Camogie Association never lost its broader social ambition. As early as October 1913, camogie officers Lady Fingall, Elizabeth Hamilton,

Máire de Buitléir, Bertha Bryan, Cáit Ní Dhonnchada and Tomás Mac Aodha were listed as officers of an Irishwomen's Athletic Association. In the absence of any attempt by J. J. Keane's NACA to organise women's athletics, from 1926 the Camogie Association began organising athletic events, two years before modesty famously became an issue in relation to athletics in 1928, when Pope Pius XI cautioned that 'in the case of girls it is extremely unbecoming for them to display themselves before the public gaze', and *The Irish Times* responded with a defence that modern researchers have judged archaic and sexist in its own right. A women's hundred-yard race was eventually held in Croke Park in 1929 as part of the NACA programme. In response to a negative reaction to women's athletics from John Charles McQuaid in 1934, camogie was to step in to organise women's athletics again.[33]

The political dimension of 1910s camogie presents itself easily to a modern researcher, but can easily be overstated. The most famous of the marchers at O'Donovan Rossa's funeral, three members of Na Fianna Camogie Club – Eileen Conroy, Nellie Kelly and May Chadwick – were arrested. The pioneers that were engaged in so many social, cultural and political fronts forgot or paid less attention to the sporting struggle in which they were engaged. As a result of this decline, Crokes took back the leadership positions of the Camogie Association in 1923. Crokes and Inghinidhe na hÉireann member Máire 'Mollie' Gill became Camogie Association President. A printer with the Yeats sisters' Cuala Press in Baggot Street, she served as President for nineteen years, and captained Dublin teams from the mid-1910s until their success in the first All-Ireland championship in 1932. Kathleen Ryan became Vice-President and Áine Ryan became Secretary.

Camogie's association with Cumann na mBan and the anti-Treaty movement was cemented in the public mind by a very public controversy over the 1924 Tailteann Games. The Camogie Association did not participate, for what it said were political reasons. J. J. Walsh, the organiser and Cumann na nGaedheal Minister for Posts and Telegraphs, accused the Association of boycotting the event for political purposes and the Tailteann Games organisers recruited Wicklow to field a team on behalf of Ireland. The heated correspondence between Tailteann Games director Walsh and Camogie Association Secretary Áine Ryan is testimony to the tensions of the age, as can be seen in the extract below (from Walsh):

There is no use whatever in you trying to deceive me with the story that the Camogie Association of Dublin would not be able to take a team to Terenure to play an English team on the score of expense. Nobody but a fool could be expected to believe stuff of that kind. We have given you an opportunity of fielding a team and you have failed to take it. If, however, at any time you care to change this foolish ruling, and cut politics out of this national organisation, the Council will be quite pleased to permit the selection to revert to your association.[34]

The day when the President and the Secretary of the Association, Mollie Gill and Esther Ryan, were arrested together on the premises of Cuala Press on 23 May 1923 must give camogie one of the most unusual records for a sporting body worldwide. A photograph may tell the story best. If, as Walter Benjamin said, 'History decomposes into images, not into narratives,' the photograph of Mollie Gill in jodhpurs with a revolver carries a near-hypnotic echo of the spirit of Ireland's revolutionary women, the coincidence of image and history.[35] If anything represents the Crokes era of camogie it is this, the President of the Association, a woman of action in battle dress, juxtaposed with the neat gymslip and black-stockinged knees of the team captain.

CHAPTER 12

The GAA, Nationalism and the Irish Diaspora in the United States, 1913–23

PAUL DARBY

Part of flyer for the 1917 All-Ireland hurling final.

THE TEN-YEAR PERIOD BETWEEN 1913 AND 1923 was a tumultuous one in Irish history. The great set-piece historical events of that decade resonated in the four corners of Ireland. However, they also impacted on the lives of Irish communities far beyond the territorial borders of the nation. This was particularly the case in the United States, where the meaning of what it was to be Irish and how one should express this Irishness were greatly influenced by events 'back home'. As an important cultural resource that Irish immigrants drew on to preserve and promote their ethnic distinctiveness in the US, the development of the Gaelic Athletic Association (GAA) there represents a useful barometer to gauge the ways in which the tremors of the Home Rule crisis, the Easter Rising, partition and the Civil War were felt and experienced overseas, and how they shaped identity politics among the Irish diaspora. This chapter seeks to examine the development of Gaelic games in this period, with a particular focus on the varying forms of Irish nationalist expression that coalesced around the GAA in four centres of transatlantic emigration: Boston, New York, Chicago and San Francisco. The chapter begins by briefly accounting for the status and profile of Gaelic games among the Irish diaspora in the US in the early twentieth century. Thereafter, the analysis centres on how Gaelic games served as a platform for politically conscious immigrants to express themselves in highly visible

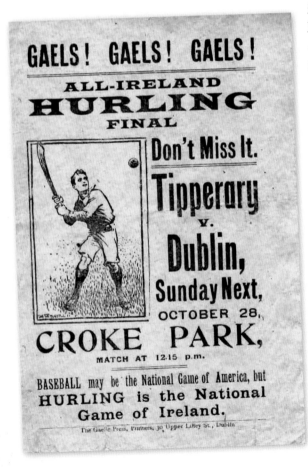

Flyer for the 1917 All-Ireland hurling final with the caption 'Baseball may be the National Game of America, but Hurling is the National Game of Ireland'.

ways as Irish nationalists in the period under consideration. This reveals that support for constitutional nationalism amongst US-based Gaels was supplanted by a hardening of attitudes and the expression of a much more belligerent, revolutionary brand of nationalism. This was a direct consequence of political events in Ireland, particularly the Home Rule crisis and the Easter Rising.

• • •

By the beginning of the twentieth century, the GAA had registered a not insignificant presence in those major American cities that had at first endured and subsequently embraced Irish immigrants. In the latter decades of the nineteenth century, the Irish in these cities had shown a great enthusiasm and propensity for sport. This extended to the games of their homeland, and while it is unlikely that they were as popular as, for example, baseball, Gaelic football and hurling were important ingredients in the diet of sports that nourished sections of America's Irish Catholic population. The connections between the GAA and Irish nationalism were clearly significant in the sports' early development, and did much to encourage politically motivated immigrants to get involved in the activities of the Association. Steven Reiss, in his brief assessment of the birth of traditional Irish sports in Boston, is correct in his assertion that 'Irishmen living in the United States quickly adopted these sports to show solidarity with revolutionaries'.[1] His description of the GAA in Boston in the late nineteenth century as '… an ethnic sub-community that gave members dignity, pride, and a heightened sense of nationalism' applies equally to the Gaels of New York, Chicago and San Francisco.[2] However, the fact that Gaelic games continued to grow and develop in the last decade of the nineteenth century, despite the decline in support amongst Irish Americans for aspects of political nationalism, illustrates that there were other reasons why America's Irish communities engaged in and consumed these sports.

Part of the explanation for the appeal of Gaelic games can be found in the same reasons why other sports that catered for the urban working classes throughout the industrial world in the late nineteenth century were so popular. Put simply, hurling and Gaelic football provided sections of the Irish diaspora with an enjoyable and often exciting escape from the rigours of work, and allowed them to give vent to their masculinity in a boisterous and at times aggressive manner. This, however, is only part of the reason behind the popular appeal of Gaelic games in this period. Beyond the identity-forming and purely sporting functions of Gaelic games, the emerging GAA culture in some of America's key industrial metropolises performed a number of other important social, economic and psychological functions for those who engaged with it. The role of the Gaelic football or hurling club in smoothing the transition from Ireland to cities that more often than not possessed a hostile Anglo-Saxon Protestant establishment cannot be overstated. The GAA afforded Irish Catholics opportunities to sustain themselves in the face of discrimination. It enabled them to rekindle old friendships, forge new ones, mix with their 'own' and simply be in a social and cultural setting resonant of 'home', however that was defined in the minds of individual immigrants. In doing so, the Association helped alleviate the feelings of dislocation and alienation that the Irish in America often felt. Crucially, immersion in Gaelic games also provided entrance into the social networks that allowed newly arrived immigrants to find work and accommodation, and hence supported their first steps in the New World.[3]

All of this ensured that, as the twentieth century entered its second decade, Gaelic games in the US were in rude health. By 1914, local Gaels in New York had become sufficiently organised to establish their own governing body, the Gaelic Athletic Association of the United States.[4] Commenting on the significance of this for the city's nineteen clubs, Byrne observed that the meeting in Snow's Hall in the Bronx at which this body was founded 'was to New York what the Thurles meeting was to Ireland'.[5] In the same period, the foundations that had been laid for Gaelic games in Boston in the latter stages of the previous century were further strengthened with the addition of new clubs and the development of formally constituted competitions, particularly the New England Championship, which attracted clubs from Boston and other parts of New England.

Gaelic games in Chicago were also thriving. By 1906, GAA field days were regularly attracting crowds of 5,000,[6] and in 1907 the local GAA acquired a long-term lease on a plot of land for what came to be known as Gaelic Park. Under the patronage of Father John Fielding, a Kilkenny native, member of Chicago's Catholic clergy since 1895 and, according to newspaper reports of the time, a skilled athlete and hurler,[7] Gaelic games went from strength to strength and the city's first inter-city hurling match,

Young Ireland hurling team at the Panama-Pacific International Exposition on St Patrick's Day, 1915. LIAM REIDY

against St Louis in 1907, drew a crowd of 12,000.[8] The work of a number of Catholic churchmen did much to set the GAA in San Francisco on a sound footing at the beginning of the twentieth century. The tireless efforts of Father Peter Yorke in particular were hugely significant, and his role in the establishment of a governing body to oversee Gaelic games helped to firmly embed these pastimes in the cultural life of sections of the city's Irish population. However, the devastating earthquake and subsequent fires in the city in April 1906 brought any growth in Gaelic games in San Francisco to a halt, and it was not until the showcasing of the GAA during San Francisco's hosting of the Panama-Pacific International Exposition in San Francisco in 1915 that the games recovered.

As will be discussed shortly, turbulent political events in Ireland did much to influence the political visage of US branches of the GAA in this period. As Irish-American backing for Irish independence grew during the Home Rule crisis and the lead-up to the Easter Rising, the Association became deeply implicated in both the groundswell of Irish nationalist sentiment and the emergence of conflicting strands of nationalism. However, there were other affairs that impacted on the quantitative development of Gaelic games in the US in this period. The disruption of the Great War of 1914–18 and America's decision to involve itself in hostilities in 1917 did much to check the impressive growth of the games, albeit temporarily. The war, and the rush of young Irish-American men to join the US Army, brought a virtual halt to the development of Gaelic football and hurling in Boston. With many hurlers and footballers volunteering for the famous 'Fighting' 69th Regiment, matches were only played on an ad hoc and infrequent basis in the late 1910s, and it was not until the early 1920s that Gaelic sports clubs once again began to cater for the sporting, recreational and cultural needs of Boston's Irish community in any sort of sustained way. A similar trend was also evident in Chicago, with fixtures played only sporadically at Gaelic Park and other venues throughout the city, and it was not until the end of the war that a full resumption of Gaelic games occurred.

In New York, however, the war had much less of an effect, at least in terms of the ability of the GAA to generate healthy attendances at matches. It is difficult to determine the precise reasons for this. Aside from the popularisation of Gaelic games on the back of their increasingly close association with Irish nationalism, discussed shortly, part of the explanation might be found in the ways that Irish involvement in America's war effort was woven into the activities and ethos of the GAA fraternity in New York at that time. For example, in August 1917, the city's Irish newspaper, *The Advocate*, began a campaign to raise funds to send equipment for hurling and Gaelic football to the training camp of the US Army's 69th Regiment, one that had traditionally comprised Irish volunteers. The rationale behind the campaign, duly named 'The Advocate Gaelic Athletic Fund', was set out in the following terms:

> There are scores of football players and hurlers from every county in Ireland in the famous Sixty-ninth. Baseball, tennis, and other such American sports do NOT appeal to those boys, consequently they will feel the loss of the Caman and Gaelic football unless the Irishmen and women of this city get up the necessary funds to supply them.[9]

The fundraising effort was undoubtedly motivated by a genuine desire to furnish Irish soldiers in the US Army with opportunities for physical activity and enjoyment amid the rigours of war. However, *The Advocate* was a long established proponent of Gaelic games in the city and it was not lost on the newspaper's publishers and editor that these sports and the organisation that governed them were likely to receive favourable publicity and exposure on the back of the campaign. This was a point specifically made in the newspaper; '… it will be a big boost for Gaelic games. When the members of this far-famed Irish regiment play those games in camp and in France, it will mean that the Irish pastimes are in for a great deal of notoriety.'[10] As might have been expected, the city's Gaelic football and hurling clubs were very much to the fore in generating the requisite finances, and the publicity around these fundraising efforts did much to keep Gaelic sports very much in the consciousness of Irish Americans in the city during the war. In doing so, it ensured that the decline in participation that had been seen elsewhere was not as keenly felt in the city.

As noted earlier, the extent to which the diaspora patronised Gaelic games, as players, spectators or administrators, and the meanings that they attached to this were heavily influenced by their relationship with Ireland and how they made sense of events across the Atlantic. This was particularly the case in the years between 1913 and 1923, a decade that shaped the course of Irish history and, as a by-product, influenced the versions of nationalism articulated by Irish-American Gaels. We now turn to this issue, firstly by charting how the GAA became entwined with Irish nationalist politics in America in the late nineteenth and early twentieth centuries and then by examining some of the ways in which the events of 1913–23 shaped the Association's nationalist visage.

• • •

As has been noted elsewhere,[11] the ability of Gaelic games to take root in America's major cities in the late nineteenth century was due in no small measure to the fact that that these sports were an important medium for the articulation of Irish nationalism. As well as keeping Irish Catholics in touch with Ireland, culturally and psychologically, Gaelic games quickly provided a platform for Irish communities across America to construct and give vent to a distinctively Irish ethnic and national identity. The use of Gaelic games in this regard was clearly not an accidental process. Rather, nationalist-minded immigrants specifically sought to use these activities in order to galvanise the Irish community in America behind the political goal of Irish independence from Britain. The first patrons of Gaelic games in Boston, New York, Chicago and San Francisco were staunch nationalists who sought to bolster support for the broader struggle for Irish emancipation by encouraging and promoting a vibrant Gaelic culture in America. The aims of Irish nationalism were also uppermost in the minds of the founders of the early GAA clubs, who articulated and celebrated their nationalism by naming them after historical and popular nationalist personalities and organisations, a practice that continued into the subsequent century.

New York typified the close relationship between the GAA and nationalism. That this was the case should come as no surprise, given the strength of Irish nationalism in the city. Two of the key pillars of Fenianism in America, the Emmet Monument Association and Clan na Gael, were formed in the city, and a whole host of republican heroes and political refugees from Ireland, such as O'Donovan Rossa, John Mitchel, John Devoy and John O'Mahony, travelled to New York and mobilised the city's Irish community firmly behind the nationalist cause.[12] Indeed, as Brundage has commented, 'New York remained the epicentre of the movement, the main locus of activities for constitutional home rulers and separatist revolutionaries alike'.[13]

Similar close associations between leaders of Irish nationalism and the GAA were also evident further west. In Chicago, those who were directly involved in the promotion of the GAA in the city were also strong proponents of Irish independence. For example, the nationalist newspaper publisher John F. Finerty was a key figure in the drive to popularise Gaelic games among Irish Chicagoans. Although it took slightly longer for the GAA to become established on the Pacific Coast, San Francisco's Gaels were equally committed to publicly stating their support for the broader nationalist mission. For example, the venue chosen for the inaugural meeting of the GAA in the city was the meeting hall of one of San Francisco's leading nationalist associations, the Knights of the Red Branch (KRB). Beyond the aspirations of leading figures within the GAA hierarchy throughout America and the founders and patrons of the earliest clubs, the association between Gaelic games and Irish nationalism was reinforced through evocative and rousing discourse on GAA activities in the Irish-American press. For example, the accounts in the *Irish Echo* and *The Gael* of GAA field days in Boston in the early 1880s framed them as 'patriotic', imbued with the 'spirit of freedom' and part of a practical drive for 'Irish emancipation'.[14]

The place of the GAA in the psyche of Irish nationalists in America was also cemented and broadened through the fact that a range of nationalist organisations, of both the physical-force and parliamentary kinds, turned to Gaelic games as a way of attracting adherents and promoting their cultural and political agendas. In Chicago, for example, organisations such as the Irish National League, the Hibernian Rifles, the Advanced Irish Nationalists and the New Ireland Colonisation Association organised picnics and rallies during the mid- to late 1880s at which Gaelic games featured prominently.[15] This pattern was repeated on America's Pacific coast where groups such as the KRB, the Gaelic League and the Ancient Order of Hibernians all ardently got behind Gaelic games and were more than happy to be closely associated with the GAA. In Boston, too, the early picnics at which traditional Irish sports and culture featured so prominently were patronised by leading members of the city's Irish nationalist movement, who not only viewed such events as useful in encouraging a strong sense of Irishness but also as invaluable opportunities for fundraising. For example, at a number of field days from the mid-1880s onwards funds were collected from both spectators and participants for the Irish Parliamentary Fund, inaugurated by 'friends of Ireland in Boston' to enable Parnell 'to carry on the work of the redemption of Ireland to final success'.[16] Around the turn of the century, Gaelic games were increasingly used as a mechanism for raising funds for Irish nationalist organisations such as the First Regiment of the Irish Volunteers of New York and the Irish Republican Brotherhood Veterans.[17]

Of all of the nationalist groups that were associated with the GAA in the late nineteenth century, Clan na Gael had perhaps the clearest vision about how best to harness the mobilising power of Gaelic sport to garner support for their militant agenda. This is a point noted by Reiss, who is correct in his assertion that 'Irish sport was … promoted by overtly political organisations, most notably the Clan na Gael, a secret revolutionary society that arranged athletic meets to gain favourable publicity, attract new adherents, and promote Irish nationalism'.[18] This process began almost as soon as the organisation was formed. Indeed, as

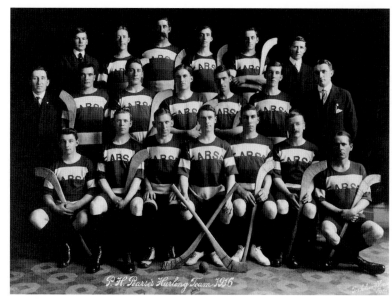

early as 1871, just four years after its inception, Gaelic games featured prominently at the annual carnival and games of Clan na Gael in New York. Branches of the organisation in Chicago also used Gaelic games as a way of recruiting young men to physical-force nationalism, a fact evidenced in a series of advertisements that ran in the *Citizen* throughout the summers of 1885, 1886 and 1887 promoting Clan na Gael picnics and rallies at which hurling and football matches took place.

By the turn of the century, the nationalist credentials of the Association were well established. This is not to say that the nationalism that the GAA did so much to foster among Gaelic sport-playing immigrants was monolithic or remained static through time. At various junctures during the late nineteenth and early twentieth centuries, the Association provided a platform on which some engaged in what they saw as a predominantly cultural act, one that allowed them to keep in touch with the traditions and heritage of their homeland. At other points, however, membership of the GAA and involvement in Gaelic games provided sections of the diaspora with an opportunity to express themselves politically, and in ways concomitant with their broader desire for and commitment to an Ireland free of British influence. Even within the latter, there were discernible schisms, with some supporting constitutional means and others advocating a more revolutionary, physical-force approach. The extent to which these strands of nationalism came to the fore within US branches of the GAA was dependent largely on political events in Ireland.

• • •

Those who took up the baton of progressing the GAA in America at the outset of the twentieth century were well aware of the significance of Gaelic sports as important markers of Irish ethnic identity. However, they did not seek to link their activities to combative or belligerent expressions of Irish nationalism to the same degree as their predecessors had at various stages during the late nineteenth century. This was largely a consequence of developments in nationalist politics in Ireland. The reunification of the IPP at the turn of the century, after years of infighting following the death of Parnell in 1891, did much to restore confidence in and a sense of solidarity with constitutional Irish nationalism in Ireland and America.[19] Almost as soon as John Redmond became leader of the party in 1900, he sought to re-galvanise Irish America behind the constitutionalist position, and helped to establish the United Irish League of Ireland to raise funds from the diaspora and generate support from US politicians.[20] Throughout the first decade of the new century, Gaelic sports clubs contributed to these efforts.[21] This was important not only for the advancement of constitutional nationalism in Ireland but also because it was useful in allowing clubs to attract nationalist-minded members.

The association of the GAA with cultural nationalism served a similar purpose. While Gaelic games clearly did much to promote a sense of cultural Irishness among the diaspora, the connection between the two was made explicit to Irish Americans by the visit of Douglas Hyde, founder of the Gaelic League, to San Francisco in February 1906 as part of a forty-city tour of the US. The aim of this tour was primarily to raise funds for the Gaelic League and garner support for Hyde's calls for the de-anglicisation of Ireland. As a by-product, however, Hyde's visit and his powerful oratory raised the profile of attempts to promote Irish cultural forms and language on American shores. Specific comments on the role of the GAA as a medium for resisting the anglicisation of Ireland and the Irish during his speech at San Francisco's Tivoli Theatre on 19 February were particularly welcome for San Francisco's Gaelic games enthusiasts and did much to confirm, in the minds of those who either listened to or read Hyde's words, the relationship between the GAA and Irish nationalism.[22]

While the GAA espoused support, financial and political, for Hyde's cultural agenda and Redmond's brand of political nationalism in the opening years of the twentieth century, as hopes for Irish independence grew following the introduction of the third Home Rule Bill to the British parliament in 1912, there was less evidence in the Irish-American press of Gaelic games being used specifically to further this agenda. Instead, sporting rivalries, often rooted in county affiliations, and a desire to preserve what was on the whole a benign, culturally oriented Irish identity, replaced more politicised expressions of nationalism for a time as the key driving forces behind the GAA's growth in America.

This is not to say that the political dimension was completely absent from Gaelic games in this period. Indeed, at this time a range of Irish nationalist organisations followed the precedent set in the late 1870s of incorporating these sports into their annual picnics and field days. For example, the programme of activities at the United Irish Societies of Chicago's celebration of Hugh O'Donnell's late-sixteenth-century victory over the army of Queen Elizabeth featured a number of 'championship' matches between the city's leading teams,[23] thus allowing the connections between the nationalist agenda and the GAA to be expressed publicly. This trend continued intermittently into the early 1910s when a number of *feiseanna* organised by the Gaelic League at various venues in the US, but particularly in New York, included hurling and football matches in their programme alongside speeches by various Gaelic orators, some of whom spoke specifically, *as Gaeilge*, about 'the Irish question'.[24]

While a thin thread of nationalist sentiment continued to weave its way loosely through the fabric of the GAA in the opening years of the century, by 1914 the association between Gaelic games in America and more belligerent expressions of Irish nationalism once again began to gather strength and become more centrally incorporated into the affairs and activities of its members. This was largely a response to events in Ireland. The slowdown in the progress of parliamentary nationalism, particularly the political procrastination surrounding the passage of the third Home Rule Bill, quickly increased levels of popular support for militant separatism in Ireland. The formation of the Irish Volunteers in 1913, in response to the signing of the Ulster Covenant and the formation of the Ulster Volunteers by Unionists in the north-east of Ireland, was the clearest manifestation of a growing feeling that force was the only solution to Ireland's relationship with Britain.[25] Although funds continued to flow across the Atlantic to support the constitutional platform, this more combative position increasingly found currency in Irish-American circles. With the possibility of civil war between nationalists and unionists looming in Ireland, concrete plans were put in place for a military uprising against British control, and many Irish Americans were only too willing to demonstrate their support politically and financially. Redmond's decision to support Britain at the outset of the Great War and his encouragement of Irishmen to enlist in the British Army hardened this willingness and added further impetus to Irish-American backing of militant separatism.

This support became very apparent within US branches of the GAA whose members sought to demonstrate their patriotism by sending money back across the Atlantic to arm and equip the Irish Volunteers. With a long-standing tradition of engaging in fundraising efforts for various nationalist causes behind them, supporters of the GAA in New York, a city historically positioned at the centre of Irish-American nationalism, began to urge the local hurling and football clubs to respond to appeals coming from Ireland for financial support. For example, a letter to the editor of the New York Irish newspaper *The Advocate* in July 1914 implored the city's most prominent clubs to organise a series of fundraising matches at Celtic Park with the following emotive and evocative plea: 'We ought to do it, if not for Ireland's sake, at least for shame-sake. Ireland when in need always looks to America, and New York in particular for aid. Let us not be found wanting in this crisis.'[26]

Although the clubs responded positively to these appeals and continued to back other nationalist organisations and causes, such as Clan na Gael and St Enda's School in Dublin, there was agreement that additional support was entirely appropriate. Thus, when the Irish National Volunteer Committee of New York approached ten leading clubs with a view to organising a fundraising day at Celtic Park on 7 September 1914, there was unanimous approval. The clubs' agreement to offer their services gratis and the decision of the Irish American Athletic Club (IAAC), the leaseholders of Celtic Park, to provide the venue free of charge were further evidence of the commitment and unity of purpose in GAA circles on 'the Irish question'.[27] In its promotion of the event, *The Advocate* made explicit the politicisation that the GAA in New York was undergoing at this time:

> The Gaelic athlete here never forgets his national honour. He was ever in the van when Ireland called for arms or money. Today Ireland is undergoing a trying ordeal. Thousands of Irishmen have volunteered to defend IRELAND FOR IRELAND, and in this way

they must be armed. The Irishmen of Greater New York can show their appreciation of Ireland's National Volunteers by turning out in their thousands at Celtic Park on Labor Day … It's an occasion that the Gael should make the most of and show the hated Saxon that at least there are a few Irishmen in New York who are not willing to 'hold Ireland for England'. Monday next will be a great day for Ireland, a great day for the games of the Gael and a greater day for the Irish National Volunteers of Ireland, the savers of the Irish nation.[28]

Rallied by this call, the event was attended by over 10,000 spectators, each paying 25 cents for admission. Further funds were solicited through the selling of volunteer's tags, subscriptions and a programme that contained articles on the Irish Volunteer movement as well as the words and music of patriotic Irish songs.[29] The radical tone of the event was further highlighted when a group of supporters of Redmond's parliamentary nationalism attempted to raise 'three cheers' during a break between games. The result, described in the *Gaelic American* as 'melancholy and weak as the death rattle in the throat of a dying call',[30] illustrates that a more militant brand of Irish nationalism was the position most favoured by the majority of New York's Gaels.

Fundraising for the Irish Volunteers was not specific to the New York GAA, however. Indeed, 3,000 miles away on the Pacific coast of the US, the Association's members in San Francisco were engaged in similar activities. For example, in December 1914, the MacBride Gaelic Football Club organised a tournament at St Ignatius Stadium to raise finances for the Volunteers. In advertising this event in the local Irish press, the organising committee employed the same sort of rousing, nationalistic rhetoric as their counterparts in New York:

No individual or club of men claiming to be Irish should at this critical moment refuse to aid … the young men at home who will have to fight for the freedom of their native land. Wake up you indifferent Gaels! … The blood of the patriots and martyrs of your ancestors must not be shed in vain, while you are alive today to take up the cause of freedom for which they died.[31]

The use of this sort of language was not new in San Francisco's Irish newspapers in this period, nor was it entirely motivated by Irish politics.

Indeed, members and supporters of the Association recognised that linking involvement in Gaelic games with a sense of belonging to the 'old country' as well as the ongoing struggle for independence from Britain could be useful in helping to bolster the flagging ranks of the GAA. Thus, 'a spectator' wrote to the editor of *The Leader* in April 1913, imploring the city's Irish community to 'be either a Gael or a "shoneen"', before going on to challenge them by saying that 'no Irish man or woman can afford to be called the latter'.[32] With a more militant version of Irish nationalism re-establishing itself on American soil in the years preceding the Easter Rising, Gaelic games in San Francisco continued to be closely intertwined with the Irish nationalist agenda and senses of Irishness that were intensely ethnic, hostile to the British presence in Ireland and supportive of a physical-force solution to that issue. This continued to be the case in the aftermath of the failed 1916 Rising. For example, leading figures in the city's GAA emphasised that involvement in Gaelic games should be considered the 'duty' of those who called themselves Irish, while individual clubs donated money to, and organised benefit matches for, a fund for 'the widows and orphans of the Irish Martyrs'.[33]

While the response of Irish Americans in joining the US Army in such large numbers, following President Woodrow Wilson's decision to enter the First World War in 1917, revealed a growing sense of patriotism towards America,[34] a commitment to Irish revolutionary nationalism continued to colour large swathes of Irish-American opinion. The work of the Friends of Irish Freedom (FOIF) and the American Association for the Recognition of the Irish Republic (AARIR) in 1916 and 1920 respectively, coupled with Éamon de Valera's tour of America in 1919 to generate finances for the IRA and gain US recognition for the Irish government, did much to keep the struggle for Irish independence at the centre of the consciousness of Irish Americans.[35] During the War of Independence in Ireland (1919–21) financial and political support for Sinn Féin and the IRA flowed freely from sections of the Irish diaspora.[36] However, the outcome of this war and the political negotiations with the British government, which ultimately led to the partition of Ireland in 1920 and the establishment of the Irish Free State, effectively resolved 'the Irish question' for much of Irish America.[37] Despite some lingering resentments around the failure to achieve independence for the whole of the island of Ireland, most viewed partition, with the possibility of full sovereignty further down the line, as a reasonable outcome and therefore felt little need to continue to donate their dollars or continue to agitate for full Irish independence.

The Irish Civil War (1922–3) hastened a declining interest in Irish political affairs, not least because most Irish Americans struggled to comprehend what was driving Irishmen 'at home' to kill their compatriots. Many were also bemused and felt increasingly alienated by some dimensions of post-partition Irish nationalism, particularly what some perceived as its isolationist Gaelic and socialist leanings. Other factors in the first half of the century, including the Depression of the 1930s and a shift in the focus of Irish emigration towards Great Britain, further lessened the inclination of Irish Americans to express their Irishness with the same intensity and vigour as they had in the late nineteenth century and in the period leading up to the Easter Rising. While there remained some support for a campaign for complete reunification of the country, events in Ireland, combined with greater levels of social mobility and cultural assimilation into American society, ultimately led to less of a preoccupation with the affairs of the 'old country' and hence a more general decline in Irish nationalism as an expression of Irish Catholic identity. As McCaffrey succinctly put it, 'As the Irish achieved success and respectability in the United States, they became more American and less Irish.'[38]

Alongside dire economic conditions and reduced levels of Irish immigration to the US, this Americanisation of the Irish diaspora and a diminishing concern for Irish politics undoubtedly fed into the decline of the GAA in Depression-era America. Conversely, those who remained committed during the lean years of the Association, especially from the 1930s through to the 1940s, did so not only because of their love of hurling and Gaelic football but also because of their politics and their continued aspirations for an Ireland free of British influence. In Chicago, for example, for much of the 1920s, the AARIR sponsored organised Gaelic football and hurling matches, thereby helping to develop a close relationship with the GAA.[39] The establishment of a GAA club in 1925 named after Harry Boland, the prominent republican and Easter Rising veteran who had been shot dead by members of the National Army of the Irish Free State three years previously, was a further indication of the political inclinations of the city's Gaels. Chicago was not alone in this regard, however, and despite the broader waning of Irish-American nationalism in this period, leading figures within the GAA elsewhere

Sinn Féin
Gaelic
football
team, San
Francisco,
1923/4.
LIAM REIDY

J.J.CONWAY.,J.CUNNINGHAM., A.WALSH, J.MCBRIDE., J.PARLEY., M COSTELLO., W.MCHUGH., J.CROWLEY., D.O'CONNOR.
A.J.FALLON., E.O'FLAHERTY., D.MCCARTHY., CAPT.J.BRADY., P.O'CONNELL., P.ROAN., J.DENNEHY.
J.LAFFERTY., E.O'FLAHERTY,JR., W.MCCARTHY., MASCOT J.T.CONWAY., J.F.CONWAY., A.VAUGHAN.

remained vociferous and steadfast in their support for physical-force nationalism and were only too eager to use Gaelic games as a way of encouraging others to revive what had become for the majority a largely dormant element of their identity. This support for the physical-force tradition within the GAA and in pockets of Irish America more generally was aided by the presence in America, particularly in New York, of Irish republicans who had fought on the anti-Treaty side in the Irish Civil War.[40] This did much to ensure that, from the mid-1920s until well into the 1950s, the GAA in New York and elsewhere in the US was favourably predisposed to lending support to political and military agitation for a united Ireland.

• • •

As was the case with the GAA in Ireland, the early years of the Association's development in the US were fraught with difficulties that ranged from internal politicking and factionalism to broader obstacles in popularising Gaelic games and attracting players, administrators and supporters.[41] However, these difficulties were ultimately overcome, which is evidence of the resolve of those who sought to preserve and promote the sports of the 'old country' in America. The fact that Gaelic games became so intrinsically linked to Irish nationalism in the US was also important in this regard, and clearly helped the GAA to take root among Irish immigrant communities in cities such as Boston, New York, Chicago and San Francisco. Gaelic games and Irish nationalism in these cities shared a symbiotic relationship, particularly during the Home Rule crisis and in the build-up to the Easter Rising. A range of nationalist organisations at this time recognised the mobilising power of Gaelic games and were eager to develop connections with the GAA and patronise these sports. For the GAA, being linked to organisations such as Clan na Gael or the Irish National Volunteers at a time of intense nationalist fervour in Ireland did much to allow them to recruit politically conscious immigrants into their ranks. While the extent to which the GAA remained connected to Irish nationalist causes and organisations fluctuated post-1923,[42] at the very least, the place of Gaelic games among Irish immigrants and second- and subsequent-generation Irish in America would continue to be linked to the ethnic distinctiveness and inherent Irishness of these sporting pastimes.

CHAPTER 13

Image and Impact: Representing and Reporting the GAA, 1913–23

SEÁN MORAN

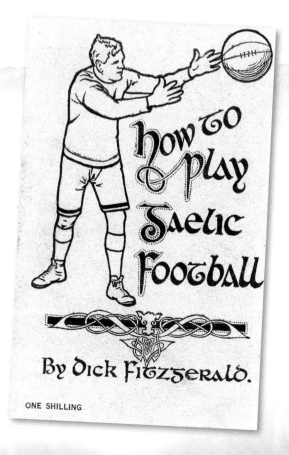

Cover of the 1915 publication
How to Play Gaelic Football
by Dick Fitzgerald.

THE LATE BREANDÁN MAC LUA, later founder of the *Irish Post* newspaper in London but then an Executive Officer in the GAA administration in Croke Park, contextualised the Association's ban on foreign games for Peter Lennon's 1968 documentary *Rocky Road to Dublin*.[1] The film portrayed the Association as one of the pillars of a failed state. Yet Mac Lua was confident and lucid in his justifications of the prohibition (the same year, he published a pamphlet, 'The Steadfast Rule', defending the ban). This was a significant juncture in the history of the GAA – and the high point for views such as Mac Lua's – coming just twelve months after the commemoration of the fiftieth anniversary of the Easter Rising and before the eruption of the Troubles in Northern Ireland. At the time, it was an orthodox self-projection by the GAA to emphasise the vital role of the membership of the Association in the Irish independence struggle; it was, after all, less than fifty years since the Association's own stark trauma on Bloody Sunday in 1920. Modern historians have scrutinised and come to question this narrative. And, when we turn back to the revolutionary years in which these events took place, we find that the Association's then image of itself was more complex.

The years from 1913 to 1923 can be depicted as the most influential decade in the GAA's history. How the Association saw itself and how others saw it during this period established the publicly perceived character of the organisation that arguably lasted for the remainder of the twentieth century and still influences perceptions today. In the unfolding turmoil of the time – the First World War, the Easter Rising, the War of Independence and the Civil War – the organisation had to steer a course that kept on board as many members as possible and gave offence to as few as possible.

In the introduction to his immense study of early Gaelic games in Kerry, Richard McElligott argues that histories of the GAA were for a long time overly focused on the Association's role in the national struggle for independence, and in consequence often Dublin-centric and lacking social context.[2] In the period under review, that orientation was hard to avoid. National events created obstacles for the GAA and administrators were aggrieved at the lack of recognition in much of the national media. Government decree would restrict the public transport vital for moving supporters around the country to matches and try to control the very staging of matches by requiring permits.[3] These were the big issues on which the GAA as an organisation allowed itself to campaign.

Yet the momentous political events of these years and the evolution of Gaelic games from the recreational expression of the broad nationalist movement into the established sports of a new state – in whose political and civil infrastructures many of the Association's best-known members would be prominent[4] – tend to obscure the GAA's essential role as the promoter and organiser of its games. All of these challenges had to be played out in public and necessarily made demands on what would now be routinely described as a 'public relations strategy', or the wish to influence or direct society's perceptions of the Association.

. . .

It is ironic, given all that was to come, that the GAA experienced arguably its most successful year as a sports body in 1913. The games were rising in popularity up to that point and gradually the focus was sharpening on those core activities, with the long-running difficulty over the administration of athletics apparently resolved.[5]

There were a number of reasons for this promising state of affairs. The games were attracting big crowds, and the quality of the spectacle of football was improved by advancing training techniques and the decision of the GAA's Central Council that year to cut the number of players per team from seventeen to fifteen.[6] This was not welcomed by everyone. A correspondent wrote to *The Gaelic Athlete* within days of the above meeting to question part of the rationale behind the initiative: the reduction of foul play by making the pitch less congested. 'It seems to me an amazing thing that the motion should have been passed upon such an argument,' wrote Seaghan Ó hÉigeartaigh from Cork, 'giving as it does the idea of 34 players thirsting to foul one another, while the removal of 4 is going to make fouling a thing of the past.'[7] The other major influence on the status of Gaelic games was the decision at the end of 1913 to purchase Croke Park as a stadium and headquarters for the GAA.

One event that contributed to both of these developments was a match – not an All-Ireland, but the 1913 final of the Croke Memorial Tournament, a competition that was inaugurated that year to raise funds for the commemoration of the GAA's first patron. So successful did it prove that sights were raised higher than the original plan of simply commissioning a monument in Thurles, and the decision was taken in late 1913 to buy a headquarters in Dublin. The reason for the success of this tournament was the coming together of Louth and Kerry in the football final. These two big rivals of the era had not contested a final for four years. In the 1912 All-Ireland semi-final, Kerry had been sensationally beaten by Antrim.[8] A day after Louth had won the ensuing All-Ireland final, the Kerry county board issued a public challenge to the new champions. The final of the Croke Memorial Tournament between the counties did not disappoint in any respect. The contest went to a replay, and under the new fifteen-a-side rules – reluctantly accepted by Louth, as the tournament had begun as seventeen-a-side[9] – the standard of play would live in the memory for a long time. Kerry won the replay decisively, 2–4 to 0–5.[10]

From the GAA's perspective, the crowds attending – estimated at 26,000 and 35,000 for the respective matches – both established the games as the pre-eminent attractions in Irish sport and generated sufficient income (£1,183 in profit from Kerry versus Louth alone) to enable Jones' Road to be bought for £3,500 and refurbished with the aid of a £2,000 loan from the Munster and Leinster Bank.[11] News that the deal had been concluded was broken in *The Gaelic Athlete* at the end of October and welcomed in the same pages a week later:

> The purchase of Jones's Road Grounds by the Central Council, as announced in our issue of last week, has removed what was little short of a reproach upon the GAA. For many years the Gaelic Athletic Association occupied the remarkable position of being the largest users of football and hurling grounds in the country, without the Central body being the possessor of a square yard which it could call its own.[12]

Now that the Association was on a firm footing, it became a priority to publicise its success and maintain the virtuous cycle of heightened public interest, gate revenues and investment. Two years previously, the importance of promoting big matches was recognised by the Central Council in advance of the 1911 All-Ireland hurling final between Limerick and Kilkenny (ironically, as the match had to be postponed because of heavy rain at the venue in Cork, and Limerick withdrawing in a dispute over the re-match): 'The Council, recognising the importance of the contest, spared no expense in perfecting arrangements for the match advertising being carried out on a very extensive scale all over the country.'[13]

However, there was also unhappiness with what was seen as a lack of commensurate coverage in the national media. A motion to the 1912 Annual Convention called for a three-man delegation to be appointed to 'wait on the proprietors of the *Irish Independent* relative to the partial boycott of the nation's games by that organ'.[14] During debate on an amendment to include *The Freeman's Journal* on the list, there were contributors defending that newspaper's record. By this stage, in any case, it was the *Irish Independent* that mattered more, as the revived title acquired by William Martin Murphy and relaunched in 1905 was well on its way to hastening the end (which duly arrived in 1924) of *The Freeman's Journal*.[15] A cheaper cover price, plus more modern production with an emphasis on photography, had shot its circulation up to 40,000 within three years,[16] and that figure would inexorably rise to 100,000 by 1915.[17]

By 1913, the GAA had the added publicity of a dedicated magazine, *The Gaelic Athlete*. Although there had been previous ventures into the business of publishing specialist Gaelic games periodicals, this was the first to be published on a weekly basis. Although not an in-house publication, *The Gaelic Athlete* was very supportive of the GAA and was published by Joe Stanley, proprietor of the Gaelic Press (established in 1913) and member of the IRB and Irish Volunteers. Commissioned by Pearse in 1916 to commandeer a printing press and publish a bulletin, Stanley seized O'Keeffe's Printing Works in Halston Street and produced the *Irish War News,* the official organ of the Easter Rising. He was afterwards interned in Frongoch, where he wrote poetry and songs, including 'The Frongoch Roll Call'.[18]

The Gaelic Athlete provided detailed coverage of GAA affairs and in-depth treatment of big events, most obviously All-Ireland finals. Correspondents reported from both contesting counties, providing, *inter alia,* interviews with the captains. Match coverage for the November 1913 All-Ireland hurling final between Kilkenny and Tipperary included 'Plan of the Field', a diagram of team selections, and 'By The Clock', a chronological detail of the lead-up to and progress of the match, complete with 'colour' writing, such as: '1.30 p.m.: ... Also, "the fair sex are here in attendance and in the display of fashion the Horse Show is quite a back number."'[19]

The publication unabashedly viewed its advent as a means of ratcheting up pressure on national newspapers to improve coverage of Gaelic games. Reflecting at the end of 1913 on improved coverage elsewhere of the upcoming All-Ireland football final, it observed, 'A sign of the times is that

Pictured are (l–r): Arthur Griffith, Éamon de Valera, Lord Mayor Laurence O'Neill and Michael Collins at Croke Park for the 6 April 1919 Irish Republican Prisoners' Dependants Fund match between Wexford and Tipperary.

two Dublin newspaper concerns are already inaugurating competitions in connection with the match, which in former days would have received scant notice after the game had been played and none to speak of beforehand.'[20] The charge was not unfounded, certainly in the case of the *Irish Independent*. For example, the two All-Ireland football finals in 1912 – the 1911 final was played in January 1912 and the 1912 final in December – gathered previews of fewer than a hundred words, plus team selections. Nor could such coverage be described as proportionate, as the 1912 final between Louth and Antrim drew a crowd of 18,000 and took a record gate of £510.[21]

By the end of 1913, however, the landscape had changed. Earlier in the year, the *Irish Independent* had even offered to present gold medals to the winners of the Kerry versus Louth final of the Croke Memorial Tournament[22] – an offer that was accepted. In December, whether it was due to the representations to the newspaper of the previous year combined with the obvious popularity of the games, or the arrival on the scene of *The Gaelic Athlete*, the *Irish Independent* gave the Wexford versus Kerry All-Ireland football final extensive coverage. The day before the game, there was a substantial preview, plus pictures of the respective captains. Two days later, a sizeable report was accompanied by a bank of seven pictures, including one of IPP MP John Dillon – conspicuously in attendance at the final of the Croke Memorial Tournament earlier in the year, with his party leader John Redmond – who was deemed 'a stranger until then to Gaelic arenas'.[23] Dillon could hardly have been accused of pretending otherwise, and is quoted in the match coverage in *The Freeman's Journal* as saying, 'It is so long since I attended a match that I didn't know how the game was to be started.'[24]

As detailed by Mark Duncan, the growing use of photography was also helping to build for the first time a national culture of celebrity. At this time, the most famous Gaelic sportsman was Kerry football captain Dick Fitzgerald.[25] A year after the watershed final of the Croke Memorial Tournament, Fitzgerald launched *How to Play Gaelic Football*, the first GAA coaching manual. This was a pioneering publication, as few books had been produced about the GAA in its first thirty years. The book marks the beginning of modern football – not because previous analyses of the game were crude, but because the game that Fitzgerald analysed was modern football, with the outside posts removed, a goal worth three points and fifteen players on each side. *How to Play Gaelic Football* is

Dick Fitzgerald demonstrating football skills.

still fascinating, with its breakdown of the duties of various positions and illustrative photographs. It also includes the author's thoughts on the applicability of his insights to hurling and an early advocacy of the thirteen-man game, with the centre back and centre forward positioned as the sole players on either half line.

Camera crews filming the opening of the 1924 Tailteann Games. The filming of
Gaelic games became popular between 1913 and 1923.

The Kerry team of the period also featured in the early emergence of another hugely significant means of mass communication, with the screening in Tralee's Theatre Royal of highlights of the Croke Memorial Tournament replay victory over Louth. Denis Condon has written about the ventures of the Gaelic games into cinema of this period, explaining how cinema owners such as James T. Jameson organised the filming of matches for audiences, boosted by the nationalist sentiment of the time as well as the growing popularity of Gaelic games.[26] Dublin and Cork staged the first viewings of the Croke Memorial Tournament replay, but the gala event was in Tralee; players from the east of the county, including Fitzgerald, were driven to the Theatre Royal for the screening.

The bright horizons for the GAA were, however, to become clouded fairly quickly. The outbreak of the First World War probably had limited effect on the Association in areas where there was little likelihood of significant enlistment,[27] but overall, the conflict had a major impact. Wartime restrictions would create friction between the GAA and state authorities. But at the levels of the individual and the local community, research that would allow us to gauge the effect is still at an early stage. The Ulster Council launched a nine-month research project in 2014 on GAA participation in the war. Publicising the project, the Council recalled, for instance, that William Manning from Belfast, who played for Antrim in the 1912 All-Ireland football final, was shot dead while serving as a Lance Sergeant with the Royal Dublin Fusiliers in France in 1918.

It presumably did not cause Association Secretary Luke O'Toole and the national administration to lose much sleep that the First World War gave the then unionist *Irish Times* a couple of opportunities to scold the GAA for the affront of young men playing in and attending matches when they could be in the trenches. In November 1916, when restrictions on railway travel were being imposed, the GAA lobbied John Redmond and MPs on the matter in advance of that year's All-Ireland football final, provoking the newspaper to protest in an editorial:

We invite thoughtful nationalists to consider the effect on British and Allied opinion of an incident in London yesterday. Ireland is at war and her government has stopped 'railway excursion traffic not necessary to the national interest'.

This decision interferes with the convenience of the GAA which is arranging a large football match in Dublin. At Westminster yesterday this body put its grievance before the nationalist members. It explained that its football matches are sometimes attended by as many as 40,000 people. Is there any other belligerent, Allied or enemy, against which this scandalous charge – an army corps of men watching football in wartime – could be laid?[28]

That same year, of course, had already seen turmoil closer to home, with the aftermath of the Easter Rising bringing an uncomfortable focus on to the GAA. The complex question of how the Association navigated the shifting electoral fortunes within nationalism is dealt with in depth elsewhere in these pages (see Chapters 5 and 8), but the question of the Association's self-image is another crucial consideration. By and large, although the IRB featured many prominent senior GAA figures, such as Harry Boland, J. J. Walsh, Austin Stack, Dan McCarthy and Eoin O'Duffy,[29] the Association was careful not to take sides as the character of political nationalism changed. David Fitzpatrick makes the point that, 'what the [Gaelic] League and GAA had to offer the politicians they offered indiscriminately to Sinn Féiners and Redmondites alike: zest for Ireland, tangible rather than rhetorical reminders of Irish nationality, Irish reels, sets, jigs, a few words of Irish, aggressively un-English games.'[30]

At the meeting immediately after the Easter Rising, the Central Council was quick to release a public statement distancing itself from the insurrection. Emphasising the Association's 'strictly non-political and non-sectarian' nature, the statement denied the evidence given to Lord Hardinge's Royal Commission, set up to investigate the Rising, by Sir Matthew Nathan, Under-Secretary for Ireland. Nathan, perhaps unsurprisingly, had confused the involvement of key GAA personalities in the Irish Volunteers with an organisational imprimatur. This allowed the Central Council to deny that the Association had, as alleged, signed a manifesto attacking John Redmond for his efforts to get the Irish Volunteers to enlist in the war.[31]

For all this caution in managing the projected image of the Association, it could not keep the world at arm's length. Rail travel restrictions led to poor attendances at the following year's All-Ireland finals, while the War of Independence and later the Civil War eventually made completing the championship in a coherent timeframe impossible. When Dublin beat Cavan in September 1920's All-Ireland football semi-final, the second semi-final between Tipperary and Mayo did not take place for nearly two years. Without well-organised match schedules, the media coverage that had been so carefully nurtured a few years previously became as erratic as the fixtures. For their part, newspapers had their own problems, with routine military raids – from either side – disrupting the print flows in many publications.[32]

There is an abiding irony in the GAA's media engagement between 1913 and 1923. Despite a strong desire to stay out of the political arena as an organisation, and to prioritise and promote the games, the Association ended the period shrouded in the mythologies of the independence struggle because of the involvement therein of so many of its key personnel and the iconic event of Bloody Sunday, which was memorably and starkly headlined in *The Freeman's Journal,* 'Amritsar repeated in Dublin' – referencing the 1919 British Army massacre in India.[33] The development of the games as public attractions was set back by nearly the whole ten years, and arguably the media focus did not recover the momentum of 1913–14 until the arrival of Radio 2RN in 1926 and of *The Irish Press* six years later.

CHAPTER 14

Social Life and the GAA in a Time of Upheaval in Ireland: A Retrospect

DIARMAID FERRITER

Harry Boland at Croke Park for the 11 September 1921
Leinster hurling final.

WHEN HE WAS IN THE UNITED STATES serving as Éamon de Valera's private secretary during the War of Independence, Harry Boland began to feel flabby and unfit. One of his diary entries lamented the loss of the physical intensity of his GAA days, the youthful endeavours that had earned him a place on the Dublin team for the All-Ireland senior hurling final in 1909: 'Oh for a good hurling match.' Much of his socialising during his American trip was very far removed from the earthiness of his recreational youth and he made numerous other references to his declining fitness; as his biographer, David Fitzpatrick, has recorded, 'memories of hurling provided a whole-some antidote to the enticements of the saloon and the dancehall.'[1]

The GAA was also of material advantage to Harry; it organised a benefit hurling match at Croke Park in late 1917 that assisted him in establishing his own tailoring business in Dublin city. Harry's father, Jim, also had an interesting and extensive relationship with the GAA; he was not renowned as a player, 'but fabled for his organisational skills' and had served as Dublin county chairman, a position Harry was also to hold.[2] There is little doubt that for the two generations of Bolands, the GAA performed an essential political function. Jim was a dedicated Fenian and Harry was vocal in his support for the GAA's ban on foreign games; for him, 'Gaelic purity mattered more than popularity.' But that political side was only one aspect of the Bolands' involvement with the GAA and its appeal to them. It is clear in Fitzpatrick's description that the GAA, as well as providing an important outlet for physical energy, discipline and honing of administrative skills, was central to Harry's 'political, social and imaginative life'; in his prison letters during his incarceration in various prisons after the 1916 Rising, the GAA 'becomes a shorthand for youth, friendship and romance'.[3] Likewise, when employed as a clerk in London before his return to Ireland in 1915, Michael Collins threw himself into the GAA for reasons that were not just political: 'Collins loved the sport, but he also very early on showed an interest in and aptitude for organisation.'[4]

Recognising such nuances is essential if the role and impact of the GAA are to be properly contextualised for the revolutionary period of 1913 to 1923. Had the GAA during this era been solely about playing, or promoting politics, or exclusively identified with the IRA and the War of Independence, it is unlikely it would have endured, adapted, survived and ultimately thrived the way it did. Had its members and followers seen it in very narrow terms, it may well have splintered like Sinn Féin in 1921 and 1922, dividing into rival groups, but 'it never had to endure a major or lasting split'. While it was politicised in a variety of ways during its formative decades, its shift over time to 'a more civic nationalism' was facilitated by a degree of ambiguity about where it fitted into the revolutionary experience and landscape.[5]

While some of the recollections of GAA members who were also active republicans in the political or military spheres during the revolutionary era might be exaggerated – Cornelius Murphy, active in the Irish Volunteers in Cork, maintained 'ninety percent of the GAA was just GAA, the other 10% was good [meaning active in the IRA]' – those who were 'just GAA' were undoubtedly very numerous, just as a majority of the population at large was not active in the IRA's campaign.[6] The preoccupation with 'earnest nationality', referred to by T. F. O'Sullivan, the first historian of the GAA, had to compete with another issue O'Sullivan referred to – the need 'to develop Irish bone and muscle'.[7] The GAA endured – a number of witnesses to the Bureau of Military History refer to the determination to 'keep going' despite the revolutionary upheaval[8] – because it served a lot more functions than a heroic, nationalist narrative would suggest, and because it was part of a wider social landscape.

In 1966, during the fiftieth anniversary commemorations of the 1916 Rising, traditional narratives were prominent; the GAA commissioned a memorial pageant in Croke Park, and speaking at the Association's annual congress in Dublin, GAA President Alf Murray insisted that the importance of the organisation in the years surrounding the 1916 Rising was its quasi-spiritual role, which made 'the fight for freedom something more than a mere attempt at changing the form of government and turned it into a people's struggle for identity'. And yet, the same year, the Kerry board of the GAA issued a statement declaring the right of all GAA members to determine their own way of commemorating the Rising's jubilee; it was not appropriate, the argument went, for the Association to be seen to be endorsing either official or unofficial celebrations.[9] There would be no single voice in 1966. There was controversy in Drogheda over the banning of rugby and soccer clubs from a commemorative parade, to the extent that Cumann na mBan withdrew its two delegates from the committee overseeing the commemorations in protest, while at the Football Association of Ireland soccer cup final in Dalymount in Dublin, President de Valera was in attendance as 200 veterans paraded. Donogh O'Malley, then Minister for Health, also met them.[10]

Clearly, there was more to the Irish nationalist sporting narrative than the GAA, and O'Malley and others were keen to embrace this broadness. O'Malley was a critic of the GAA's ban on foreign sports (not rescinded until 1971) and in 1968, shortly before his death, he expressed defiance in opening a rugby pavilion, by contending that 'rugby and soccer people were sick and tired of having the finger pointed at them as if they were any worse Irishmen for playing these games. When Ireland was asked for sons to call to the colours we were there and were not asked what shape of a ball we used.'[11]

The important point about these observations is that they represented a continuance of the challenges that had always existed to assertions that the GAA was just the sporting wing of Irish nationalism. Historians, journalists and other writers have been busy in recent years elaborating on the nuances of the GAA's historic identity and appeal, and have rightly expressed scepticism about traditional narratives that do little to foster an appreciation of the many layers to the organisation and its reach; they have worked to build on the assertion of historian W. F. Mandle, over thirty years ago, that the GAA 'saw itself as having a wider responsibility to itself as a popular sporting organisation'.[12] In prisons during the War of Independence, the playing of GAA games was not just about a commitment to nationalism but also cementing group identity. It was a crucial physical outlet, which both prison guards and prisoners recognised the importance of, but it had other advantages: 'I shall be quite young again when I am permitted to return to you,' Denis McCullough, who spent much of the War of independence in various prisons in England and Ireland, informed his wife.[13]

It has been much more common in recent years to assert that the GAA's relationship with nationalism during this period was complex and that a strong GAA was not a prerequisite for a county to develop into a strong IRA county.[14] According to Richard McElligott's history of the GAA in Kerry, 'the rising tide of Sinn Féin nationalism did not lift all GAA boats'.[15] Like the rest of the Irish public in 1916, the Easter Rising 'caught the GAA completely by surprise' and it showed 'no immediate empathy'.[16] Vincent Comerford asserts that the participation of the GAA in the revolution after 1916 was 'as mixed and patchy as that of the nationalist collectivity in general'. It also shared an attachment to a patriarchal society and when women began to play camogie, despite the obvious nationalism of many of its participants, 'promoting female autonomy was not a concern of the early GAA'.[17]

William Murphy posed the following question in 2009: 'has the grand narrative changed?' and provided this convincing answer: 'The GAA appears to have been a playground of the revolution more often than it was a player in the revolution.'[18] Such conclusions have been facilitated by a greater determination to analyse the GAA from the 'inside', and recognition of the shortcomings of dismissing 'two thirds of the iceberg … with the word grassroots'.[19] The 'grassroots' were living through a time of upheaval and GAA membership was not the only issue pervading their lives and experiences. Nor should it be accepted without question that the GAA 'was more directly confrontational' than the Gaelic League when it came to separatist sentiment.[20] The Gaelic League receives a lot more space and attention in histories of the revolutionary period than the GAA. The GAA does not merit a single mention in one of the most acclaimed accounts of this period, Ernie O'Malley's *On Another Man's Wound*,[21] nor does it feature at all in Colm Ó Gaora's *Mise*, one of the best-known Irish-language accounts of IRA activities in the west of Ireland, first published in 1943, which contains nearly forty references to the Gaelic League.[22]

Patrick Pearse maintained there would have been no 1916 Rising without the Gaelic League, not an accolade he offered to the GAA. But the Gaelic League was also undermined by its very success and 'began to lose its charm when it became powerful. It was then worth capturing and people … set out to do so.'[23] The GAA was not 'captured' in this way because its appeal was more broadly defined and more flexible; indeed, it could also provide 'a welcome distraction from violent events unfolding elsewhere'.[24] GAA membership, crucially, could accommodate both those who were apolitical and those who were advanced or moderate nationalists, 'as illustrated by the name of [Cork city's] leading hurling club, Redmonds', named after the leader of the IPP, John Redmond.[25]

Some of the GAA's defiant gestures during the revolutionary period seemed to imply common cause being made with the political and militarist republicans – most obviously Gaelic Sunday in August 1918, when it flouted a government prohibition on public meetings, but it could be contended that this act of rebellion was just as much about sport as politics. The GAA has to be seen in the context of the 'birth of modern sport' and the need to transform sport into a spectacle 'geared to the turnstile'.[26] Any government prohibition was going to impact on the business of sport and spectacle, thus galvanising the Association's leadership into mobilising the grass roots.[27] Money earned as a result of sporting fixtures was a key part of the local economy.[28] The Mayo county board during this period, for example, appealed against the practice of Connacht finals usually being played in Tuam, as 'it felt Tuam was used as the location for the Connacht final too often. This benefited the Galway GAA financially to the detriment of other Western counties.'[29] What the GAA was involved in was 'no simple revival of traditional pastimes. Both hurling and Gaelic football, as developed by the GAA were essentially spectator sports of a new kind, exhibitions of skill laid on for the mass audiences made possible by the railway, the newspaper and the spending power of an emerging consumer society.'[30]

GAA stalwarts were active in other areas, too, and not just the Gaelic League. A variety of sporting endeavour, language, temperance and fitness campaigns, student societies and summer schools were part of the wider social context for the Ireland the GAA evolved in.[31] Enniscorthy's Pádraig Doyle and Frank Boggan endorsed the temperance slogan 'no true Gael should touch intoxicating drink.'[32] Battles over the sacredness of Sunday were also relevant; advocates of sabbatarianism in Terenure in Dublin, for example, persuaded the Flood family to terminate the GAA's lease of local grounds. For others, Sundays were very much about converging; the availability of sports pitches at the Phoenix Park in Dublin, for example, provided places where 'spectators could congregate and migrants unattached to a Dublin club could make their way on Sunday mornings and get absorbed.'[33] This was part of a wider process of social and political mobilisation; 'it is often overlooked,' remarks Joe Lee, 'how much social history can be found in the accounts of political events; the gatherings of the Irish Volunteers, for example, were often festive events, enlivening somewhat drab daily routines with their parades often headed by bands.'[34]

Jeremiah Murphy, in his memoir of growing up in Kerry in the first decade of the twentieth century, places the GAA 'and concerts and dances' in the same sentence. He describes the GAA as providing 'a highly refined type of entertainment', and the local handball court was 'one source of entertainment that never seemed to lose its edge'.[35] There was an emphasis, not just on political nationalism, but on 'the manly, the virtuous, the temperate', which encouraged some contemporary journalists to make plaster saints of GAA supporters. Fearghal McGarry quotes a *Dundalk Democrat* newspaper report after a Monaghan versus Cavan GAA final in

1916; the journalist challenged 'any other association, society or body to get together voluntarily a gathering of over 5,000 young men and women and afterwards truthfully chronicle that not an untoward incident occurred, not an appearance of drink, not an obscene expression'.[36] Allowing for exaggeration (after all, some of the same saints were ordered to stop betting on GAA matches, a practice 'long frowned on' by the GAA[37]), this still points to the way in which the GAA-inspired mobilisation needs to be fitted onto a broader canvas than the solely political, and that canvas was indeed crowded.

In his seminal *Politics and Irish Life: Provincial Experience of War and Revolution*, first published in 1977, David Fitzpatrick made much of the 'diversity and sheer density of active social and political organisations in the provinces'; by analysing Clare newspaper reports from 1913 to 1916, he concluded that 'no less than 82 villages in that county of 100,000 people had active branches of some sort of political or social organisation'. Significantly, he also identified the GAA as 'on the periphery' of politics and social agitation, grouping it with 'race committees … pipe and drum bands … amateur dramatics'.[38] The GAA, like other organisations, had to compete for free time; Liam Deasy, later active in an IRA flying column in Cork, was so involved in the GAA that it delayed his joining the Volunteers, and there were complaints that too many young men demonstrated a preference for football over drilling.[39] This reality has to be balanced against the testimony of veterans who recall GAA rooms being used for meetings of the IRB and the use of matches to mobilise the Irish Volunteers.[40] However, the assertion that 'politics rather than sport dominated people's lives' is too sweeping.[41]

Social life in Ireland a hundred years ago was vibrant and varied, and people were on the move. There were 330 trams in Dublin in 1911, for example, operating on lines that ran for 60 miles around the city as part of a public transport system that was one of the most impressive of any city in the world. Bicycles had also become a very popular mode of transport nationwide.[42] Alongside sport and language, there was a great interest in music, dance, conversation and theatre. Fair days, race meetings and religious holidays were honoured traditions. In rural areas, house visiting was the most common form of social interaction, and matchmaking was a priority in January and February as there was little work to be done in the fields during winter. Lough Derg pilgrimages provided a mixture of prayer and penance, as did another popular ritual, climbing Croagh

Patrick on the last Sunday of July.[43] The first Irish cinema, the Volta Electric Theatre, had opened in Dublin in 1909 and in 1910 the first film made in Ireland was a tale of emigration, *The Lad from Old Ireland*. Music hall comedy and pantomime were also popular.

While hunting, shooting and fishing were more conspicuous displays of leisure for the better-off, blood sports like cock fighting, though illegal, survived in working-class areas. Soccer was the most popular sport in Dublin and by 1911 there were thirty-one pitches in use in the Phoenix Park; it has been asserted that, in 1907, 'only 3 of the 32 playing fields in the Phoenix Park were required for Gaelic games, the rest being used for soccer.'[44] In 1914 in Cork city there were twelve hurling teams, eleven football clubs, three rugby clubs, seven soccer teams and three camogie teams; Gaelic games 'routinely drew thousands to the Cork athletic grounds'. It is hardly surprising that the Cork county board introduced turnstiles, referee standardisation and 'transparent accounting'.[45] Cricket was more popular in the wealthier Dublin suburbs, but Tom Hunt has convincingly challenged the perception of cricket players as elitist and anti-nationalist, as well as establishing that GAA games were more common in Westmeath among farmers than farm labourers.[46] In other counties, however, labourers were more dominant.[47] Golf was also becoming popular with the upper classes, while in 1910, the Five Nations rugby tournament was inaugurated and Ireland joined the English, Scots, Welsh and French in the competition. Spontaneous dances took place in houses, at crossroads and in other public places, while in some parts of the country the Irish tradition of the *cuaird*, where men would meet regularly in a neighbouring house for storytelling, gossip and cards, or reading aloud from newspapers, remained an important part of social interaction.[48]

Where does the GAA fit into this dispensation? Extensive rail travel facilitated the development of national GAA competitions and bedding-down of the organisational structures of the Association. Most people had little disposable cash, but rail and bicycle made people mobile; as one man recalled in the *Limerick Rural Survey*, published in 1964, 'long ago, we thought nothing of cycling ten miles to play in a match.'[49] As well as in the spread of the GAA, railways played a major role in the broadening of personal travel experience: 'many country youth first came to Dublin to watch their county play in an all-Ireland competition' and there were special trains to take Dublin fans to Thurles, Cork and Kilkenny.[50] Regular competitions meant 'the community was deeply involved in the fate of its hurling team'; inter-parish matches were 'a safety-valve'. It was one place where a community 'which had few opportunities for sublimation could give vent to its emotions'. Sport was also an outlet for the young men for whom emigration was not possible; *The Kerryman* newspaper, for example, noted that the fundamental reason for the success of GAA town and district leagues in 1919 was because emigration had ceased to be the option it had previously been.[51]

Dressing up and showing colours was a product of social and cultural as well as political forces. Fearghal McGarry has made the point, in looking at the motivations of those who would eventually be involved in the 1916 Rising, that not all participants were consumed by debates or thoughts about ideology or notions of the continuity of the republican struggle they supposedly embodied; although many joined the Irish Volunteers because they regarded the continued anglicisation of Ireland as retrograde and akin to slavery, some were more focused on their pleasure and pride in looking 'swank' in their new Volunteer uniforms, and being able to hold weapons for the first time made them feel authentic and like 'the real thing'.[52] Likewise, at a reception for released republican prisoners in Cork in 1917, GAA teams were prominent: 'the men wore their brightly coloured jerseys and bore their hurls on their shoulders, while the female hurlers wore green blouses and carried their sports sticks.'[53] Of course this was about identification with a transformed political opinion after the Rising, but it was also about socially and sartorially being part of a new collective. In a similar vein, after the Rising, some began wearing 'small badges in the colours of the new flag at GAA tournaments and other meetings'.[54]

Even for those GAA members who were committed revolutionaries, loyalty to the fate of their GAA team could sometimes take precedence over revolutionary activity; one IRA member involved in weapons smuggling and who was supposed to be a participant in manoeuvres the day after the All-Ireland football final in 1915, 'spent much of the Sunday night drowning his sorrows' over Kerry's defeat against Wexford and was not fit for military purpose the following day.[55] The match may have been used as a cover for mobilising these volunteers, but they were not always able to detach themselves from their county and sporting loyalties. Perceived bias and lack of fairness in the administration and oversight of GAA games were also taken very seriously; for those involved in administration there were 'endless rows about disputed results, biased referees, poached players and unpaid fines'.[56] Some of the long letters from Fenian Tom Clarke, later executed as a 1916 leader, to John Daly in Limerick in 1913 were 'about that Kilkenny and Limerick match' and the strained relations it gave rise to, which were afforded the status of a serious crisis, 'all dating back to that match in Dublin which [Mick] Crowe refereed a year ago when Limerick was marked defeated'.[57]

In relation to the Irish Volunteer movement that evolved into the IRA, Edward MacLysaght in Clare, whose heart was with the 1916 republicans though his head was against them, wondered if it would prove to be a 'transient flame kindled by curiosity and fed by sheepism … which will die out when the novelty is no longer in it'.[58] This happened to some organisations; it did not happen to the GAA because it had planted different and more robust roots. Fitzpatrick comments that 'Volunteering, of course, took second place to games'; a county inspection of the Volunteers in Clare had to be postponed for a week as it clashed with the All-Ireland hurling final between Dublin and Clare in 1914. Fitzpatrick also noted that the GAA never became 'as subservient as the Gaelic League to the political organisation'; Sinn Féin made use of matches rather than organised them, and 'suffocated' the Gaelic League but not the GAA.[59] That was also because the GAA was sufficiently stubborn and independent to keep a degree of autonomy. It was advised to call off the calamitous game played on Bloody Sunday in 1920, but refused 'on the grounds that a last-minute cancellation would confirm British suspicions that the organisation was a front for the IRA'.[60]

It was undoubtedly difficult for the GAA to weather the Civil War from 1922 to 1923, and there were 'severe limits to the GAA's powers of healing', but the determination to look forward was strong. Eoin O'Duffy, who, like Harry Boland, saw the GAA as performing a variety of different functions, urged his men, as the commissioner of the new Civic Guard in 1922, to use Gaelic sports to 'play their way into the hearts of the people'.[61] That was ultimately what was done by sufficient numbers of GAA players all over Ireland. During the revolutionary decade, the GAA survived, and was able to move on after it, because it managed to transcend the divisions and limitations of the upheaval.

ENDNOTES

1. Introduction

1   See, for clear evidence of the changing historiography, the bibliographies of such recent volumes as: Marie Coleman, *The Irish Revolution 1916–1923* (Abingdon, 2014); Diarmaid Ferriter, *A Nation and Not a Rabble: The Irish Revolution 1913–1923* (London, 2015); Fearghal McGarry, *The Rising: Ireland, Easter 1916* (Oxford, 2010); Charles Townshend, *Easter 1916: The Irish Rebellion* (London, 2005); *idem, The Republic: The Fight for Irish Independence* (London, 2013).

2   Dan Breen, *My Fight for Irish Freedom* (Dublin, 1924); Tom Barry, *Guerilla Days in Ireland* (Dublin, 1949).

3   Ernie O'Malley, *On Another Man's Wound* (London, 1936) is one such exception. See also, Richard English, *Ernie O'Malley: IRA Intellectual* (Oxford, 1998).

4   For the raw emotions present in its immediate aftermath, see Dorothy Macardle, *Tragedies of Kerry* (first published 1924).

5   F. X. Martin, '1916 – Myth, Fact, and Mystery', *Studia Hibernica* 7 (1967), pp. 7–126.

6   The changing pattern of public commemoration of the Great War in Ireland has been examined by Keith Jeffery, most recently in 'Irish Varieties of Great War Commemoration', in John Horne and Edward Madigan (eds), *Towards Commemoration: Ireland in War and Revolution 1912–1923* (Dublin, 2013), pp. 117–25.

7   See Coleman, *op. cit.*; David Fitzpatrick (ed.), *Revolution? Ireland 1917–1923* (Dublin, 1990); and essays by Townshend, Hart and Garvin in Joost Augusteijn (ed.), *The Irish Revolution 1913–1923* (Basingstoke and New York, 2002).

8   See, in particular, J. M. Regan, *The Irish Counter-Revolution, 1921–1936* (Dublin, 1999).

9   The journal *Irish Economic and Social History* began publication in 1974; *Saothar*, the journal of the Irish Labour History Society, dates from 1975.

10   F. X. Martin (ed.), 'Select Documents: Eoin MacNéill on the 1916 Rising', *Irish Historical Studies*, 12 (March, 1961), pp. 226–71; Breandán MacGiolla Choille (ed.), *Intelligence Notes 1913–16* (Dublin, 1966); Pádraig Ó Snodaigh, *Comhghuaillithe na Réabhlóide 1913–1916* (*Baile Átha Cliath*, 1966); Leon Ó Broin, *Dublin Castle and the 1916 Rising* (London, 1966); *idem, The Chief Secretary: Augustine Birrell in Ireland* (London, 1969).

11   David Fitzpatrick (ed.), *Terror in Ireland: 1916–1923* (Dublin, 2012).

12   Recent contributions include Cormac Ó Comhraí, *Ireland and the First World War: A Photographic History* (Cork, 2014), and Pádraig Óg Ó Ruairc, *Revolution: A Photographic History of Revolutionary Ireland 1913–1923* (Cork, 2014).

13   David Fitzpatrick, *Politics and Irish Life, 1913–1921: Provincial Experience of War and Revolution* (Dublin, 1977).

14   The Gaelic League was established by Douglas Hyde and others in 1893 and sought to revive Irish as a spoken language and literary movement.

15   Coleman, *op. cit.*, offers a useful survey of these aspects, pp. 67–94; for longer-term analysis of social origins of revolutionaries, see Tom Garvin, *Nationalist Revolutionaries in Ireland 1858–1928* (Oxford, 1987); also, Joost Augusteijn, *From Public Defiance to Guerrilla Warfare: The Experience of Ordinary Volunteers in the Irish War of Independence, 1916–1923* (Dublin, 1996).

16   Cal McCarthy, *Cumann na mBan and the Irish Revolution* (Cork, 2007); Margaret Ward, *Unmanageable Revolutionaries: Women in Irish Nationalism* (London, 1995); Sinéad McCoole, *No Ordinary Women: Irish Female Activists in the Revolutionary Years, 1900–1923*

(Dublin, 2003); Anne Matthews, *Renegades: Irish Republican Women 1900–1922* (Dublin/Cork, 2010); Senia Paseta, *Irish Nationalist Women 1900–1918* (Cambridge, 2014); Margaret Ó hÓgartaigh, *Kathleen Lynn: Irishwoman, Patriot, Doctor* (Dublin, 2006); also Margaret Ward, 'Gender: Gendering the Irish Revolution', in Augusteijn (ed., 2002), *op. cit.*, pp. 168–85.

17 A major project, involving a comprehensive calculation and directed by Eunan O'Halpin, is in progress as *The Dead of the Irish Revolution*: see, as an example, 'Counting Terror: Bloody Sunday and The Dead of the Irish Revolution', in Fitzpatrick (ed., 2012), *op. cit.*, pp. 141–57.

18 David Fitzpatrick (ed.), *Ireland and the First World War* (Dublin, 1988); Keith Jeffery, *Ireland and the Great War* (Cambridge, 2000); John Horne (ed.), *Our War: Ireland and the Great War* (Dublin, 2008); Horne and Madigan (eds), *op. cit.*

19 The series was republished in 2009, with introductory essays by distinguished historians, under the general editorship of Brian Ó Conchubhair: see, for example, *Limerick's Fighting Story 1916–21*, introduction by Ruán O'Donnell (Cork, 2009).

20 See Jennifer Doyle, Frances Clarke, Eibhlis Connaughton and Orna Somerville, *An Introduction to the Bureau of Military History 1913–1921* (Dublin, 2002); Diarmaid Ferriter, '"In such deadly earnest": The Bureau of Military History', *Dublin Review*, 6 (Winter 2001–2); also Fearghal McGarry, *Rebels: Voices from the Easter Rising* (London, 2011), pp. ix–xx.

21 Catriona Crowe (ed), *Guide to the Military Service (1916–1923) Pensions Collection* (Dublin, 2012); Diarmaid Ferriter, 'Throwing Light on the Silent State', *The Irish Times* (Special Supplement), 3 October 2014.

22 McGarry (2011), *op. cit.*, and *idem*, '1916 and Irish Republicanism: Between Myth and History', in Horne and Madigan (eds), *op. cit.*, pp. 46–53.

23 Patrick Maume, *The Long Gestation: Irish Nationalist Life, 1891–1918* (Dublin, 1999); P. J. Mathews, *Revival* (Cork and Notre Dame, 2003); R. F. Foster, *Vivid Faces: The Revolutionary Generation in Ireland, 1890–1923* (London, 2014).

24 For police casualties, see Richard Abbott, *Police Casualties in Ireland, 1919–1922* (Dublin, 2000); Anthony J. Gaughan, *Memoirs of Constable Jeremiah Mee, RIC* (Dublin, 1975); Stephen Ball (ed.), *A Policeman's Ireland: Recollections of Samuel Waters, RIC* (Cork, 1999).

25 J. A. Mangan, *The Games Ethic and Imperialism: Aspects of the Diffusion of an Ideal* (Middlesex, 1986); Richard Holt, *Sport and the British: A Modern History* (Oxford, 1989); Neil Tranter, *Sport, Economy and Society in Britain, 1750–1914* (Cambridge, 1998); Patrick F. McDevitt, *'May the Best Man Win': Sport, Masculinity, and Nationalism in Great Britain and the Empire, 1880–1935* (New York and Basingstoke, 2004).

26 For an insightful perspective of cultural geography, see Kevin Whelan, 'The Geography of Hurling' in *History Ireland*, I, no.1 (1993), pp. 25–8.

27 Examples might include Séamus Ó Ceallaigh, *Gaelic Days* (Limerick, 1944) and *idem*, Gaelic *Athletic Memories* (Limerick, 1945). In a category of its own is Breandán Ó hEithir, *Over the Bar: A Personal Relationship with the GAA* (Dublin, 1984).

28 Art Ó Maolfabhail, *Camán: Two Thousand Years of Hurling in Ireland* (Dundalk, 1973).

29 Marcus de Búrca, *The GAA: A History of the Gaelic Athletic Association* (Dublin, 1980).

30 Liam P. Ó Caithnia, *Scéal na hIomána* (*Baile Átha Cliath*, 1980); *idem*, *Báirí Cos in Éirinn* (*Baile Átha Cliath*, 1984).

31 W. F. Mandle, *The Gaelic Athletic Association and Irish Nationalist Politics 1884–1924* (Dublin, 1987).

32   Mark Tierney, *Croke of Cashel* (Dublin, 1976); Liam P. Ó Caithnia, *Micheál Cíosóg* (*Baile Átha Cliath*, 1982); Séamus Ó Riain, *Maurice Davin* (Dublin, 1994); Pádraig Ó Baoighill, *Nally as Muigh Eo* (*Baile Átha Cliath*, 1998).

33   For Sports History Ireland Society, see the website of *History Ireland:* www.historyireland. com. See number XXXXI (2014) of *Irish Economic and Social History* – in contrast, Ó Caithnia's major publications of the early 1980s were not reviewed in the journal. See also the special edition of *Éire-Ireland* (2013) cited in full in note 36.

34   In addition to the works already cited, an impressive excavation of local source material is William Nolan (ed.), *The Gaelic Athletic Association in Dublin, 1884–2000* (Dublin, 2005).

35   Mike Cronin, *Sport and Nationalism in Ireland* (Dublin, 1999); for particular codes, see Neal Garnham, *Association Football and Society in Pre-Partition Ireland* (Belfast, 2004) and Liam O'Callaghan, *Rugby in Munster: A Social and Cultural History* (Cork, 2011); for an exemplary regional study, see Tom Hunt, *Sport and Society in Victorian Ireland* (Cork, 2007).

36   Mike Cronin, William Murphy and Paul Rouse (eds), *The Gaelic Athletic Association 1884–2009* (Dublin and Portland Or., 2009); see, also, special issue on Ireland and Sport (edited by Mike Cronin and Brian Ó Conchubhair) of *Éire-Ireland, Volume 48: 1 & 2* (Spring/Summer 2013).

37   Ian McBride (ed.), *History and Memory in Modern Ireland* (Cambridge, 2001).

38   Gabriel Doherty and Dermot Keogh (eds), *1916: The Long Revolution* (Cork, 2007); Máirín Ní Dhonnchadha and Theo Dorgan (eds), *Revising the Rising* (Derry, 1991); Roisín Higgins, *Transforming 1916: Meaning, Memory and the Fiftieth Anniversary of the Easter Rising* (Cork, 2012); Mary E. Daly and Margaret O'Callaghan (eds), *1916 in 1966: Commemorating the Easter Rising* (Dublin, 2007); Mark McCarthy, *Ireland's 1916 Rising: Explorations of History-Making, Commemoration & Heritage in Modern Times* (Farnham, UK and Burlington, VT, 2012).

39   See the titles cited in note 16. The commemorative issues of the magazine *History Ireland* give an indication of the interest in these historical anniversaries among the general public.

2. The Triumph of Play

1   Tim Carey, *Croke Park: A History* (Dublin, 2004), pp. 42–95.

2   See W. F. Mandle, *The Gaelic Athletic Association and Irish Nationalist Politics 1884–1924* (Dublin, 1987), p. 151; Malachy Clerkin and Gerard Siggins, *Lansdowne Road* (Dublin, 2010), pp. 96–100; and Neal Garnham, *Association Football and Society in Pre-Partition Ireland* (Belfast, 2004), pp. 115 and 129.

3   See Mandle, *op. cit.*, p. 151; Malachy Clerkin and Gerard Siggins, *Lansdowne Road* (Dublin, 2010), pp. 96–100; and Garnham, *op. cit.*, pp. 115 and 129.

4   *Enniscorthy Echo*, 30 November 1912.

5   *The Irish Times*, 17 May 1914.

6   *Enniscorthy Echo*, 18 July 1914 and 13 March 1915.

7   *Enniscorthy Guardian*, 21 September 1912.

8   Tom Hunt, *Sport and Society in Victorian Ireland: The Case of Westmeath* (Cork, 2007), p. 210.

9   *Enniscorthy Echo*, 10 January 1914 and *Enniscorthy Guardian*, 17 October 1914.

10   Seán Whelan, *The Ghosts of Bygone Days: An Enniscorthy GAA History* (1998), p. 60.

11   *Enniscorthy Guardian,* 12 October 1912; see also, NAI, 1911 census returns.

12   *Enniscorthy Guardian,* 3 January 1914.

13   *Enniscorthy Echo,* 12 December 1914.

14   Ross O'Carroll, 'The Gaelic Athletic Association 1914–1918' (UCD, MA Thesis, 2010), p. 21.

15   *National Volunteer,* 15 May 1915.

16   *The Gaelic Athlete,* 27 December 1913.

17   *Limerick Leader,* 3 April 1914.

18   William Murphy, 'The GAA during the Irish Revolution, 1913–23' in Mike Cronin, William Murphy and Paul Rouse (eds), *The Gaelic Athletic Association 1884–2009* (Dublin, 2009), pp. 61–76, 70.

19   NLI, MS 22, 114., J. J. O'Connell papers.

20   GAA Museum and Archives, Leinster Council Minutes, 14 February 1915, 16 March 1915 and 11 April 1915.

21   GAA Museum and Archives, Central Council Minutes, 28 May 1916.

22   *HC Debates,* Vol. 81, 17 April 1916, Cols 2146–50.

23   *Ibid.,* 12 April 1916, Cols 1825–35.

24   *Ibid.,* Vol. 81, 3 May 1916, Cols 2597–98.

25   Clare GAA Circular re: Hurling Championship semi-final for the Championship of Munster, Ennis, July 1914, Clare County Museum; Circular letter asking people of Laois to contribute to the Training Fund, 29 August 1914, GAA Museum and Archives, GAA/Laois/2.

26   *Limerick Leader,* 4 February 1914.

27   *Ibid.*

28   See for example, *Cork Weekly Examiner,* 6 February 1915; *Limerick Leader,* 9 October 1914; *The Mayo News,* 12 May 1917.

29   *Limerick Leader,* 12 October 1914.

30   *The Clare Champion,* 24 October 1914.

31   *Ibid.,* 17 and 24 October 1914.

32   *Ibid.,* 24 October 1914.

33   Tomás Mac Conmara, '"Tip and slashin" – Clare's hurling victories of 1914', *Clare Association Yearbook, 2006.* Later, two men involved in the preparation of the Clare team for this success – Stephen Clune and Jim O'Hehir – wrote to the GAA asking that they too should receive All-Ireland medals for their part in the success. Their request was denied.

34   *The Clare Champion,* 10 September 1914.

35   *Ibid.,* 24 October 1914.

36   *Ibid.,* 10 September 1914.

37   Dónal McAnallen, '"The Greatest Amateur Association in the World"? The GAA and Amateurism' in Cronin, Murphy and Rouse, *op. cit.,* p. 165.

38   *The Clare Champion,* 22 August 1914.

39   *Ibid.,* 3 October 1914.

40   Mac Conmara, *op. cit.*

41   Anonymous letter to the Laois County Secretary, *c.* October 1914, GAA Museum and Archives, GAA/Laois/74.

42 Letter from M. J. Sheridan and John J. Higgins, Honorary Secretaries to the Training Fund Sub-Committee, to each of the officers of the county committee and to club secretaries, 6 March 1914, GAA Museum and Archives, GAA/Laois/1(2).

43 Circular letter asking for contributions to the training fund, 29 August 1914, GAA Museum and Archives, GAA/Laois/2.

44 See for example, misc. subscriptions, GAA Museum and Archives, GAA/Laois/5–44.

45 Receipt card, September 1914, GAA Museum and Archives, GAA/Laois/5.

46 See for example, misc. subscriptions, GAA Museum and Archives, GAA/Laois/5–44.

47 E. Fitzgerald to John J. Higgins, 25 November 1914, on Wynn's Hotel headed notepaper, GAA Museum and Archives, GAA/Laois/ 88.

48 John Phelan, *In the Shadow of the Goalpost* (2004), p. 18.

49 Robert O'Keeffe to John J. Higgins, 7 September 1914, GAA Museum and Archives, GAA/Laois/4.

50 E. P. McEvoy to John J. Higgins, 22 October 1914, GAA Museum and Archives, GAA/Laois/4.

51 Schedule on amounts needed to pay substitute workers, undated, GAA Museum and Archives, GAA/Laois/45.

52 J. Quigley to John J. Higgins, 19 September 1914, GAA Museum and Archives, GAA/Laois/59.

53 Mrs Lalor to John J. Higgins, 29 October and 30 November 1914, GAA Museum and Archives, GAA/Laois/68–69.

54 See Arnold Mahon, 'An analysis of the development of sport in Laois/Queen's County within the context of the period 1910–1920' (UCD, MA Thesis, 2007).

55 Ballygeeghan went on to win five championships in a row between 1914 and 1918. See Phelan, *op. cit.*

56 Robert O'Keeffe to John J. Higgins, 18 November 1914, GAA Museum and Archives, GAA/Laois/178.

57 GAA Museum and Archives, GAA/Laois/165–75.

58 *Sport*, 30 October 1915.

59 Letter from John Finlay, John Phelan (Hon. Sec., Ballygeeghan Hurling Club) and John Phelan (Hon. Treas., Ballygeeghan Hurling Club), 22 March 1915, GAA Museum and Archives, GAA/Laois/96.

60 *Irish Independent*, 1 September 1976.

61 Notes on training methods, *c.* 1914, GAA Museum and Archives, GAA/Laois/73.

62 P. Daly to John J. Higgins, 11 October 1915, GAA Museum and Archives, GAA/Laois /91.

63 Letter from Fr J. J. Kearney, 11 October 1915, GAA Museum and Archives, GAA/Laois/97.

64 *Sport*, 23 October 1915.

65 Teddy Fennelly, *One Hundred Years of GAA in Laois* (Laois, 1984), p. 31.

66 Jim Doyle to Fr J. J. Kearney, 1 October 1915 and Dick 'Drug' Walsh to John J. Higgins, 15 October 1915, GAA Museum and Archives, GAA/Laois/94–95.

67 'Notes for players previous to match', undated, GAA Museum and Archives, GAA/Laois/71.

68 *United Ireland*, 11 July 1885.

69 See *United Ireland*, February 1885.

70   *Western News*, 17 October 1885.

71   Dick Fitzgerald, *How to Play Gaelic Football* (1914), p. 13.

72   *Ibid.*, p. 15.

73   *Ibid.*, p. 15.

74   P. J. Devlin, 'Celt', *Our Native Games* (Dublin, 1935).

75   *Gaelic Athletic Annual and County Directory, 1907–8*, p. 19.

76   *The Freeman's Journal (FJ)*, 19 July 1915.

77   *FJ*, 19 July 1915.

3.   Croke Park

1   Most recently, David Dickson, *Dublin: The Making of a Capital City* (London, 2014), pp. 424–60; also Jacinta Prunty, *Dublin Slums, 1800–1925: A Study of Urban Geography* (Dublin, 1999); and Francis Devine, Mary Clarke and Máire Kennedy (eds), *A Capital in Conflict: Dublin City and the 1913 Lockout* (Dublin, 2013).

2   Jacinta Prunty, 'From City Slums to City Sprawl: Dublin from 1800 to the Present', in Howard B. Clarke (ed.), *Irish Cities* (Cork and Dublin, 1995), p. 116.

3   *Ibid.*, Report of the Departmental Committee Appointed to Enquire into the Housing Conditions of the Working Class in Dublin (1914).

4   Richard McElligott, '"Quenching the Prairie Fire": the Collapse of the Gaelic Athletic Association in 1890s Ireland', *Irish Economic and Social History*, XXXXI (2014), pp. 53–73.

5   Marcus de Búrca, *The GAA: A History of the Gaelic Athletic Association* (Dublin, 1980), p. 88.

6   Mary Moran, *A Game of Our Own: Camogie's Story* (Dublin, 2011); see, also, essay by Eoghan Corry in this volume.

7   De Búrca, *op. cit.*, p. 107.

8   *Ibid.*, p. 113.

9   For a biographical profile of Dinneen, see Paul Rouse, 'Frank Brazil Dinneen, 1863–1916', *Dictionary of Irish Biography*, volume 3 (Dublin and Cambridge, 2009), pp. 327–8.

10   For an engaging account, see Tim Carey, *Croke Park: A History* (Cork, 2004), especially pp. 29–43.

11   Central Council Minutes, 6 July 1913 (GAA Museum and Archives, Croke Park).

12   *Ibid.*, 27 July 1913.

13   *Ibid.*, 17 August 1913.

14   *Ibid.*, 7 September, 14 September 1913.

15   *Ibid.*, 4 October 1913.

16   *Ibid.*, 1 November 1913.

17   *Ibid.*, 4 January 1914.

18   Local issues, including the exact site of the monument, contributed to the delay, rather than any difficulty with the funding.

19   Central Council Minutes, 27 June 1914.

20   Annual Convention (attached to Central Council Minutes), 23 April 1916.

21   De Búrca, *op. cit.*, p. 121.

22 See chapters in this volume by Cormac Moore and Richard McElligott.

23 *FJ*, 5 August 1918, p. 4.

24 See chapter in this volume by Mike Cronin.

25 Annual Convention report (attached to Central Council Minutes), 23 April 1916.

26 Minutes of Grounds Sub-Committee, 5 January, 18 January 1920.

27 Central Council Minutes, 26 May 1917.

28 Central Council Minutes, 11 October 1919.

29 *Ibid.*

30 Minutes of Grounds Sub-Committee, 12 inst. (probably December) 1919.

31 See essays by Cormac Moore and Mike Cronin in this volume; also Michael Foley, *The Bloodied Field: Croke Park 21 November 1920* (Dublin, 2014).

32 De Búrca, *op. cit.*, p. 148; thirteen spectators, one of whom died later in hospital, and one player were killed in the attack.

33 *Ibid.*, pp. 150–1.

34 The extent to which Croke Park had become busy with major inter-county games was reflected in the decision of the Dublin county board to seek a ground in the south of the city for a fixture list that was experiencing difficulty finding available grounds. Minutes of Dublin Senior Board Convention, 28 January 1923: '…[we] had to rely principally on Croke Park, and this was only available when not required by other Councils'.

35 Minutes of Standing Committee, 21 April 1922.

36 Central Council Minutes, 22 October 1922.

37 Central Council Minutes, 3 March 1923.

4. Luke O'Toole: Servant of the GAA

1 See Marcus de Búrca, 'Luke O'Toole', in James McGuire and James Quinn (eds), *Dictionary of Irish Biography*, Volume 7 (RIA/Cambridge, 2009), pp. 1003–4.

2 Pádraig O'Toole, *The Glory and the Anguish* (Galway, 1984), p. 15.

3 Thomas F. O'Sullivan, *Story of the GAA* (Dublin, 1916), p. 147.

4 Lawrence William White, *Dictionary of Irish Biography*, available from dib.cambridge.org; accessed on 30 November 2014.

5 W. F. Mandle, *The Gaelic Athletic Association and Irish Nationalist Politics 1884–1924* (Dublin, 1987), p. 130.

6 *Ibid.*, p. 134.

7 For studies on the ban rules, see Paul Rouse, 'Sport and the Politics of Culture: A History of the GAA Ban 1884–1971', (UCD, MA Thesis, 1991) and Cormac Moore, *The GAA v Douglas Hyde: The Removal of Ireland's First President as GAA Patron* (Cork, 2012).

8 *Longford Leader*, 10 December 1921, p. 3.

9 Marcus de Búrca, *The GAA: A History of the Gaelic Athletic Association* (Dublin, 1980), p. 68.

10 O'Toole, *op. cit.*, p. 39.

11 *The Gaelic Athlete*, 10 January 1914, p. 4.

12 O'Toole, *op. cit.*, p. 20.

13   *Ibid.,* p. 70.

14   GAA Annual Convention Meeting Minutes, 16 April 1911.

15   GAA Central Council Meeting Minutes/GAA/CC/01/02, 1 December 1913.

16   *The Anglo-Celt (AC),* 12 July 1913, p. 11.

17   *The Gaelic Athlete,* 7 February 1914, p. 2.

18   *The Kerryman,* 12 July 1913, p. 1.

19   GAA Central Council Meeting Minutes/GAA/CC/01/02, 27 July 1913.

20   *The Gaelic Athlete,* 11 January 1913, p. 5.

21   *AC,* 26 July 1913, p. 3.

22   GAA Annual Convention Meeting Minutes, 7 April 1912.

23   GAA Central Council Meeting Minutes/GAA/CC/01/02, 12 December 1912.

24   De Búrca, *op. cit.,* p. 95.

25   GAA Central Council Meeting Minutes/GAA/CC/01/02, 6 July 1913.

26   De Búrca, *op. cit.,* p. 93.

27   O'Toole, *op. cit.,* p. 19.

28   *Irish Independent,* 26 November 1913, p. 5.

29   De Búrca, *op. cit.,* p. 98.

30   *The Gaelic Athlete,* 27 December 1913, p. 3.

31   *Ibid.,* 17 January 1914, p. 4.

32   *Ibid.,* 18 April 1914, p. 4.

33   De Búrca, *op. cit.,* p. 94.

34   GAA Central Council Meeting Minutes/GAA/CC/01/02, 7 September 1913.

35   *The Gaelic Athlete,* 17 October 1914, p. 2.

36   William Murphy, 'The GAA during the Irish Revolution, 1913–1923', Mike Cronin, William Murphy, Paul Rouse (eds), *The Gaelic Athletic Association 1884–2009* (Dublin, 2009), p. 66.

37   *Ibid.,* p. 67.

38   GAA Annual Convention Meeting Minutes, 4 April 1915.

39   *The Gaelic Athlete,* 27 March 1915, p. 2.

40   GAA Central Council Meeting Minutes/GAA/CC/01/02, 3 October 1914.

41   *The Gaelic Athlete,* 31 October 1914, p. 2.

42   *Ibid.,* 3 October 1914, p. 2.

43   De Búrca, *op. cit.,* p. 99.

44   *The Gaelic Athlete,* 29 August 1914, p. 1.

45   De Búrca, *op. cit.,* p. 100.

46   *The Gaelic Athlete,* 15 May 1915, p. 2.

47   *Ibid.,* 1 January 1916, p. 4.

48   GAA Annual Convention Meeting Minutes, 23 April 1916.

49   Bureau of Military History (BMH), Witness Statement 1005: Liam Walsh, Waterford, p. 5.

50   Jim Walsh, *The Alderman and the GAA in his Time* (Kilkenny, 2013), p. 88.

51   *HC Debates*, 29 May 1916 vol. 82 cc 2381–6, available from hansard. millbanksystems.com; accessed on 14 December 2014.

52   O'Toole, *op. cit.,* p. 95.

53   *Ibid.,* p. 97.

54   GAA Central Council Meeting Minutes/GAA/CC/01/02, 28 May 1916.

55   De Búrca, *op. cit.,* p.104.

56   GAA Annual Convention Meeting Minutes, 8 April 1917.

57   GAA Central Council Meeting Minutes/GAA/CC/01/02, 3 December 1916.

58   De Búrca, *op. cit.,* p. 102.

59   GAA Central Council Meeting Minutes/GAA/CC/01/02, 28 May 1916.

60   *HC Debates*, 10 May 1916 vol. 82 cc 630–6, available from hansard. millbanksystems.com; accessed on 14 December 2014.

61   GAA Central Council Meeting Minutes/GAA/CC/01/02, 6 November 1916.

62   O'Toole, *op. cit.,* p. 101.

63   De Búrca, *op. cit.,* p. 106.

64   GAA Central Council Meeting Minutes/GAA/CC/01/02, 26 November 1916.

65   Mandle, *op. cit.,* p. 188 and *Meath Chronicle,* 13 April 1918, p. 1.

66   David Fitzpatrick, *Harry Boland's Irish Revolution* (Cork, 2003), p. 97.

67   GAA Central Council Meeting Minutes/GAA/CC/01/02, 26 November 1916.

68   *The Kerryman,* 2 December 1916, p. 1.

69   *Sunday Independent,* 26 November 1916, p. 4.

70   De Búrca, *op. cit.,* p. 110.

71   *Irish Independent,* 20 September 1919, p. 6.

72   O'Toole, *op. cit.,* p. 100.

73   *FJ,* 30 May 1917, p. 6.

74   GAA Central Council Meeting Minutes/GAA/CC/01/02, 6 August 1917.

75   O'Toole, *op. cit.,* p. 101.

76   *Meath Chronicle,* 13 April 1918, p. 1.

77   *The Gaelic Athlete,* 8 April 1916, p. 1.

78   GAA Annual Convention Meeting Minutes, 31 March 1918.

79   J. J. Walsh, *Recollections of a Rebel* (Tralee, 1944), pp. 16–17.

80   De Búrca, *op. cit.,* p. 111.

81   GAA Central Council Meeting Minutes/GAA/CC/01/02, 20 July 1918.

82   *Ibid.,* 20 July 1918.

83   *Ibid.,* 20 July 1918.

84   *FJ,* 2 August 1918, p. 3.

85   O'Toole, *op. cit.,* p. 109.

86   Mandle, *op. cit.,* p. 185.

87   Murphy, 'The GAA during the Irish Revolution, 1913–1923', Cronin, Murphy, Rouse (eds), *op. cit.,* p. 72.

88 GAA Central Council Meeting Minutes/GAA/CC/01/02, 17 November 1918.

89 *Ibid.*, 7 December 1918.

90 *The Kerryman*, 29 March 1919, p. 5.

91 Mandle, *op. cit.*, p. 187.

92 *Ibid.*

93 See O'Toole, *op. cit.*, p. 153, Fitzpatrick, *op. cit.*, p. 72, Fearghal McGarry, *Eoin O'Duffy: A Self-Made Hero* (Oxford, 2005), p. 26 and Michael Foley, *The Bloodied Field* (Dublin, 2014), p. 103.

94 McGarry, *op. cit.*, p. 26.

95 Fitzpatrick, *op. cit.*, p. 93.

96 *The Washington Post*, 27 August 1922, p. 14.

97 O'Toole, *op. cit.*, p. 117.

98 *Irish Independent*, 4 November 1921, p. 7.

99 David Leeson, 'Death in the Afternoon: The Croke Park Massacre, 21 November 1920', *Canadian Journal of History*, XXXVIII (April, 2003), p. 47.

100 Foley, *op. cit.*, p. 169.

101 *The Irish Press*, 14 February 1963, p. 8.

102 BMH, Witness Statement 679: John Shouldice, Dublin, p. 27.

103 Foley, *op. cit.*, p. 171–2.

104 *The Irish Times*, 28 October 2009, p. A7.

105 O'Toole, *op. cit.*, p. 126.

106 *FJ*, 23 November 1920, p. 4.

107 Tim Carey and Marcus de Búrca, 'Bloody Sunday 1920: New Evidence', *History Ireland*, Vol. 11 No. 2 (Summer, 2003), p. 10.

108 *The Irish Press*, 15 February 1963, p. 8.

109 *FJ*, 30 May 1921, p. 3.

110 Leeson, *op. cit.*, p. 55.

111 O'Toole, *op. cit.*, p. 127.

112 De Búrca, *op. cit.*, p. 19.

113 GAA Central Council Meeting Minutes/GAA/CC/01/02, 11 September 1921.

114 *Ibid.*, 2 October 1921.

115 *Ibid.*, 26 February 1922.

116 *Ibid.*, 20 May 1922.

117 *Ibid.*, 11 September 1921, 27 September 1921, 2 October 1921, 15 October 1922, 22 October 1922, 3 March 1923.

118 *Ibid.*, 17 December 1922.

119 Murphy, 'The GAA during the Irish Revolution, 1913–1923', Cronin, Murphy, Rouse (eds), *op. cit.*, p. 75.

120 GAA Central Council Meeting Minutes/GAA/CC/01/02, 17 December 1922.

121 *Ibid.*, 7 January 1923.

122 *Ibid.*, 23 January 1923.

123 O'Toole, *op. cit.*, p. 137, p. 146.

124 *Ibid.*, p. 152.

125 *Ibid.*, p. 171.

126 Marie Coleman, *Dictionary of Irish Biography,* available from dib.cambridge.org; accessed on 15 December 2014.

127 De Búrca, *op. cit.*, p. 145.

5. The GAA and the Irish Parliamentary Party, 1913–18

1 Stephen Gwynn, *John Redmond's Last Years* (London, 1919), p. 16.

2 Mike Cronin, 'Fighting for Ireland, Playing for England? The Nationalist History of the Gaelic Athletic Association and the English Influence on Irish Sport', *International Journal of the History of Sport*, 15, 3 (1998), 36–56; Neal Garnham, 'Accounting for the Early Success of the Gaelic Athletic Association', *Irish Historical Studies*, 34, 133 (2004), pp. 65–78.

3 Alvin Jackson, *Ireland, 1798–1998* (Oxford, 1999), p. 181.

4 Pádraig Puirséal, *The GAA in its Time* (Dublin, 1982), p. 35.

5 *Ibid.*, p. 48.

6 Paul Rouse, 'The Politics of Culture and Sport in Ireland: A History of the GAA Ban on Foreign Games, 1884–1971. Part One: 1884–1921', *International Journal of the History of Sport*, 10, 3 (1993), 336.

7 Michael Wheatley, *Nationalism and the Irish Party: Provincial Ireland, 1910–1916* (Oxford, 2005), p. 67.

8 Marcus de Búrca, *Michael Cusack and the GAA* (Dublin, 1989), pp. 110–12, 120, 124.

9 W. F. Mandle, 'Sport as Politics: the Gaelic Athletic Association, 1884–1916', in Richard Cashman and Michael McKernan (eds), *Sport in History: The Making of Modern Sporting History* (Queensland, 1979), p. 101; Pat Coen, *A History of the GAA in Killererin* (Killerin, 1984), pp. 9–12.

10 Puirséal, *op. cit.*, p. 83; Marcus de Búrca, *The GAA: A History of the Gaelic Athletic Association* ([1980] Dublin, 2000), p. 29; W. F. Mandle, *The Gaelic Athletic Association and Irish Nationalist Politics, 1884–1924* (Dublin, 1987), p. 66.

11 J. P. Kelly, *History of the Limerick GAA from Earliest Times to the Present Day* (Tralee, 1937), pp. 34, 64–5; Mandle, *op. cit.*, p. 35. Joyce's opposition to the resolution reflected the fact that he was also a founding member and treasurer of the Garryowen Rugby Football Club, and played in the first fifteen for both Garryowen and County Limerick. See Brian Donnelly, 'Michael Joyce: Squarerigger, Shannon Pilot and MP', *Old Limerick Journal*, 27 (1990), p. 43.

12 Puirséal, *op. cit.*, p. 83; de Búrca, *op. cit.*, p. 29.

13 Mandle, *op. cit.*, p. 66.

14 *Ibid.*, p. 102.

15 De Búrca, *op. cit.*, pp. 51–2.

16 Mandle, *op. cit.*, p. 130.

17 *The Tuam Herald*, 31 January 1903.

18 *Irish Examiner*, 27 October 1902; Mandle, *op. cit.*, p. 8, 17, 132; *The Connacht Tribune*, 14 August 1909.

19 Patrick Meehan, *The Members of Parliament for Laois and Offaly, 1801–1918* (Portlaoise, 1983), p. 64; *Limerick Leader*, 3 November 1951.

20 *HC Debates,* 22 May 1914, cols. 2272–4.

21 Patrick Maume, *The Long Gestation: Irish Nationalist Life, 1891–1918* (Dublin, 1999), pp. 105, 108.

22 John Redmond to John Dillon, Trinity College Dublin Archive, John Dillon Papers, Ms 6747/72; P. P. Sutton to John Redmond, NLI, Redmond Papers, Ms 15,239/3.

23 Wheatley, *op. cit.,* p. 66.

24 De Búrca, *op. cit.,* p. 72.

25 *Meath Chronicle*, 14 November 1903; *Sunday Independent*, 7 January 1906; *FJ,* 7 March 1910.

26 *Irish Independent*, 15 January 1906.

27 *FJ,* 19 October 1914.

28 *FJ,* 7 March 1910; Donal McGahon, '"The Light of the Village": William Field MP', *Blackrock Society Proceedings*, 9 (2001), 88.

29 De Búrca, *op. cit.,* p. 73; *FJ,* 7 March 1910.

30 *FJ,* 9 April 1910.

31 De Búrca, *op. cit.,* pp. 72, 87.

32 Secretary Connacht Council to Daniel Boyle, Trinity College Dublin Archive, John Dillon Papers, Ms 6752/63.

33 *The Times*, 15 January 1906.

34 Richard McElligott, *Forging a Kingdom: The GAA in Kerry, 1884–1934* (Cork, 2013), pp. 216, 220.

35 Wheatley, *op. cit.,* p. 67, 256. Also see David Fitzpatrick, *Politics and Irish Life, 1913–1921: Provincial Experience of War and Revolution* (Dublin, 1977), p. 112.

36 *FJ,* 15 December 1913.

37 *Ibid.*

38 De Búrca, *op. cit.,* p. 96.

39 James McConnel, *The Irish Parliamentary Party and the Third Home Rule Crisis* (Dublin, 2013), pp. 222–41; *FJ,* 15 December 1913.

40 *The Gaelic Athlete*, 2 March 1912.

41 Central Council Minutes, 1911, GAA/CC/01, GAA Library and Archive, Dublin; Central Council Minutes, 1912, GAA/CC/01, GAA Library and Archive, Dublin.

42 *Limerick Leader*, 15 April 1912.

43 *Limerick Leader*, 29 June 1912.

44 *The Gaelic Athlete*, 2 March 1912, p. 8.

45 *FJ,* 15 December 1913.

46 McElligott, *op. cit.,* p. 223, 225.

47 *FJ,* 19 October 1914.

48 Mandle, *op. cit.,* p. 168.

49 De Búrca, *op. cit.,* p. 99.

50 McConnel, *op. cit.,* p. 279.

51 De Búrca, *op. cit.,* p. 98.

52 McElligott, *op. cit.,* p. 230.

53   Mandle, *op. cit.*, p. 167; McElligott, *op. cit.*, p. 227, 230–1.

54   Fearghal McGarry, *The Rising: Ireland, Easter 1916* (Oxford, 2010), pp. 53–4; *The Times*, 30 December 1913.

55   McElligott, *op. cit.*, p. 234.

56   *FJ*, 1 February 1915; de Búrca, *op. cit.*, p. 99.

57   De Búrca, *op. cit.*, p. 99.

58   M. J. Kelly, *The Fenian Ideal and Irish Nationalism, 1882–1916* (Woodbridge, 2006), p. 160; Frank Dinneen to John Redmond, 30 September 1907, NLI, John Redmond Papers, Ms 15,247/8.

59   *Irish Examiner*, 22 April 1916; *Irish Independent*, 21 April 1916.

60   *Irish Examiner*, 10 December 1915.

61   *Ibid.*, 23 January 1915.

62   *Ibid.*, 6 September 1915.

63   *FJ*, 29 December 1916.

64   McConnel, *op. cit.*, p. 112.

65   *FJ*, 13 April 1916; *Irish Independent*, 13 April 1916.

66   *FJ*, 16 April 1916.

67   *Ibid.*

68   *Limerick Leader*, 19 April 1916.

69   *The Times*, 18 April 1916.

70   *The Connacht Tribune*, 22 April 1916.

71   *Limerick Leader*, 19 April 1916.

72   William Murphy, 'The GAA during the Irish Revolution', in Mike Cronin, William Murphy, and Paul Rouse (eds), *The Gaelic Athletic Association, 1884–2009* (Dublin, 2009), p. 68; de *Búrca, op. cit.*, p. 102.

73   Central Council Minutes, May 1916, GAA/CC/01, GAA Library and Archive, Dublin.

74   Mandle, *op. cit.*, pp. 178–9; de Búrca, *op. cit.*, p. 104.

75   Mandle, *op. cit.*, p. 180.

76   Mandle, *op. cit.*, p. 180.

77   De Búrca, *op. cit.*, p. 105.

78   Central Council Minutes, Nov. 1916, GAA/CC/01, GAA Library and Archive, Dublin; L J. O'Toole to John Redmond, 28 Nov. 1916, NLI, John Redmond Papers, Ms 15,262/9.

79   *Irish Independent*, 30 November 1916; *Irish Examiner*, 1 December 1916; Central Council Minutes, December 1916, GAA/CC/01, GAA Library and Archive, Dublin.

80   *Irish Examiner*, 15 December 1916.

81   Annual Convention Minutes, 3 March 1918, GAA/CC/01, GAA Library and Archive, Dublin.

82   De Búrca, *op. cit.*, p. 110.

83   Mandle, *op. cit.*, p. 181.

84   Fitzpatrick, *op. cit.*, p. 112; Peter Hart, *The IRA at War, 1916–1921* (Oxford, 2003), p. 55. Also see Peter Hart, *The IRA and its Enemies: Violence and Community in Cork, 1916–1923* (Oxford, 1999), pp. 211–12.

85   Fergus Campbell, *Land and Revolution: Nationalist Politics in the West of Ireland, 1891–1921* (Oxford, 2005), p. 223; Fergal McCluskey, *Fenians and Ribbonmen: The Development of Republican Politics in East Tyrone, 1898–1918* (Manchester, 2011), pp. 199–200.

86   Mandle, *op. cit.*, p. 177; *AC*, 15 April 1916.

87   *Longford Leader*, 9 June 1917; 8 September 1917.

88   *HC Debates*, 25 July 1918, col. 1978. 8 August 1918, col. 1641.

89   *HC Debates*, 1 August 1918, col. 801.

90   *The Munster Express*, 5 November 1926.

91   Fitzpatrick, *op. cit.*, p. 112.

6.   The GAA and the First World War, 1914–18

1   See for example, Richard McElligott, *Forging a Kingdom, The GAA in Kerry 1884–1934* (Dublin, 2013).

2   *The Gaelic Athlete*, 28 March 1914.

3   Secretary's Report, GAA Annual Convention 1914.

4   *The Gaelic Athlete*, 21 February 1914.

5   *Limerick Leader*, 26 January 1914.

6   *The Connacht Tribune*, 4 April 1914.

7   *FJ*, 13 April 1914.

8   *The Gaelic Athlete*, 14 February 1914.

9   See for example, *FJ*, 5 September 1914.

10   Tom Johnstone, *Orange, Green and Khaki: The Story of the Irish Regiments in the Great War, 1914–1918* (Dublin, 1992), p. 89; Paul Maguire, *Follow Them up from Carlow: Carlow's Lost Generation* (Naas, 2002), p. 89.

11   *Irish Independent*, 17 September 1914.

12   *Clonmel Chronicle*, 5 August 1914.

13   *Sport*, 15 August 1914.

14   *Clonmel Chronicle*, 8 August 1914.

15   *Sunday Independent*, 16 August 1914.

16   *Irish Independent*, 1 October 1915.

17   *Irish Independent*, 15 September 1914.

18   Edmund Van Esbeck, *One Hundred Years of Irish Rugby: The Official History of the IRFU* (Dublin, 1974), pp. 92–3.

19   *Irish Independent*, 12 September 1914.

20   *Sport*, 20 September 1914.

21   Neal Garnham, *Association Football and Society in Pre-Partition Ireland* (Belfast, 2004), pp.159–71.

22   *Irish Independent*, 24 February 1915.

23   *Ibid.*

24   *Ibid.*

25   *Cork Examiner*, 7 August 1914.

26   *The Gaelic Athlete,* 15 August 1914.

27   *Limerick Leader,* 12 August 1914.

28   See for example, *The Mayo News,* 15 August 1914.

29   *The Mayo News,* 21 November 1914.

30   *Limerick Leader,* 14 August 1914; 14 September 1914.

31   *Ibid.,* 28 September 1914.

32   *Cork Examiner,* 19 August 1914.

33   See Dónal McAnallen, '"The Greatest Amateur Association in the World"? The GAA and Amateurism', in Mike Cronin, William Murphy and Paul Rouse (eds), *The Gaelic Athletic Association 1884–2009* (Dublin, 2009), p. 165.

34   *The Clare Champion,* 29 August 1914.

35   Letter from M. Collier to Fr J. J. Kearney, 15 October 1914, in Bob O'Keeffe collection, GAA Museum, Croke Park.

36   *The Gaelic Athlete,* 15 August 1914.

37   *Kilkenny Journal,* 15 August 1914.

38   *The Gaelic Athlete,* December 1914, 'Xmas Double' Edition.

39   See for example, *Clonmel Chronicle,*12 August 1914; *Sport,* 15 August 1914; *Tipperary Star,* 4 September 1914.

40   *Sunday Independent,* 16 August 1914.

41   *Cork Examiner,* 31 August 1914.

42   *The Kerryman,* 20 February 1915.

43   *Sport,* 23 January 1915.

44   *The Gaelic Athlete,* 23 January 1915.

45   *FJ,* 8 March 1915.

46   *Sport,* 13 February 1915.

47   *Kilkenny Journal,* 14 April 1915.

48   *The Gaelic Athlete,* 10 April 1915.

49   *FJ,* 5 April 1915.

50   *Kilkenny Journal,* 10 March 1915.

51   *The Gaelic Athlete,* December 1914, 'X Mas Double' Edition.

52   See Marcus de Búrca, *The GAA: A History of the Gaelic Athletic Association* (Dublin, 1980), p. 100; *The Gaelic Athlete,* 20 December 1915; *Enniscorthy Echo,* 18 September 1915.

53   Neal Garnham, 'Accounting for the Early Success of the Gaelic Athletic Association', in *Irish Historical Studies,* 34, 133 (2004), p. 69.

54   T. F. O'Sullivan, *The Story of the GAA* (Dublin, 1916), p. 1.

55   *Meath Chronicle,* 26 September 1914.

56   *National Volunteer,* 8 May 1915.

57   *The Irish Times,* 29 April 1915.

58   *Cork Weekly Examiner,* 25 August 1917.

59   *Ibid.,* 9 June 1917.

60   *Ibid.,* 24 June 1917.

61 *Ibid.*, 19 May 1917.

62 *Ibid.*, 16 June 1917.

63 *FJ*, 13 December 1913.

64 *FJ*, 19 November 1915.

65 *The Mayo News,* 6 March 1915.

66 British Army Medal Index Card 1914–1920, *The National Archives,* Image Reference 20953.

67 *The Mayo News,* 31 July 1915.

68 James McGuinn, *Sligo Men in the Great War 1914–1918* (Cavan, 1994), p. 13.

69 Seán Kierse, *History of Smith O'Brien GAA Club, Killaloe 1886–1987* (Killaloe, 1991), p. 139.

70 *The Clare Champion,* 19 February 1916.

71 *The Gaelic Athlete,* 2 October 1915.

72 *The Clare Champion,* 22 January 1916.

73 *Ibid.*, 22 January 1916.

74 *Ibid.*, 5 December 1914.

75 *Ibid.*, 14 November 1914.

76 *Tipperary Star,* 23 October 1914; *Limerick Leader,* 21 September 1914.

77 Daniel McCarthy, *Ireland's Banner County: Clare from the Fall of Parnell to the Great War 1890–1918* (Ennis, 2002), p. 106.

78 John Fox (grand-nephew), interviewed by Ross O'Carroll (August, 2014).

79 Fox, *op. cit.*

80 Fox, *op. cit.*

81 Fox, *op. cit.*

82 *The Southern Star,* 11 September 1915.

83 *Ibid.*, 17 April 1915.

84 *The Gaelic Athlete,* 19 December 1914.

85 Dónal McAnallen, 'The Radicalisation of the Gaelic Athletic Association in Ulster, 1912–23: The Role of Owen O'Duffy', 31, 7, *The International Journal of the History of Sport* (2014), p. 708.

86 McAnallen, *op. cit.,* p. 710.

87 McAnallen, *op. cit.,* pp. 704–23.

88 McAnallen, *op. cit.,* p. 710.

89 *FJ*, 8 October 1918.

90 *FJ*, 25 October 1915.

91 *Cork Weekly Examiner,* 10 August 1918.

92 William Murphy, 'The GAA during the Irish Revolution, 1913–23', in Mike Cronin, Murphy and Rouse, *op. cit.,* p. 64.

93 *Cork Weekly Examiner,* 25 May 1918.

94 *The Clare Champion,* 3 July 1915.

95 *Irish Examiner,* 4 January 1915.

96 *Cork Examiner,* 19 August 1914.

97 *The Connacht Tribune,* 12 April 1919.

98   *Ibid.,* 12 April 1919.

99   *Ibid.,* 12 April 1919.

100 Paul Rouse, 'Empires of Sport: Enniscorthy, 1880–1920', cited in Colm Toibín (ed.), *Enniscorthy: A History* (Wexford, 2010), p. 16.

101 *Enniscorthy Echo,* 24 October 1914.

102 *Enniscorthy Echo,* 31 October 1914.

103 *The Irish Times,* 9 February 1915.

104 *Enniscorthy Echo,* 24 October 1914.

105 *The Irish Times,* 26 June 1914.

106 *The Gaelic Athlete,* 27 March 1915.

107 *Ibid.,* 3 April 1915.

108 *The Nenagh Guardian,* 24 October 1914.

109 British Army Victoria Cross report, National Archives, Image reference 299.

110 *Cork Weekly Examiner,* 27 February 1915.

111 *Ibid.,* 3 April 1915.

112 *Limerick Leader,* 19 April 1916.

113 *Cork Weekly Examiner,* 13 April 1918.

114 Phil O'Neill, *History of the GAA 1910–1930* (Kilkenny, 1931), p. 99.

115 Jim Cronin, *Munster GAA Story* (Ennis, 1984), p. 103.

116 *AC,* 21 November 1914.

117 *The Irish Times,* 3 August 1915; *The Leitrim Observer,* 7 August 1915.

118 McGuinn, *op. cit.,* p. 10.

119 *The Mayo News,* 25 January 1919.

120 Annual Convention, 20 April 1919.

121 Rouse, *op. cit.,* p. 20.

122 See for example, *Donegal News,* 7 August 1915; and Paul Melia 'Recruit, Recruit, Recruit: Why the Irish Volunteered', in *Irish Independent,* 11 May 2014.

123 *Donegal News,* 19 September 1914.

124 Irish Census 1911.

125 Seamus and Joe Seery, 'World War 1 – The Wexford Casualties', available from taghmon. com/vol3/chapter6/chapter6.htm; accessed 18 August 2014.

126 British Army Medal Card, The National Archives, Image reference 4483.

127 Irish Census 1911.

128 *Ibid.*

129 *Skibbereen Eagle,* 1 May 1915.

130 McAnallen, *op. cit.,* p. 708.

131 Irish Census 1911.

132 Fox, *op. cit.*

7. The GAA Unionism and Partition, 1913–23

1   In this chapter, 'Unionism/t' will be capitalised for references to the political party or its representatives, and will appear in lower case for references to ordinary citizens and their unionist sentiments.

2   United Kingdom House of Commons debates (*Hansard*), 5th series vol. 44, cols 2118–2119, 31 July 1912; *IN*, 30 July 1912, 1 August 1912.

3   *BNL*, 26 August 1912; *IN*, 26 August 1912; *Ulster Guardian*, 31 August 1912.

4   *DD*, 19 February 1916. See also *AC*, 30 September 1911, 22 March 1913.

5   *AC*, 21 April 1917.

6   *UKHC*, 5th series vol. 62, cols 2227–2228, 22 May 1914.

7   *Derry People*, 27 June 1914; *AC*, 18 July 1914.

8   *IN*, 28 July 1914.

9   *AC*, 3 October 1914. See also W. F. Mandle, *The Gaelic Athletic Association and Irish Nationalist Politics, 1884–1924* (Dublin, 1987), pp. 171–5.

10 *The Gaelic Athlete*, 27 March 1915.

11 *UKHC*, 5th series vol. 71, cols 704–705, 28 April 1915.

12 *AC*, 24 July 1915.

13 *The Times*, 18 April 1916.

14 *UKHC*, 5th series vol. 81, cols 2597–2598, 2 May 1916.

15 *Ibid.*, vol. 82, cols. 20–22, 3 May 1916; *ibid.*, vol. 83, col. 1519, 5 July 1916. See also *ibid.*, vol. 86, col. 553, 18 October 1916.

16 Marcus de Búrca, *The GAA: A History of the Gaelic Athletic Association* (Dublin, 1980), pp. 102–3.

17 *DD*, 3 June 1916.

18 *AC*, 10 June 1916.

19 *AC*, 1 July 1916.

20 *AC*, 5 August 1916.

21 *DD*, 17 February 1917.

22 David McGuinness, Witness Statement 417, BMH, NAI, p. 8; Thomas Fox (BMH WS 365), p. 1. 23 *IN*, 11 April 1917, 16 April 1917, 16 May 1917; *ISN*, 21 July 1917.

24 *UKHC*, 5th series vol. 93, cols 2464–2465, 2480, 24 May 1917.

25 Report of County Inspector, RIC, for Monaghan, March 1918, PRO CO 904/105; cited in Fearghal McGarry, *Eoin O'Duffy: A Self-Made Hero* (Oxford, 2005), p. 35.

26 *IN*, 2 April 1918.

27 *DD*, 2 February 1918; John McCoy (BMH WS 492), p. 26.

28 *AC*, 6 July 1918, 10 August 1918, 19 October 1918, 2 November 1918; Francis Tummon (BMH WS 820), pp. 6–7.

29 *Armagh Guardian*, 7 June 1918. See also Ulster Council GAA Minutes, convention of 16 March 1918, Cardinal Ó Fiaich Library and Archive.

30 *UKHC*, 5th series vol. 109, col. 152, 29 July 1918.

31 *DD,* 10 August 1918. See also *UH*, 24 August 1918.

32 *FJ*, 13 March 1919; *AC,* 16 August 1919.

33   *ISN*, 29 March 1919, 12 April 1919.

34   *FS*, 21 August 1920.

35   Pearse Lawlor, *The Burnings 1920* (Cork, 2009), pp. 116, 119; *IN*, 23 April 1904, 8 November 1940.

36   Jim McDermott, *Northern Divisions: The Old IRA and the Belfast Pogroms 1920–22* (Belfast, 2001), pp. 60–1, 285; *IN*, 27 September 1920.

37   *UKHC*, 5th series vol. 135, cols 39–42, 22 November 1920; *FJ*, 23 November 1920; *BNL*, 23 November 1920.

38   *FS*, 29 January 1921.

39   McDermott, *Northern Divisions*, p. 101; *BNL*, 11 July 1921; *IN*, 12 July 1921.

40   *Irish News*, 5 September 1921.

41   *DJ*, 20 May 1921.

42   Seamus McCluskey, *The GAA in County Monaghan: A History* (Monaghan, 1984), pp. 39–41.

43   Robert Lynch, *The Northern IRA and the Early Years of Partition 1920–22* (Dublin, 2006), p. 100. See also *FJ*, 17 January 1922; *IN*, 17 January 1922.

44   *IN*, 17 January 1922.

45   Northern Ireland House of Commons debates (*Hansard*; hereafter NIHC), vol. 2, col. 26, 14 March 1922. See also PRONI CAB 4/20.

46   *UKHC*, 5th series vol. 150, cols 1009–10, on 15 February 1922. See also House of Lords debates (*Hansard*), 5th series vol. 49, cols. 135–136, 14 February 1922.

47   Patrick Buckland, *The Factory of Grievances: Devolved Government in Northern Ireland 1921–39* (Dublin, 1979), p. 209; minutes of Cabinet meeting, 14 February 1922, and draft conclusion of Cabinet meeting, 13 March 1922, PRONI CAB/4/32/12.

48   Ewing Gilfillan, District Inspector, on behalf of Inspector-General, RUC, to secretary, Ministry of Home Affairs, 6 April 1923, PRONI HA/32/1/366.

49   D. I.'s Office, RUC Dungannon, to County Inspector, County Tyrone, RUC, 15 February 1923, PRONI HA/5/1237, refers to 'a Gaelic League convention in Dublin', probably alluding to the GAA congress that week.

50   Denise Kleinrichert, *Republican Internment and the Prison Ship* Argenta*, 1922* (Dublin, 2001), pp. 23, 33, 52, 62, 136, 335–368 *passim*.

51   Intelligence file on recommended internment of Daniel Dempsey, *c.* June 1922, PRONI HA/32/1/155.

52   RUC intelligence file on John Henry King, *c.* 15 February 1923, PRONI HA/5/2325; W. F. Curry, District Inspector's Office, RUC Newcastle, to CI, County Down, 24 March 1923, *ibid.*

53   See Kleinrichert, *op. cit.*, pp. 337, 341, 353, 360, 362.

54   RUC intelligence file on Peter Tohall, no date (n. d.), 1923, Peter Tohall, Moy, County Tyrone: application to return to Northern Ireland from Gormanston Camp, PRONI HA/5/1237.

55   Joe Connellan, 'Down's Early Days' in *Ulster Games Annual*, 1966, p. 121.

56   *DJ*, 18 August 1922.

57   *Irish Independent*, 2 April 1923.

58 *Ardchomhairle, Cumann Lúthchleas Gael, An Treoraí Oifigúil*, 1922–3 edn; c. f. 1919–20 edn, pp. 30–1.

59 GAA Central Council Minutes, meeting of 19 October 1923, GAA Museum and Archive, Croke Park, GAA/CC/01/02.

60 Inspector-General's Office, RUC, to Ministry of Home Affairs, 18 March 1925, PRONI HA/8/237.

61 *NIHC*, vol. 2, col. 1081, 19 October 1922.

62 *NIHC*, vol. 3, col. 273, 27 March 1923.

63 *NIHC*, vol. 2, col. 1050, 17 October 1922.

64 UC Minutes, meeting of 27 October 1923, CÓFLA.

65 *UH*, 16 February 1924.

66 *Tyrone Courier*, 7 February 1924; UC Minutes, meeting of 16 February 1924, CÓFLA.

67 UC Minutes, 9 June 1923, CÓFLA.

68 *Frav-lio Queen's*, vol. 1 no. 1 (June 1922), p. 6; *ibid.*, vol. 2 no. 2 (March 1923), pp. 3, 5; vol. 2 no. 3 (June 1923), pp. 7–8.

69 Dáil Éireann debates, vol. 1, cols 2125–2126, 16 November 1922.

70 Dónal McAnallen, *The Cups that Cheered: A History of the Sigerson, Fitzgibbon and Higher Education Gaelic Games* (Cork, 2012), pp. 128–33.

71 Minutes of Belfast Corporation Cemeteries and Parks Committee, meetings of 16 November 1921, 1 March 1922, 13 September 1922, 11 October 1922, PRONI LA/7/11AB/9.

72 *Ibid.*, meeting of 22 November 1922, PRONI LA/7/11AB/9.

73 *DJ*, 11 February 1921.

74 *Ibid.*, 15 August 1923.

75 *UH*, 10 March 1923, 6 October 1923.

76 *AC*, 28 July 1923.

77 *AC*, 28 July 1923.

78 Con Short, *The Crossmaglen GAA Story 1887–1987* (Crossmaglen, 1987), p. 80.

79 *Dungannon Democrat*, 22 August 1923.

80 Síghle Nic An Ultaigh, *Ó Shíol go Bláth: An Dún – The GAA Story*, p. 101.

81 *FJ*, 30 October 1923.

8. The GAA, the 1916 Rising and its Aftermath to 1918

1   W. F. Mandle estimated from contemporary police reports that the GAA had a national membership of over 17,000, spread across 500 clubs. However, Mandle admitted that police records for early 1916 were not comprehensive and hence very conservative in their estimates. Considering the Association mobilised at least 45,000 people for its 'Gaelic Sunday' demonstration in August 1918, the suspicion is that the GAA's membership was far higher. W. F. Mandle, *The Gaelic Athletic Association and Irish Nationalist Politics 1884–1924* (Dublin, 1987), p. 175.

2   MacNeill set out his argument in an article entitled the 'The North Began' published in the Gaelic League's newspaper, *An Claidheamh Soluis*, 1 November 1913.

3   *Dublin Leader*, 25 October 1913.

4   NAI, The British in Ireland Collection CO 904, Microfilm Archive (MFA), 54/53: Inspector General & County Inspector (IG & CI) Monthly Confidential Reports September–December 1913, IG Monthly Confidential Report November 1913, 15 December 1913, 4950/S.

5   *FJ*, 26 November, 1913.

6   Mike Cronin, Mark Duncan, and Paul Rouse (eds), *The GAA: A People's History* (Cork, 2009), p. 148.

7   See Richard McElligott, *Forging a Kingdom: The GAA in Kerry 1884–1934* (Cork, 2013), pp. 226–36.

8   *Irish Independent*, 21 September 1914.

9   NAI, CO 904, MFA 54/55: IG & CI Monthly Confidential Reports July–December 1914, IG Confidential Monthly Report November 1914, 12 December 1914, 7424/S.

10   Pat O'Shea, *Trail Blazers: A Century of Laune Rangers 1888–1988* (Killorglin, 1988), p. 54.

11   *The Gaelic Athlete*, 3 October 1914.

12   These included the Kerry, Limerick, Armagh, Belfast, Cavan, Derry, Down, Tyrone, Kildare, Kilkenny, Meath and Roscommon county boards. Mandle, *op. cit.*, p. 174; Dónal McAnallen, 'The Radicalisation of the Gaelic Athletic Association in Ulster, 1912–1923: The Role of Owen O'Duffy', in *The International Journal of the History of Sport*, Vol. 31, No. 7 (2014), p. 707.

13   Charles Townshend, *Easter 1916: The Irish Rebellion* (London, 2006), p. 94.

14   T. Ryle Dwyer, *Tans, Terror and Troubles: Kerry's Real Fighting Story 1913–23* (Cork, 2001), p. 60.

15   By 1890, the IRB was said to hold every position on the Kerry GAA county board, while a reformed board in 1900 was said to contain seven IRB members. NAI, Crime Branch Special (CBS) Index, RIC South Western Division, Connection between the IRB and GAA in Clare and Kerry, 15 April 1890, 126/S; CBS, Precis Box No. 2, Home Office Crime Department Special Branch, Precis of Information on Secret Societies January 1898–December 1899, 22189/S.

16   Anthony J. Gaughan, *Austin Stack: Portrait of a Separatist* (Dublin, 1977), p. 30.

17   NAI, BMH Interviews, Witness Statement (WS) 135: Tadgh Kennedy, Tralee, pp. 3–4.

18   *Ibid.*, WS 132: Michael Spillane, Killarney, p. 2.

19   Mandle, *op. cit.*, p. 175.

20   NAI, CO 904, MFA 54/58, 10893/S.

21   NAI, CO 904, MFA 54/58, 10664/S.

22   F. S. L. Lyons, *Ireland Since the Famine* (London, 1985), p. 353.

23   Gaughan, *op. cit.*, p. 45.

24   *The Kerryman*, 11 March 1916.

25   Townshend, *op. cit.*, p. 131.

26   William Murphy, 'The GAA during the Irish Revolution, 1913–23', in Mike Cronin, William Murphy and Paul Rouse (eds), *The Gaelic Athletic Association, 1884–2009* (Dublin, 2009), pp. 63–4.

27   CPA, GAA/CC/01/02, Central Council Minute Books: 1911–1925: 23 April 1916.

28   Curiously, however, Walsh stated that Nowlan and the others were now aware of what was going to transpire and had wished him luck. J. J. Walsh, *Recollections of a Rebel* (Tralee,

1944), p. 36. 29 Marcus de Búrca, *The GAA: A History of the Gaelic Athletic Association* ([1980] Dublin, 1999), p. 101.

30   William Nolan (ed.), *The Gaelic Athletic Association in Dublin 1884–2000, Vol. 1 1884–1959* (Dublin, 2005), pp. 149–61.

31   *Ibid.*, p. 128.

32   Edmundo Murray, 'Éamon Bulfin [Eduardo, Ned] (1892–1968) Irish republican and diplomatist', in *Irish Migration Studies in Latin America*, Vol. 2, No. 1 (2004), p. 5.

33   Nolan, *op. cit.*, p. 130.

34   Townshend, *op. cit.,* p. 177.

35   *The Irish Times*, 3 May 1916.

36   Seán Ó Lúing, *I Die in A Good Cause* (Tralee, 1970), p. 80.

37   From the *Daily Sketch*, reprinted in *Kerry Sentinel*, 6 May 1916.

38   Fergus Campbell, 'The Easter Rising in Galway', in *History Ireland*, Vol. 14, No. 2 (2006), p. 24.

39   Robert Brennan, *Allegiance* (Dublin, 1950), pp. 51, 64.

40   *FJ*, 6 May 1916.

41   They were Pádraig Pearse, Seán McDermott, Con Colbert, Michael O'Hanrahan and Eamonn Ceantt. Mandle, *op. cit.*, p. 178.

42   Mike Cronin, 'Defenders of a Nation? The Gaelic Athletic Association and Irish Nationalist Identity', in *Irish Political Studies*, No. 11 (1996), p. 7.

43   Stack, for example, was a prominent member of the Gaelic League's Tralee branch. *Kerry Sentinel*, 6 February 1909.

44   For example, in 1911, the future GAA President Dan McCarthy stated he wanted GAA men 'to train and be physically strong [so that] when the time comes the hurlers will cast away the camán for the steel that will drive the Saxon from our land'. *Wicklow People*, 21 January 1911.

45   De Búrca, *op. cit.*, p. 96.

46   Alvin Jackson, *Ireland 1798–1998, Politics and War* (Oxford, 1999), p. 206.

47   NAI, CBS, District Inspectors' Crime Special (DICS) Reports Box 2, South Western Division: Monthly Report of DI Jones, January 1892, 1 February 1892, 521/S/8031.

48   *Kerry Sentinel*, 29 April 1916.

49   Michael Laffan, *The Resurrection of Ireland: The Sinn Féin Party, 1916–1923* (Cambridge, 1999), p. 53.

50   *FJ*, 8 May 1916.

51   Lyons, *op. cit.*, p. 376.

52   NLI, J. J. O'Connell Papers, Autobiographical Account of events leading to 1916, MS 22, 117, p. 3.

53   NAI, BMH, WS 801: William Mullins, Tralee, p. 1.

54   Joseph E. A. Connell, 'Sport in Frongoch', in *History Ireland*, Vol. 20, No. 4 (July/August 2012), p. 66.

55   Mandle, *op. cit.*, p. 178.

56   Thomas B. Looney, *A King in the Kingdom of Kings: Dick Fitzgerald* (Cork, 2008), p. 123.

57   *Kerry Sentinel*, 22 July 1916.

58 Murphy, *op. cit.*, p. 71.

59 NLI, *The Royal Commission on the Rebellion in Ireland, Minutes of Evidence and Appendix of Documents*, Ir 94109 12, p. 3.

60 *Ibid.*, p. 58.

61 De Búrca, *op. cit.*, p. 102.

62 The Central Council stated it 'strongly protests against the misrepresentations of the aims and objects of the Gaelic Athletic Association as tendered to the Commission by Sir Matthew Nathan and other witnesses. And thinks that all such allegations should, at least, be accompanied by definite proofs.' CPA, GAA/CC/01/02, Central Council Minute Books: 1911–1925: 28 May 1916.

63 De Búrca, *op. cit.,* p. 103.

64 *Kerry Sentinel,* 7 June 1916.

65 *Kerry Sentinel*, 12 August 1916.

66 Paul Bew, 'The Real Importance of Sir Roger Casement', in *History Ireland*, Vol. 2, No. 2 (1994), p. 45.

67 NAI, CO 904, MFA 54/58, 11179/S.

68 Joost Augustine, *From Public Defiance to Guerrilla Warfare: The Radicalisation of the Irish Republican Army – A Comparative Analysis, 1916–1921* (Amsterdam, 1994), p. 252.

69 Mandle, *op. cit.*, p. 180.

70 NAI, MFA CO 904, 54/60, 12427/S.

71 As a consequence, a Special Meeting of the Central Council was called at which the Association decided to send a deputation to the Inspector General of the RIC to ascertain under what grounds members of the force felt they were entitled to force entry into GAA events. CPA, GAA/CC/01/02, Central Council Minute Books: 1911–1925: 22 September 1916.

72 Sinn Féin was formed in 1905 as a political grouping that advocated the establishment of an independent Ireland. Kevin Rafter, *Sinn Féin 1905–2005: In the Shadow of Gunmen* (Dublin, 2005), p. 43.

73 J. J. Lee, *Ireland 1912–1985 Politics and Society* (Cambridge, 1989), p. 38.

74 Diarmaid Ferriter, *The Transformation of Ireland 1900–2000* (London, 2004), p. 155.

75 NAI, CO 904, MFA 54/60, 12427/S.

76 *Kerry Sentinel,* 13 January 1917.

77 McAnallen, *op. cit.*, p. 710.

78 *Kerry Sentinel,* 23 June 1917.

79 *Ibid.*, 11 August 1917.

80 *FJ*, 26 November 1917.

81 *Kerry Sentinel,* 25 August 1917; *FJ*, 1 September 1917.

82 *The Death of Thomas Ashe: Full Report of the Inquest* (Dublin, 1917), p. 84.

83 Dwyer, *op. cit.*, p. 121.

84 *FJ*, 29 September 1917.

85 *Ibid.*, 1 October 1917.

86 NAI, CO 904, MFA 54/62, 17685/S.

87 Peter Hart, *The IRA at War, 1916–1923* (Oxford, 2003), p. 55; David Fitzpatrick, *Politics and Irish Life, 1913–1921: Provincial Experience of War and Revolution* (Cork, 1998), p. 112.

88   NAI, CO 904, MFA 54/62, 14679/S.

89   Fitzpatrick, *op. cit.*, p. 130.

90   Jim Cronin, *Munster GAA Story* (Ennis, 1986), p. 107.

91   De Búrca, *op. cit.*, p. 109.

92   *Kerry Sentinel*, 13 October 1917.

93   Terence Dooley, *The Land for the People: The Land Question in Independent Ireland* (Dublin, 2004), pp. 31–4.

94   Maurice O'Connor, *Keel GAA: A Club History* (Naas, 1991), p. 74.

95   *DD*, 10 August 1918.

96   Murphy, *op. cit.*, p. 69.

97   Fitzpatrick, *op. cit.*, p. 169. Such an example in Kerry was Michael Leen, captain of the Castleisland hurling team, who reorganised the local Volunteer company in 1917. NAI, BMH, WS 1190: Michael Pierce, Castleisland, pp. 2–3

98   *FJ*, 8 April 1918.

99   CPA, GAA/CC/01/02, Central Council Minute Books: 1911–1925: 14 April 1918.

100 *FJ*, 23/24 April 1918.

101 *The Kerryman*, 4 May 1918.

102 NAI, CO 904, MFA 54/63, 18085/S.

103 *FJ*, 5 July 1918.

104 Murphy, *op. cit.*, p. 68.

105 Quoted in *Kerry Sentinel*, 13 July 1918.

106 Andrew McGuire and David Hassan, 'Cultural Nationalism, Gaelic Sunday and the Gaelic Athletic Association in Early Twentieth Century Ireland', in *The International Journal of the History of Sport*, Vol. 29, No. 6 (2012), p. 916.

107 In Down and Offaly, several games were dispersed by RIC baton charges. In Cootehill, the Ulster semi-final between Armagh and Cavan had to be abandoned when local police took possession of the field and warned that forcible methods would be resorted to if any attempt was made to play the game. Under duress, the 3,000-strong attendance returned to the town where the local parish priest, Fr O'Connell, addressed them, calling for self-restraint and for the crowds to return home quietly. In Tuam, the police were reported to have taken the names of all players and officials involved in local club ties. Meanwhile, in Kildare, a match between Milltown and Rathangan was abandoned when the police entered the field and took down the goalposts to prevent the match taking place. *Sport*, 13 July 1918.

108 CPA, GAA/CC/01/02, Central Council Minute Books: 1911–1925: 5 November 1918.

109 De Búrca, *op. cit.*, p. 107.

110 *Sport*, 17 February 1917.

111 Murphy, *op. cit.*, p. 70.

112 CPA, GAA/CC/01/02, Central Council Minute Books: 1911–1925: 20 July 1918. The GAA's Secretary, Luke O'Toole, told those assembled that after visiting Dublin Castle he was informed that GAA events would only be allowed to proceed if a permit was first obtained from the local police and military authorities. The meeting unanimously decided that no permit would be sought under any circumstances. The Central Council order that 'no member of the Association shall take part in any competition where such a permit has been obtained … Anyone that disobeyed this rule would be automatically and indefinitely suspended.'

113 The arrangements were exhaustive, and upwards of 54,000 Gaels were expected to participate. Sixteen games in separate locations were organised in north Tipperary. In Cavan, seventeen matches were planned, while in Monaghan twenty-seven matches were fixed. Dublin arranged to host twenty-five matches, Cork forty, Wexford forty-two and Kildare seventeen. *Sport*, 3/10 August 1918.

114 Matches were also reported to have been played between nationalist prisoners in a Belfast jail. *Sport*, 10 August 1918.

115 Indeed, there were reports in *The Freeman's Journal* that Dublin Castle, possibly fearful that any attempt to interfere with the protest could lead to further unrest and bloodshed, had sent a circular on 31 July instructing local police not to interfere. *FJ*, 1 August 1918.

116 De Búrca, *op. cit.*, p. 111.

117 Murphy, *op. cit.*, p. 72.

118 Laffan, *The Resurrection of Ireland*, pp. 164–6.

119 *Kerry Weekly Reporter*, 12 April 1919.

120 CPA, Annual Congress Minute Books 1911–1927: 20 April 1919.

121 Murphy, *op. cit.*, p. 65.

9. The GAA in a Time of Guerrilla War and Civil Strife, 1918–23

1 Breandán Ó hEithir, *Over the Bar: A Personal Relationship with the GAA* (Dublin, 1991), p. 20.

2 For an assessment of the GAA Museum see Mike Cronin, 'Croke Park: Museum, Stadium and Shrine for the Nation' in Murray Phillips (ed.), *Representing the Sporting Past in Museums and Halls of Fame* (London, 2012).

3 Mike Cronin, Mark Duncan and Paul Rouse, *The GAA: A People's History* (Cork, 2009), p. 154. Specifically on Bloody Sunday, see Michael Foley, *The Bloodied Field: Croke Park 21 November 1920* (Dublin, 2014).

4 William Murphy, 'The GAA during the Irish Revolution, 1919–23' in Mike Cronin, William Murphy and Paul Rouse (eds), *The Gaelic Athletic Association 1884–2009* (Dublin, 2009), p. 61.

5 Clearly, the near disastrous effects of the Parnell split on the GAA are an important legacy when it comes to the thinking of the organisation during the Irish revolutionary period. Internal cohesion and maintenance of the organisation and its games are the key objectives.

6 The numbers of Irishmen serving in and dying during the First World War are highly complex and not commonly agreed. For details, see *The Irish Times*, 2 August 2014, p. 4.

7 The numbers in relation to deaths during these conflicts have varied, but the best recent figures have emerged from Eunan O'Halpin's project, *The Dead of the Irish Revolution*, which lists 2,141 deaths in the years 1917–21.

8 For an assessment of where the Irish revolutionary violence was most intense geographically, see Peter Hart, *The IRA at War, 1916–23* (Oxford, 2003), chapter 2.

9 *Irish Independent*, 6 December 1922, p. 11.

10 *Irish Examiner*, 8 November 1919, p. 5.

11 David Fitzpatrick (ed.), *Terror in Ireland: 1916–1923* (Dublin, 2012), pp. 8–9.

12   Hart, *op. cit.,* p. 55.

13   *Irish Independent,* 22 December 1919, p. 7.

14   *Irish Examiner,* 31 August 1923, p. 4.

15   *Irish Independent,* 28 October 1920, p. 7.

16   Murphy, *op. cit.,* p. 76.

17   Diarmaid Ferriter, *The Transformation of Ireland, 1900–2000* (London, 2004), p. 354.

18   *Irish Independent,* 28 February 1923, p. 8.

19   *Ibid.,* 28 March, 1921, p. 7.

20   *Meath Chronicle,* 4 May 1919, p. 1.

21   *Irish Independent,* 27 July 1923, p. 10.

22   *Ibid.,* 27 March 1923, p. 8.

23   For the early struggles of Donegal, for example, see Conor Curran, *Sport in Donegal: A History* (Dublin, 2010).

24   See, for example, the report on the 1920 Annual Convention and a motion for a GAA organiser to be appointed to Donegal to promote the games, *UH,* 10 April 1920, p. 6. Also see *Fermanagh Herald,* 5 May 1923, p. 6, for discussion at an Ulster Provincial Council meeting of the relative strength of the games in Ulster and the need for support from Central Council. At the meeting, the Tyrone representative stated that, while there were twenty-four active clubs in the county, there was no county board. The situation was the same in Fermanagh and Down.

25   *The Irish Times,* 15 July 1918, p. 3.

26   Andrew McGuire and David Hassan, 'Cultural Nationalism, Gaelic Sunday and the Gaelic Athletic Association in Early Twentieth-Century Ireland', *International Journal of the History of Sport,* 1: 12 (2012), p. 7.

27   Some later estimates ranged as high as 100,000; Marcus de Búrca, *The GAA: A History of the Gaelic Athletic Association* (Dublin, 1980), p. 142.

28   McGuire and Hassan, *op. cit.,* pp. 9–10.

29   *Irish Independent,* 21 April 1919, p. 5.

30   *Connacht Tribune,* 26 April 1919, p. 5.

31   *Irish Independent,* 21 April 1919, p. 3.

32   *Ibid.,* 19 April 1919, p. 5.

33   On Bloody Sunday, see Anne Dolan, 'Killing and Bloody Sunday, November 1920', *Historical Studies,* 49 (2006), pp. 789–810 and David Leeson, 'Death in the Afternoon: The Croke Park Massacre, 21 November 1920', *Canadian Journal of History,* 38 (2003), pp. 43–67.

34   Jane Leonard, 'English Dogs or Poor Devils? The Dead of Bloody Sunday Morning' in Fitzpatrick, *op. cit.,* p. 105.

35   It was notable in 2007 when the English rugby team played at Croke Park that they were given a historical lecture about the events of Bloody Sunday so that they could understand and respect the ground that they would play on and the sensibilities involved. See *The Irish Times,* 28 February 2009, p. 24.

36   On prisons, see Murphy, *op. cit.,* pp. 70–1.

37   De Búrca, *op. cit.,* p. 151.

38   De Búrca, *op. cit.,* pp. 155–7, and W. F. Mandle, *The GAA and Irish Nationalist Politics, 1884–1924* (London, 1987), pp. 203–7.

39   On Kerry and the complexity of Civil War politics in the GAA in the county, see Richard McElligott, *Forging a Kingdom: The GAA in Kerry, 1884–1934* (Cork, 2013).

40   On the Tailteann Games, see Mike Cronin, 'Projecting the Nation through Sport and Culture: Ireland, Aonach Tailteann and the Irish Free State', *Journal of Contemporary History,* 38, 3 (2003), pp. 395–411.

10. The GAA and Irish Political Prisoners, 1916–23

1   Parnell was imprisoned in Kilmainham Jail in 1881 under the terms of Protection of the Person and Property Act, 1881. Davitt was imprisoned on two occasions: in 1870 he was convicted of 'Treason Felony' and served seven years of a fifteen-year sentence in Dartmoor Prison; following an outspoken speech against the Chief Secretary of Ireland, Davitt's ticket of leave was revoked in 1881 and he spent one year in Portland Prison. Seán McConville, *Irish Political Prisoners, 1848–1922, Theatres of War* (London, 2005).

2   At the 1887 Convention it was Edward Bennett's refusal to pass a motion of sympathy with the imprisoned William O'Brien that caused most consternation among constitutional nationalists; at the 1888 Convention the IRB proposed the imprisoned John Mandeville as president as a means of stopping Davin's return to the post. W. F. Mandle, *The Gaelic Athletic Association and Irish Nationalist Politics 1884–1924* (Dublin, 1987).

3   See Chapter 3 of Fergus Campbell, *Land and Revolution: Nationalist Politics in the West of Ireland 1891–1921* (Oxford, 2004).

4   1909 Annual Convention Minutes, Central Council Minute Book 1899–1911, p. 453.

5   *The Kerryman,* 29 July 1916.

6   Tom Looney, *Dick Fitzgerald: King in a Kingdom of Kings,* (Dublin, 2008), pp. 122–4.

7   *The Kerryman,* 29 July 1916.

8   *Irish Independent,* 25 January 1921.

9   Dublin County Board Minutes, 12 October 1921, Dublin County Board Minute Book 1917–23, p. 261.

10   *Kildare Observer,* 14 October 1922.

11   John Feehan, *The Curragh of Kildare,* (Dublin: UCD School of Biology and Environmental Science/Department of Defence, n. d.), p. 64.

12   Brian Hanley, 'Irish Republican Attitudes to Sport since 1921' in *The Evolution of the GAA: Ulaidh, Éire agus Eile* (Armagh, 2009), pp. 175–84.

13   *The Kerryman,* 26 August 1916.

14   Central Council Minutes, 13 May 1921, Central Council Minute Book 1911–25, pp. 541–2.

15   Central Council Minutes, 3 July 1921, Central Council Minute Book 1911–25, pp. 542–3.

16   *Ibid.,* p. 543.

17   Leinster Council Minutes, 1 October 1921, Leinster Council Minute Book, 1915–22, p. 191.

18 William Murphy, 'The GAA during the Irish Revolution, 1913–1923', in Mike Cronin, William Murphy and Paul Rouse (eds), *The Gaelic Athletic Association 1884–2009* (Dublin, 2009), pp. 61–76.

19 *The Kerryman*, 29 July 1916.

20 *Ibid.*

21 Dublin County Board Minutes, 23 June 1924, Dublin County Board Minute Book 1923–28, p. 82.

22 *FJ*, 30 June 1924.

23 *Westmeath Examiner*, 5 July 1924.

24 Dublin County Board Minutes, 28 July 1924, Dublin County Board Minute Book 1923–28, p. 87.

25 *The Kerryman*, 16 February 1924.

26 *Ibid.*, 29 March 1924.

27 Richard McElligott, *Forging a Kingdom: The GAA in Kerry 1884–1934* (Cork, 2013), pp. 307–9.

28 *The Kerryman*, 2 August 1924.

29 Central Council Minutes, 5 November 1916, Central Council Minute Book 1911–25, pp. 384–5.

30 *Nenagh Guardian*, 6 March 1920.

31 *Ibid.*, 3 April 1920.

32 *FJ*, 5 April 1920.

33 Dublin County Board Minutes, 14 April 1920, Dublin County Board Minute Book 1917–23, p. 187.

34 *Nenagh Guardian*, 27 October 1923.

35 *Ibid.*, 27 October 1923.

36 *Irish Independent*, 5 November 1923.

37 *Ibid.*, 27 November 1923.

38 *FJ*, 12 June 1924.

39 *Irish Independent*, 16 June 1924.

40 Richard McElligott, *Forging a Kingdom: The GAA in Kerry 1884–1934* (Cork, 2013), pp. 310–1.

41 In the official Central Council Minutes, the word 'threatened' has been crossed out and replaced with 'warned'.

42 Central Council Minutes, 28 June 1924, Central Council Minute Book 1911–25, p. 726.

43 *Irish Independent*, 3 July 1925.

44 Central Council Minutes, 12 July 1924, Central Council Minute Book 1911–25, pp. 731–2.

45 *The Kerryman*, 5 July 1924.

46 *Ibid.*

47 Louth County Board Minutes, 29 June 1924. Louth County Board Minute Book 1923–26, p. 125.

48 *Irish Independent*, 11 August 1924.

49 Central Council Minutes, 17 August 1924, Central Council Minute Book 1911–25, pp. 745–6.

50   The IVDF was founded in the days after the 1916 Rising by Kathleen Clarke with the aim of distributing money given to her by her husband, Tom Clarke (before his execution), to support the dependants of the Volunteers.

51   The INAA was launched in May 1916 and appealed to a cross-section of Irish society who wished to support the prisoners without endorsing the politics of the Rising.

52   W. F. Mandle, *The Gaelic Athletic Association and Irish Nationalist Politics 1884–1924* (Dublin, 1987), p. 174.

53   *The Southern Star*, 22 July 1916.

54   The Irish National Aid and Volunteer Dependants Fund was formed in August 1916 when the Irish National Aid Association (INAA) and the Irish Volunteer Dependants Fund (IVDF) merged into one organisation.

55   Central Council Minutes, 5 November 1916, Central Council Minute Book 1911–25, p. 386.

56   Dublin County Board Minutes, 13 February 1917, Dublin County Board Minute Book 1917–23, p. 9.

57   *Irish Independent*, 30 April 1917.

58   *Ibid.*, 28 January 1918.

59   *Ibid.*, 1 April 1918.

60   *FJ*, 6 May 1918.

61   INAA and VDF Executive Committee Minutes, 13 November 1917, NLI MS 23,468.

62   Louth County Board Minutes, 8 October 1916. Louth County Board Minute Book 1916–20, p. 15.

63   The Dublin county board held their National Aid Tournament in Croke Park in March and April 1917; in total £39 13s. 5d. was raised and donated to National Aid from this tournament, which was won by Collegians (hurling) and Lawrence O'Tooles (football). Dublin County Board Minutes, 17 July 1917, Dublin County Board Minute Book 1917–23, p. 35.

64   When the Dublin county board was informed, in June 1916, that under martial law regulations, permits were necessary for holding matches and meetings, they decided to continue with their championships, without permits, and to donate the net proceeds to National Aid. This decision was later rescinded and a £10 grant given to National Aid instead. Dublin County Board Minutes, 6 June 1916, 13 June 1916, 20 June 1916, Dublin County Board Minute Book 1912–17, pp. 184–8.

65   INAA and VDF Executive Committee Minutes, 12 March 1918, NLI MS 23,468.

66   INAA and VDF Executive Committee Minutes, 11 January 1919, NLI MS 23,468.

67   Central Council Minutes, 25 January 1919, Central Council Minute Book 1911–25, p. 452.

68   Central Council Minutes, 8 February 1919, Central Council Minute Book 1911–25, pp. 453–4.

69   INAA and VDF Executive Committee Minutes, 3 February 1919, NLI MS 23,468.

70   *Irish Independent*, 10 February 1919.

71   *Ibid.*, 10 December 1917.

72   Annual Convention Minutes 1918, Central Council Minute Book 1911–25, p. 425.

73   Dublin County Board Minutes, 11 April 1916, Dublin County Board Minute Book 1912–17, p. 182.

74 Central Council Minutes, 15 February 1919, Central Council Minute Book 1911–25, p. 456.

75 *FJ*, 7 April 1919.

76 The exact purpose of the game played on Bloody Sunday is somewhat unclear – the day before the game, *The Freeman's Journal* advertised it as being a benefit game for an 'injured Gael', whereas John Shouldice, Secretary of the Leinster Council at the time, in his statement to the Bureau of Military History (1913–21), stated that it was a game in aid of the IRPDF.

77 GAA Secretary's Report to the 1922 Annual Convention.

78 *FJ*, 24 February 1922.

79 The Irish Republican Prisoners' Dependants Cup was donated to the IRPDF by the National Assurance Company. The cup was donated by the Naas GAA club in 2012 to the GAA Museum where it is currently on display.

80 *Irish Independent*, 27 February 1922.

81 *FJ*, 21 January 1924.

82 *Irish Independent*, 22 January 1924.

83 Annual Convention Minutes, 21 May 1922, Central Council Minute Book 1911–25, p. 600.

84 Central Council Minutes, 10 June 1922, Central Council Minute Book 1911–25, p. 596.

85 Central Council Minutes, 3 March 1923, Central Council Minute Book 1911–25, pp. 635–6.

86 Louth County Board Minutes, 12 August 1923, Louth County Board Minute Book 1923–26, p. 21.

87 Louth County Board Minutes, 28 October 1923, Louth County Board Minute Book 1923–26, pp. 41–2.

88 Dublin County Board Minutes, 28 January 1924, Dublin County Board Minute Book 1923–28, p. 50.

89 *FJ*, 4 February 1924.

90 William Murphy, 'The GAA during the Irish Revolution, 1913–23', in Mike Cronin, William Murphy and Paul Rouse (eds), *The Gaelic Athletic Association 1884–2009* (Dublin and Portland, Or., 2009), p. 70.

11.   Camogie and Revolutionary Ireland, 1913–23

1 *FJ*, 13 August 1913; *Killarney Echo*, 16 August 1913

2 The reference is in one of Lucky's speeches in *Waiting for Godot*: 'in spite of the strides of physical culture the practice of sports such as tennis football running cycling swimming flying floating riding gliding conating camogie skating tennis of all kinds dying flying sports of all sorts', Samuel Beckett, *Waiting for Godot* (London, 1965 [reset 2000]), pp. 36–7.

3 *The Irish Times*, 30 June 1917.

4   See, Ríona Nic Congáil, '"Looking on for Centuries from the Sideline": Gaelic Feminism and the Rise of Camogie', *Éire-Ireland*, volume XLVIII; 1–2 (Spring-Summer 2013), pp. 168–90.

5   John Arlott, *Oxford Companion to Sports and Games* (1978), p. 488.

6   Jennifer Hargreaves, *Sport and Popular Culture: A Social and Historical Analysis of Popular Sport in Britain* (Cambridge and Oxford, 1986). For sport as patriarchy, see Allen Guttman, *Women's Sports: A History* (Columbia, 1991) and note 8 below. For the myth of female frailty, see Nancy Theberge, '"It's Part of the Game": Physicality and the Production of Gender' in *Women's Hockey, Gender and Society*, Vol. 11, No. 1 (February, 1997), pp. 69–87.

7   Mary Moran, *A Game of Our Own* (Camogie Association, 2011), p. 36.

8   Allen Guttmann, 'Sport, Politics and the Engaged Historian', *Journal of Contemporary History*, Vol. 38, No 3, Sport and Politics (London, 2003), pp. 363–75.

9   Mary Moran, *A Game of Our Own* (Dublin, 2011), p. 15.

10 'Máire Ní Chinnéide and Peig' in the *Irish Independent*, 12 January 1952.

11 Liam P. Ó Caithnia, *Scéal na hIomána* (*Baile Átha Cliath*, 1980), pp. 677–92; Art Ó Maolfábhail, *Camán: 2000 years of Hurling in Ireland* (Dundalk, 1973).

12 *FJ*, 13 April 1906.

13 *FJ*, 5 April 1911.

14 The only fixtures in 1910 of which records have survived were Crokes versus Drumcondra and Kevins versus Colmcille, *FJ*, 10 October 1910.

15 *FJ*, 19 April 1911.

16 *FJ*, 23 April 1911.

17 *Ibid.*

18 *FJ*, 23 April 1912.

19 *Irish Examiner*, 31 March 1914.

20 Eoghan Corry, *Illustrated History of the GAA* (Dublin, 2005).

21 For Coachford, see *Irish Examiner*, 12 August 1913. For Cork Athletic Grounds, see *Irish Examiner*, 26 July 1913.

22 For comments on Ireland's early prominence in women's sport, see Arlott, *op. cit.*, p. 607.

23 *FJ*, 3 March 1896.

24 *Skibbereen Eagle*, 4 July 1914.

25 *Irish Examiner*, 23 August 1913.

26 *Ibid.*, 28 August 1913.

27 *Ibid.*, 29 August 1913. For discussion of the circumstances of the game, see discussion of Cork Camogie Board, *Irish Examiner* 5 September 1913.

28 *Irish Examiner*, 21 July 1913.

29 *Ibid.*, 12 July 1913.

30 For Carrigdubh and Fáinne an Lae, see *Irish Examiner*, 16 September 1914; for Toomevarra, see *Irish Examiner*, 4 May 1918; for Nenagh, see *Nenagh Guardian*, April 20 1918; for Meath, see *Meath Chronicle*, May 4 1918.

31 For Killpatrick, see *Irish Examiner*, 6 June 1914; for Shanballymore, see *Irish Examiner*, 18 August 1914.

32   *Irish Examiner,* 21 July 1913.

33   *Ibid.,* 17 October 1913; for reaction to the directive on women's athletics, see *The Irish Times,* 4 May 1928; for McQuaid's letters, see *The Irish Press,* 24 February 1934. See also, Yvonne Judge, *Chasing Gold: Sportswomen of Ireland* (Dublin, 1995), p. 9, where she notes that both camogie and women's hockey survived the century only because of the gymslip.

34   Mary Moran, *A Game of Our Own* (Camogie Association, 2011), p. 29. A comprehensive summary of the correspondence between J. J. Walsh and Áine Ryan is given in the *Meath Chronicle,* 30 August 1924.

35   Sinéad McCoole, 'Mollie Gill, 1891–1977: A Woman of Ireland' in *History Ireland,* Vol. 13, No. 2 March–April 2005, pp. 10–11.

12.   The GAA, Nationalism and the Irish Diaspora in the United States, 1913–23

1   Stephen A. Reiss, 'Sport, Race and Ethnicity in the American City, 1879–1950', in Michael D'Innocenzo and Joseph P. Sirefman (eds), *Immigration and Ethnicity: American Society – 'Melting Pot' or 'Salad Bowl'?* (Westport, CN and London, 1992), pp. 191–219.

2   *Ibid.*

3   Paul Darby, *Gaelic Games, Nationalism and the Irish Diaspora in the United States* (Dublin, 2009).

4   O'Shea, L. 'Governing Body Formed', *The Advocate,* 12 December 1914, p. 3.

5   Byrne, J. 'The New York GAA, 1914–1976', in D. Guiney (ed.) *The New York Irish* (Dublin, 1976), pp. 6–24.

6   *Chicago Daily Tribune,* 'Irish Field Day Enthuses Crowd', 10 September 1906, p. 5.

7   *Chicago Daily Tribune,* 'Donnybrook Fair was Nothing Like This; Today's the Day of the Irishmen's Picnic', 15 August 1909, p. 13.

8   *Chicago Daily Tribune,* 'Interested in Approaching Chicago-St. Louis Hurling Match', 20 October 1907, p. C3.

9   *The Advocate,* 'The Gaelic Athletes in the Old Sixty-Ninth are Calling for Hurling Sticks and Footballs', 1 September 1917, p. 5.

10   *Ibid.*

11   Darby (2009), *op. cit.*; Darby, Paul 'Playing for Ireland in Foreign Fields: The Gaelic Athletic Association and Irish Nationalism in America', *Irish Studies Review,* 18, 1 (2010), pp. 69–89.

12   Hasia S. Diner, 'The Most Irish City in the Union: The Era of the Great Migration, 1844–1877', in Ronald H. Bayor and Timothy J. Meagher (eds), *The New York Irish* (Baltimore and London, 1997), pp. 87–106.

13   David Brundage, 'In Time of Peace, Prepare for War: Key Themes in the Social Thought of New York's Irish Nationalists, 1890–1916', in Ronald H. Bayor and Timothy J. Meagher (eds), *The New York Irish* (Baltimore and London, 1997), p. 322.

14   *Irish Echo,* July 1888; *The Gael,* May 1887.

15   *Citizen,* 26 September 1885; *Citizen,* 3 July 1886; *Citizen,* 6 August 1887.

16   *Donohoe's Magazine,* 'Parliamentary Fund', April 1886, p. 180.

17 *Gaelic American*, 7 November, 1903; *Gaelic American*, 2 July 1904.

18 Reiss, *op. cit.*, p. 192.

19 Lawrence J. McCaffrey, *Textures of Irish America* (Syracuse, NY, 1992).

20 Andrew J. Wilson, *Irish America and the Ulster Conflict 1968–1995* (Belfast, 1995).

21 Darby (2009), *op. cit., passim.*

22 *The San Francisco Call*, 19 February 1906.

23 *Chicago Daily Tribune*, 9 August 1903: 5.

24 *Gaelic American*, 23 March 1912; *Gaelic American*, 7 June 1913.

25 Tim Pat Coogan, *The Troubles: Ireland's Ordeal 1966–95 and the Search for Peace*, (London, 1995).

26 *The Advocate*, 25 July 1914.

27 *Gaelic American*, 29 August 1914; *Gaelic American*, 5 September 1914.

28 *The Advocate,* 3 September 1914.

29 *Ibid.*

30 *Gaelic American*, 5 September 1914.

31 *The Leader*, 5 December 1914, p. 5.

32 *The Leader*, 'Gaelic Athletic News', 19 April 1913, p. 7.

33 *The Leader*, 'The Gaelic Ideal', 26 August 1916, p. 1.

34 McCaffrey, *op. cit.*

35 Wilson, *op. cit.*; Troy Davis, 'Éamon de Valera's Political Education: The American Tour of 1919', *New Hibernia Review,* 10, 1 (2006), pp. 65–78.

36 McCaffrey, *op. cit.*

37 *Ibid.*

38 *Ibid.*, p. 154.

39 North American County Board, *Our Story Retold: 1884–1997* (North American County Board, 1997).

40 Fergie Hanna, 'The Gaelic Athletic Association', in M. Glazier (ed.), *The Encyclopedia of the Irish in America* (Notre Dame, IN, 1999).

41 Darby (2009), *op. cit.*

42 *Ibid.*

13. Image and Impact: Representing and Reporting the GAA, 1913–23

1 Although Mac Lua is not credited by Lennon in the film and is referred to only as 'Assistant Secretary of the GAA', he was identified for this essay by Eugene McGee, author, journalist and All-Ireland-winning Offaly football manager.

2 Richard McElligott, *Forging a Kingdom: The GAA in Kerry 1884–1934* (Cork, 2013), p. 1.

3 The motion to refuse to seek permits was carried unanimously, along with the decision to stage the Gaelic Sunday national programme of matches the following month. Central Council Minutes, 20 July 1918 (GAA Museum and Archive, Croke Park).

4   J. J. Lee, *Ireland 1912–1985: Politics and Society* (Cambridge, 1989), p. 81.

5   Marcus de Búrca, *The GAA: A History of the Gaelic Athletic Association* ([1980] Dublin, 2000), pp. 84–6.

6   Central Council Minutes, 6 April 1913 (GAA Museum and Archive).

7   Letters to the Editor, *The Gaelic Athlete*, 19 April 1913.

8   McElligott, *ibid.*, p. 166.

9   Central Council Minutes, 20 April 1913.

10   Eoghan Corry, *Catch and Kick: Great Moments of Gaelic Football 1880–1990* (Dublin, 1989), pp. 91–2.

11   Central Council Minutes, 4 October 1913.

12   Editorial, *The Gaelic Athlete*, 1 November 1913.

13   Annual Convention Minutes 1912, Central Council Minute Book 1911–25, p. 45.

14   Annual Convention Minutes 1913, Central Council Minute Book 1911–25, p. 49.

15   Hugh Oram, *The Newspaper Book: A History of Newspapers in Ireland, 1619–1983* (Dublin, 1983), p. 100.

16   *Ibid.* p. 106.

17   Felix M. Larkin, '"A Great Daily Organ": *The Freeman's Journal*, 1763–1924' in *History Ireland*, issue 3, volume 14 (May/June, 2006).

18   Seán O'Mahony, *Frongoch: University of Revolution* (Dublin, 1987), p. 53.

19   *The Gaelic Athlete*, November 1913.

20   Editorial, *The Gaelic Athlete*, 22 November 1913.

21   De Búrca, *op. cit.*, p. 81.

22   Central Council Minutes, 27 April 1913.

23   De Búrca, *op. cit.*, p. 96.

24   *FJ*, 15 December 1913.

25   Mark Duncan, 'The Camera and the Gael: The Early Photography of the GAA, 1884–1914', in Mike Cronin, William Murphy and Paul Rouse (eds), *The Gaelic Athletic Association 1884–2009* (Dublin, 2009), p. 110.

26   Denis Condon, 'Watching Gaelic Games on Screen in 1913', on www.academia.edu; accessed 2013.

27   See, for example, Con Short, *The Crossmaglen GAA Story 1887–1987* (Crossmaglen, 1987), p. 67.

28   Editorial, *The Irish Times*, 30 November 1916.

29   William Murphy, 'The GAA during the Irish Revolution, 1913–23', in Cronin, Murphy and Rouse (eds), *The Gaelic Athletic Association 1884–2009* (Dublin, 2009), p. 64.

30   *Ibid.*, p. 65, citing David Fitzpatrick, *Politics and Irish Life, 1913–1921: Provincial Experience of War and Revolution* (Dublin, 1977), p. 112.

31   *The Irish Times*, 19 May 1916.

32   Oram, *op. cit.*, chapter 5.

33   Michael Foley, *The Bloodied Field: Croke Park, Sunday 21 November 1920* (Dublin, 2014).

14. Social Life and the GAA in a Time of Upheaval in Ireland: A Retrospect

1   David Fitzpatrick, *Harry Boland's Irish Revolution* (Dublin, 2003), p. 163

2   *Ibid.*, p. 22.

3   Diarmaid Ferriter, *Occasions of Sin: Sex and Society in Modern Ireland* (London, 2009), p. 91.

4   Peter Hart, *Mick: The Real Michael Collins* (London, 2005), p. 45.

5   Gearóid Ó Tuathaigh, 'The GAA as a Force in Irish Society: An Overview' in Mike Cronin, William Murphy and Paul Rouse (eds), *The Gaelic Athletic Association 1884–2009* (Dublin, 2009), pp. 237–57.

6   Irish Military Archives (IMA) BMH Witness Statement (WS) 24, Con Murphy.

7   T. F. O'Sullivan, *The Story of the GAA* (Dublin, 1916), cited in William Murphy, 'The GAA during the Irish Revolution, 1913–23' in Cronin, Murphy and Rouse (eds), *op. cit.*, pp. 61–77.

8   IMA, BMH WS 679, Jack Shouldice.

9   Roisín Higgins, *Transforming 1916: Meaning, Memory and the Fiftieth Anniversary of the 1916 Rising* (Cork, 2012), pp. 52–3.

10 *Ibid.*

11 *Gaelic Weekly*, 6 January 1968.

12 W. F. Mandle, 'The GAA and Popular Culture, 1884–1924' in Oliver MacDonagh, W. F. Mandle and Pauric Travers (eds) *Irish Culture and Nationalism, 1750–1950* (Dublin, 1983), pp. 104–121.

13 William Murphy, *Political Imprisonment and the Irish, 1912–1921* (Oxford, 2014), p. 115.

14 William Murphy, 'The GAA during the Irish Revolution, 1913–23' in Cronin, Murphy and Rouse (eds), *op. cit.*, pp. 61–77.

15 Richard McElligott, *Forging a Kingdom: The GAA in Kerry, 1884–1934* (Cork, 2013), p. 266.

16 *Ibid.* p. 251.

17 Richard Vincent Comerford, *Ireland: Inventing the Nation* (London, 2003), pp. 223–31.

18 *Ibid.*, p. 76.

19 Tom Humphries, 'Inside the Heart of the GAA', *The Irish Times*, 4 July 2009.

20 Charles Townshend, *The Republic: The Fight for Irish Independence* (London, 2013), pp. 1–15.

21 Ernie O'Malley, *On Another Man's Wound* (Dublin, 1979).

22 Colm Ó Gaora, *On The Run: The Story of an Irish Freedom Fighter* (a translation of Ó Gaora's *Mise*; translation by Mícheál Ó hAodha, Cork, 2011), p. 349.

23 Seán Moran, *Patrick Pearse and the Politics of Redemption* (Washington, 1994), p. 116.

24 Dominic Price, *The Flame and Candle: War in Mayo, 1919–24* (Cork, 2012), p. 50.

25 John Borgonovo, *The Dynamics of War and Revolution: Cork City, 1916–18* (Cork, 2013), p. 17.

26 Mandle, *op. cit.*

27 McElligott, *op. cit.*, p. 274.

28 Tom Hunt, *Sport and Society in Victorian Ireland: The Case of Westmeath* (Cork, 2007).

29 Price, *op. cit.*, p. 50.

30 Alvin Jackson (ed.), *The Oxford Handbook of Modern Irish History* (Oxford, 2014), pp. 27–45.

31 R. F. Foster, *Vivid Faces: The Revolutionary Generation in Ireland 1890–1923* (London, 2014), pp. 31–75.

32 Paul Rouse, 'Empires of Sport: Enniscorthy 1880–1970' in Colm Tóibín (ed.), *Enniscorthy: A History*, pp. 333–69.

33 William Nolan (ed.), *The Gaelic Athletic Association in Dublin, 1884–2000, Volume 1* (Dublin, 2005), p. 112.

34 Brian Ó Conchubhair (ed.), *Kerry's Fighting Story 1916–21: Told by the Men who Made It* (Cork, 2010 edition), introduction by Joe Lee, p. 10.

35 Jeremiah Murphy, *When Youth Was Mine: A Memoir of Kerry, 1902–1925* (Dublin, 1998), p. 31.

36 Fearghal McGarry, *Eoin O'Duffy: A Self-Made Hero* (Oxford, 2005), p. 17.

37 Joost Augusteijn, *From Public Defiance to Guerrilla Warfare* (Dublin, 1996), p. 310.

38 David Fitzpatrick, *Politics and Irish life, 1913–21: Provincial Experience of War and Revolution* (Dublin, 1977), p. 93.

39 Murphy, *op. cit.*

40 IMA, BMH, WS 1041, Thomas Doyle.

41 Nolan, *op. cit.*, p. 141.

42 Catríona Crowe (ed.), *Dublin 1911* (Dublin, 2011), p. 152ff.

43 Mary E. Daly, 'Two Centuries of Irish Social Life' in Brendan Rooney (ed.), *A Time and a Place: Two Centuries of Irish Social Life* (Dublin, 2006), pp. 3–12.

44 Tony Farmar, *Ordinary Lives: Three Generations of Irish Middle Class Experience, 1907, 1932, 1963* (Dublin, 1991), p. 68.

45 Borgonovo, *op. cit.*, p. 16.

46 Hunt, *op. cit.*

47 Rouse, *op. cit.*

48 Daly, *op. cit.*

49 Jeremiah Newman (ed.), *Limerick Rural Survey, 1958–1964* (Tipperary, 1964) pp. 240–1.

50 Daly, *op. cit.* and Nolan, *op. cit.*, p. 113.

51 McElligott, *op. cit.*, p. 279.

52 Fearghal McGarry, *Rebels: Voices from the Easter Rising* (Dublin, 2011), p. 64.

53 Borgonovo, *op. cit.*, pp. 62–3.

54 Augusteijn, *op. cit.*, p. 84.

55 *Ibid.,* p. 248.

56 McGarry (2011), *op. cit.,* p. 12.

57 Gerard MacAtasney, *Tom Clarke: Life, Liberty, Revolution* (Dublin, 2013), pp. 262–3.

58 Fitzpatrick, *op. cit.*, p. 102.

59 *Ibid.*, p. 155.

60 Pádraig Yeates, *A City in Turmoil: Dublin 1919–21* (Dublin, 2012), p. 195.

61 Murphy, *op. cit.*

INDEX

Higgins, George 189
hockey 16, 88, 107, 195, 200, 213, 215–16
Hogan, Dan 119
Hogan, Michael 49, 67, 166
Holland, Patrick 99
Hourigan-Purcell, Agnes 196, 215
housing 38–9
hunger strikes 144, 157, 181, 183
Hunt, Tom 20, 258
Hyde, Douglas 76, 210–11, 229

image and impact 237–50, 256
Inghinidhe na hÉireann 204
internment 24, 120–1, 139–40, 141, 168, 170,
    181, 183, 191, 192, 241
    Gaelic games 140, 170–9
Intoxicating Liquor Act (Northern Ireland)
    1923 124
IRA (Irish Republican Army) 66, 114, 115,
    118, 119, 120, 121, 127, 156, 166, 172,
    184, 233, 253, 259, 260
Ireland's Saturday Night 112
Irish Amateur Athletic Association (IAAA) 114
Irish American Athletic Club (IAAC) 231
Irish Association of Volunteer Training Corps
    137
Irish Guards 93, 94, 98, 103
Irish Independent 88, 158, 159, 241, 244
Irish National Aid and Volunteer Dependants
    Fund 61, 148–9, 152, 185–7
The Irish News 112
Irish Parliamentary Fund 227
Irish Parliamentary Party (IPP) 47, 57–8, 62,
    71–83, 111, 113, 138, 141, 144, 145,
    152, 187, 229
Irish Republican Brotherhood (IRB) 8, 55, 58,
    72, 73–4, 79, 91, 107, 114, 131–2, 133,
    138, 139, 241, 249, 257
Irish Republican Brotherhood Veterans 227
Irish Republican Prisoners' Dependants Fund
    (IRPDF) 47, 187–91
The Irish Times 112, 160, 217, 248–9
Irish Volunteers 22, 23, 46, 66, 72, 78–9, 192,
    241, 253
    1914 split 8, 46, 59, 60, 72, 78, 79, 100,
        109, 131
    1917 reorganisation of 147
    conscription 148
    Easter Rising 7–8, 130, 131, 132, 133,
        137–8, 139, 140, 249
    formation of 57, 58, 130–1
    hurling stick and drill 112
    proscribed 148
    Sinn Féin 144
    social life 256, 257
    Ulster 109, 111, 115
    United States 230–2

Jackson, Alvin 72
Jameson, James T. 248
Jordan, Stephen 99, 167
Joyce, Brian 171
Joyce, Michael 73

Keane, J.J. 181, 217
Kearney, Fr J.J. 31
Keating, Matthew 83
Kehoe, Pádraig 20, 21
Kelly, John 86
Kelly, Nellie 217
Kelly, Tom 58
Kennedy, Tadhg 132
Kerry 60, 73, 76, 155, 168, 179, 183–5, 240,
    253, 256
    aftermath of Rising 141, 144, 145–6, 148
    arms 131–3, 259
    camogie 210
    First World War 90, 145
    IPP 77, 79, 145
    IRB 132
    Irish Volunteers 60, 79, 131–3, 148
    Sinn Féin 144, 145–6, 254
Kettle, Tom 58
Kierse, Seán 94
Kilcoyne, Tom 66
Kildare 60, 168, 172, 187, 189
Kilkenny 60, 90, 183, 184, 260
    camogie 200, 210, 215
King, John H. 121

Langrishe, Mary 212
language 20, 72, 120, 178, 195, 201, 229, 256
Laois 25–30, 31–4, 59–60, 100–1, 109
    camogie 210
Larkin, James 38
Lee, Joe 256
Leinster 23, 49, 58, 62–3, 73, 86, 90, 167,
    173, 186
    see also individual counties
Leinster Regiment 94
Lennon, Peter 238
Lett, Anita 204
Limerick 22, 35, 60, 62, 73, 74, 86, 155, 158,
    184–5, 260
    camogie 210, 216
    First World War 89, 90
Limerick Leader 22, 89
Lisburn 107, 115
Lloyd George, David 111, 124
Longford 78
Longford, Countess of 20
Lonsdale, Sir John 110
Louth 146, 184, 186, 191, 240
    camogie 210, 215

Lundon, Thomas 74, 141
Lynn, Robert 119

Mac Aodha, Tomás 210, 217
Mac Lua, Breandán 238
McAnallen, Dónal 99
MacBride, John 79
McCaffrey, L.J. 234
McCarthy, Dan 66, 67, 125, 167
McCarthy, Nell 200
McCarthy, Seán 184
McCullough, Denis 254
McElgunn, P.L. 109
McElligott, Richard 238, 254
McEntee, Andy 127
McFadden, John 115
McFadden, Patrick 115, 122, 128
McGarry, Fearghal 7–8, 79, 256–7, 259
McGeough, John 93
McGrath, Frank 167, 181
McGuinn, James 102
McGuire, Andrew 160–2
McHugh, P.A. 74
Macken, Peadar 58
McKenna, Reginald 80, 110
McKenny, J.J. 121
McKillop, William 76
MacLysaght, Edward 260
McMahon, Con 168
MacManaway, J.G. 125
MacNeill, Eoin 58, 130, 131
McQuaid, John Charles 217
MacSwiney, Mary 211
MacSwiney, Terence 157, 181, 211
Maginess, Brian 125
Mandle, W.F. 11, 18, 55, 167, 254
Manning, William 99, 248
martial law 23, 110, 139, 141
Matthews, David 120
Maxwell, General Sir John 23–4, 62–3, 81, 82
Mayo 76, 89, 256
Meagher, Widger 181
Meath 60, 158, 210, 215
media engagement 237–50, 256
Meehan, P.A. 74
Midleton GAA Club 76
Mills, Kathleen 216
minute books 22, 23, 118
Mitchel, John 226
Moles, Thomas 119
Molson, John 115
Monaghan 108, 110, 119, 124–5, 210, 215
Mooney, John 99

Moran, Mary 195, 195–7, 211, 215
Moynihan, Maurice 141
Mulligan, Clare 212
Mullins, William 139–40
Munster 35, 66, 67–9, 73, 86, 88–9, 90, 133, 155, 166, 167, 181, 184
see also individual counties
Munster Fusiliers 98, 102
Murphy, Cornelius 253
Murphy, Fr 20
Murphy, Jeremiah 256
Murphy, William 22, 64, 149, 154, 157, 192, 255
Murphy, William Martin 38, 241
Murray, Alf 253

names of clubs 73, 77, 111, 128, 144, 146, 171, 201, 226, 234, 255
Nannetti, J.P. 76
Nathan, Sir Matthew 61, 81, 110, 249
National Athletic and Cycling Association of Ireland 122, 217
National League 73
National Volunteers 59, 60, 79, 100, 101, 131
Navan 108
Ní Chinnéide, Máire 197, 210
Ní Dhonnchada, Cáit 217
Nic Aitéinn, Éibhlín 210, 216–17
Nolan, William 137
Northern Ireland 4–5, 6, 115, 118–28, 144
internment 170, 171
local elections 126–7
sectarian violence 155
Nowlan, James 40, 46, 54, 55, 56, 58, 60–1, 63, 65, 66, 67, 70, 136, 163, 181

Ó Braonáin, Séamus 200
Ó Buachalla, Domhnall 137
Ó Caoimh, Pádraig 70
Ó Ceallacháin, Pádraig 201
Ó Cuiv, Shán 197
Ó Donnchadha, Tadhg 197
Ó Foghlú, Risteard 197
Ó Gaora, Colm 255
Ó hÉigeartaigh, P.S. 211
Ó hÉigeartaigh, Seaghan 239
Ó hEithir, Breandán 154
oath of allegiance to Crown 9, 65, 100, 114, 122–3, 152, 162–3, 192
O'Brien, Kendal 74
O'Brien, Pat 80
O'Brien-Twohig, Patrick 125
O'Connell, J.J. 22
O'Connor, James 73
O'Connor, John 23, 73, 80, 81